MW01272904

Can I Know What to Believe?

Beliefs to Beware Of

Paul Borthwick and Randy Petersen

"They're Not Like Us!"

Randy Petersen, Fran and Jill Sciacca

Your Bible's Alive!

Stan Campbell, Fran and Jill Sciacca

NEXGEN®

Building the New Generation of Believers

An Imprint of Cook Communications Ministries
Colorado Springs, Colorado

Can I Know What to Believe?

© 2003 Cook Communications Ministries

Published by Cook Communications Ministries
4050 Lee Vance View
Colorado Springs, CO 80918
www.cookministries.com

Editorial Manager: Doug Schmidt
Product Developer: Karen Pickering
Series creator: John Duckworth
Series editor: Randy Southern
Designer: Bill Paetzold
Cover Design: Granite Design
Interior Design: Becky Hawley Design, Inc.

Unit 1: Beliefs to Beware Of
© 2003 Cook Communications Ministries
Editor: Randy Southern
Writers: Randy Petersen, Paul Borthwick
Option writers: John Duckworth, Nelson E. Copeland, Jr.,
and Ellen Larson
Inside illustrator: Al Hering

Unit 2: "They're Not Like Us!"
© 2003 Cook Communications Ministries
Editor: Randy Southern
Writers: Randy Petersen, Fran and Jill Sciacca
Option writers: Stan Campbell, Sue Reck, Randy
Southern, and Mark Syswerda
Inside illustrator: Jackie Besteman

Unit 3: Your Bible's Alive!
© 2003 Cook Communications Ministries
Editor: Randy Southern
Writers: Stan Campbell, Fran and Jill Sciacca
Option writers: Stan Campbell, Nelson E. Copeland, Jr.,
and Sue Reck
Inside illustrator: Eric Masi

Printed in the U.S.A.

Contents

Unit Three: Your Bible's Alive!

How to Customize Your Curriculum

We know your time is valuable. That's why we've made **Custom Curriculum** as easy as possible. Follow the three steps outlined below to create custom lessons that will meet the needs of *your* group. Let's get started!

Read the basic lesson plan.

Every Custom Curriculum session in this book has four or five steps designed to meet five goals. It's important to understand these five goals as you choose the options for your group.

Getting Together

The goal for Getting Together is to break the ice. It may involve a fun way to introduce the lesson.

Getting Thirsty

The goal for Getting Thirsty is to earn students' interest before you dive into the Bible. Why should students care about your topic? Why should they care what the Bible has to say about it? This will motivate your students to dig deeper.

Getting the Word

The goal for Getting the Word is to find out what God has to say about the topic they care about. By exploring and discussing carefully selected passages, you'll help students find out how God's Word applies to their lives.

Getting the Point

The goal for Getting the Point is to make the leap from ideals and principles to real-world situations students are likely to face. It may involve practicing biblical principles with case studies or roleplays.

Getting Personal

The goal for Getting Personal is to help each group member respond to the lesson with a specific action. What should group members do as a result of this session? This step will help each person find a specific "next step" response that works for him or her.

Consider your options.

Every **Custom Curriculum** session gives you 14 different types of options. How do you choose? First, take a look at the list of option categories below. Then spend some time thinking and praying about your group. How do your students learn best? What kind of goals have you set for your group? Put a check mark by the options that you're most interested in.

 Extra Action—for groups that like physical challenges and learn better when they're moving, interacting, and experiencing the lesson.

 Media—to spice up your meeting with video, music, or other popular media.

 Heard It All Before—for fresh approaches that get past the defenses of students who are jaded by years in church.

 Little Bible Background—to use when most of your students are strangers to the Bible or haven't yet made a Christian commitment.

 Extra Fun—for longer, more "festive" youth meetings where additional emphasis is put on having fun.

 Fellowship and Worship—for building deeper relationships or enabling students to praise God together.

 Mostly Girls—to address girls' concerns and to substitute activities girls might prefer.

 Mostly Guys—to address guys' concerns and to substitute activities guys might prefer.

 Small Group—for adapting activities that might be tough with groups of fewer than eight students.

 Large Group—to alter steps for groups of more than 20 students.

 Urban—for fitting sessions to urban facilities and multiethnic (especially African-American) concerns.

 Short Meeting Time—tips for condensing the meeting. The standard meeting is designed to last 45 to 60 minutes. These include options to cut, replace, or trim time off the standard steps.

 Combined Junior High/High School—to use when you're mixing age levels but an activity or case study would be too "young" or "old" for part of the group.

 Sixth Grade—appearing only in junior high/middle school volumes, this option helps you change steps that sixth graders might find hard to understand or relate to.

 Extra Challenge—appearing only in high school volumes, this option lets you crank up the voltage for students who are ready for more Scripture or more demanding personal application.

Customize your curriculum!

Here's a simple, three-step plan to customize each session for your group:

1. Choose your options.

As you read the basic session plan, you'll see icons in the margin. Each icon represents a different type of option. When you see an icon, it means that type of option is offered for that step. The five pages of options are found after the Repro Resource student pages for each session. Turn to the option noted by the icon and you'll see that option explained.

Let's say you have a small group, mostly guys who get bored if they don't keep moving. You'll want to keep an eye out for three kinds of options: Small Group, Mostly Guys, and Extra Action. As you read the basic session, you might spot icons that tell you there are Small Group options for Step 1 and Step 3— maybe a different way to play a game so that you don't need big teams, and a way to cover several Bible passages when just a few kids are looking them up. Then you see icons telling you that there are Mostly Guys options for Step 2 and Step 4—perhaps a substitute activity that doesn't require too much self-disclosure, and a case study guys will relate to. Finally, you see icons indicating Extra Action options for Step 2 and Step 3—maybe an active way to get kids' opinions instead of handing out a survey, and a way to act out some verses instead of just looking them up.

2. Use the checklist.

Once you've picked your options, keep track of them with the simple checklist at the end of the option section (just before the start of the next session plan). This little form gives you a place to write down the materials you'll need too—since they depend on the options you've chosen.

3. Get your stuff together.

Gather your materials; photocopy any Repro Resources (reproducible student sheets) you've decided to use. And…you're ready!

Unit One: Beliefs to Beware Of

Talking to Kids about Cults

by Paul Borthwick

About 40 students from our youth group gathered together for a football game after church. Several members of the leadership team were there, but none of our adult volunteers. Three men approached the group. They came from The Way, a local cultic group that adheres to heretical teachings about Jesus, salvation, and the Holy Spirit.

As they engaged our students in conversation, they asked questions and made assertions that bothered the young people; but none of the members could quite put his finger on the problem. One student later told me, "We smelled a theological problem, but we didn't know how to uncover it."

I drove by the field, and one of the students flagged me down. He explained the situation and asked if I could help. I stopped, interacted with the cult evangelist, asked a few questions about salvation and the deity of Christ, and the three men retreated.

The students seemed excited. From their perspective, we had "won." But the experience disappointed me. It showed me that even my student leaders did not really know how to handle the situation. It reminded me that these students—many of whom would soon be on their own in college—did not know how to respond to the myriad of cults that they might face in the years ahead.

Addressing Cult Questions

Across the country and around the world, Christians face the challenge of cults—those groups whose overemphasis on one issue or error in another have led them away from the orthodox, evangelical faith. Some cults—like the Mormons, Jehovah's Witnesses, or Christian Scientists—have been around for years. Others are being formed today. Some are built on faulty doctrines like salvation through works or errant teaching on the deity of Christ. Others rest on some dynamic or charismatic leader's authoritarian style or personal interpretation of the Bible.

Equipping our students to be Christians in the world means training them to identify and respond to cults. In my group members' encounter with members of The Way, the young people knew there was something theologically wrong, but they had no idea how to uncover the error or respond to it.

Effectively equipping our high schoolers in this respect will involve versing them in the answers to questions like the following:
- Who is Jesus Christ?
- Is Jesus God?
- What is the basis for forgiveness? For salvation?
- Why did Jesus die on the cross?
- What do you believe about the resurrection?

As You Approach These Sessions

As we prepare to undertake the studies in this book, we must keep the following principles in mind.

First, we must address realistically the attractive doctrines that cults teach. Cults will sometimes attract Christians because their doctrines are easier to understand or explain than Christian doctrines.

The Jehovah's Witnesses, for example, confuse many Christians with their teaching that Jesus was created. For some people, that concept is more palatable and easier to believe than the concept of Jesus being God in a "Three-in-One" Trinity.

Cults succeed because they teach doctrines or promote ideas that often have a greater appeal than the truth. A young woman from our church joined a cult that taught that salvation was based on works. She was drawn to this group because she had never been able to accept the idea of salvation through faith alone. To her, such salvation seemed too easy. She had come from a rigid family where affection was "earned," and she never experienced unconditional love. Thus, when she was presented with the idea of needing to work hard to earn the love of a hard-to-please God, she fell prey to heresy.

Insecure men may be drawn to a cult that denigrates women. Those who need to have everything fully explained will be attracted to cults that teach that Jesus was only a man and not God incarnate. Students who are bored with "powerless" Christianity may be drawn to experiment with satanism because it appears to offer more in terms of the miraculous and dramatic.

Our task will be to explain these attractive aspects of cultic teaching and then respond with our convictions as to why orthodox and biblical faith is still the answer.

Second, we must recognize the social environment that attracts some to cults. In an age of dysfunctional families and the breakdown of authority, people's attraction to cults often stems from the social structure the cults create. Their regimented "fellowships" may provide some with a security that our church groups may never provide. People with lives in disarray will be drawn to authoritarian teaching that promises to get their lives in order. Young people may find in cults the love they never experienced at home.

The social attractiveness of some cults cannot be overlooked. This attraction should cause us to evaluate what is lacking in our own fellowships, and then try to respond. In addition, it should cause us to teach students the significance of not letting emotion rule our understanding of theology.

Be Cautious

Students may show a great interest in studying cults, but often this interest is motivated by a voyeuristic curiosity or a desire to show that "we are right and they are wrong!" As leaders, therefore, we must be cautious about some of the potential pitfalls involved in this series.

Caution #1: Exemplify "speaking the truth in love." Our experience with the evangelists from The Way illustrated an attitude that we now try to avoid. The students felt like we "won" when my questions sent the evangelists away.

But our goal is not to win arguments. Our goal is to teach students how to defend their faith so that they will be protected from heresy and able to explain the true Gospel to people lost in cultic error. If we present cult members as our enemies, we often promote in students a desire to destroy. Instead, we need to foster love so that students desire to win people out of their error to the love and mercy of Christ.

Caution #2: Don't gloss over the tough issues. In presenting the Christian perspective on cultic error, it is easy for us to want to present an "easy" understanding of the truth. As a result, we may try to oversimplify teachings on tough issues like the Trinity, the deity of Christ, or difficult passages like those in Acts, which seem to make baptism part of salvation.

If all of these issues were vividly clear and easy to understand, why would there be cults? The fact remains: Attacking the issues raised by cults leads us into some strenuous theology—like explaining the

Trinity. Be willing to take the time needed to wrestle with these issues so that we present a credible Gospel to inquiring students.

Caution #3: Don't present "our brand" of Christianity as the only option. Studies concerning cults can lead to an unfortunate spirit of "witch-hunting." Uncovering one error in one group can lead to the creation of theological detectives who dedicate themselves to uncovering error in all other groups. The net result can be the creation of another cultic group—if we get to the point where we believe that our group alone has all the truth and everybody else is mistaken.

The studies that follow attempt to avoid this error by concentrating on essential doctrines—salvation through Christ alone, the Trinity, etc.—rather than secondary doctrines about which the Christian church has always experienced a freedom to differ.

Stretch Some Minds

As this series begins, remember that our goal as teachers is to present the truth and encourage students to interact with it themselves. It is better to teach students discernment than it is to overwhelm them with dogma that they memorize without thinking. Our goal is to teach our young people how to think in addition to affirming the biblical doctrines of the Christian faith.

One of the errors of manipulative cults is the attitude that keeps group members from asking questions or challenging the teachings of the group. We can avoid that same error by encouraging interaction, listening to all of the questions that arise, and letting the Bible provide our answers.

Paul Borthwick is minister of missions at Grace Chapel in Lexington, Massachusetts. A former youth pastor and frequent speaker to youth workers, he is the author of several books, including ***Organizing Your Youth Ministry*** (Zondervan).

The images on these two pages are designed to help you promote this course within your church and community. Feel free to photocopy anything here and adapt it to fit your publicity needs. The stuff on this page could be used as a flier that you send or hand out to kids—or as a bulletin insert. The stuff on the next page could be used to add visual interest to newsletters, calendars, bulletin boards, or other promotions. Be creative and have fun!

How Much Do You Know about Cults?

How do your beliefs differ from a Jehovah's Witness? Or from Scientology? What's so dangerous about the New Age movement? We'll be looking at questions like these, and more, as we start a new series called *Beliefs to Beware Of.* Come and learn about cults, so you'll be prepared next time they come knocking on your door.

Who:

When:

Where:

Questions? Call:

Unit One: Beliefs to Beware Of

Witch Cult Is Witch?

What would you say to this guy about Jesus?

Give me one good reason. . .

(Fill in the tag with your own message.)

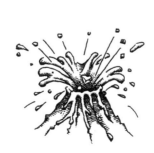

Finally, be strong in the Lord and in his mighty power.
—Ephesians 6:10

What Is a Cult?

YOUR GOALS FOR THIS SESSION:

Choose one or more

☐ To help kids recognize the dangers of cults and their false teachings.

☐ To help kids understand how to recognize cults.

☐ To help kids equip themselves to withstand the lure of cults.

☐ Other:_____

_____

Your Bible Base:

Colossians 2:1-10,
16-19; 3:1

STEP 1

Selling Out

(Needed: Paper, pencils)

Begin the session with a creative activity. Divide group members into three teams. Distribute paper and pencils to each team. Explain: **As a team, you're going to be starting a business. You're going to make and sell a certain product. First, you need to decide what that product will be. It could be something that already exists, or it could be a new invention that you make up.**

Give the teams a few minutes to decide what their product will be. Assign one person on each team to write down an explanation of the product.

When the teams have come up with their products, say: **Now you need to figure out the group of people that you want to sell your product to. How old are they? Are they male or female? Rich or poor? What interests do these people have? In the next minute or two, come up with a brief profile of your "target consumers."**

Give the teams a few minutes to profile their target consumers. Again, have someone from each team take notes during the process—on a separate sheet of paper from the product explanation notes.

After the teams have come up with products to sell and target consumers to sell them to, they will come up with TV commercials for the products, which they'll act out for the rest of the group. However, the teams won't be selling their own products. Each team will give its product explanation to the group to its right, and its consumer profile to the group to its left. So each team will have another team's product to sell to yet another team's target audience.

Give the teams about five minutes to come up with a thirty-second TV spot. Then have them perform their commercials.

Use this activity to introduce the topic of the session: cults. Explain that, in a way, cults are "selling" a particular brand of religion. Their tactics often mirror the tactics of advertising: "You are lacking something." "You need this product." "This product cures all your ills." "We offer you a way to be understood, loved, successful, etc."

Refer to some of the "sales logic" and strategies the teams used in their commercials. Then draw parallels to the logic and strategy cults use to "sell" their beliefs.

Test Case

(Needed: Copies of Repro Resource 1, pencils)

Hand out copies of "The Cult Test" (Repro Resource 1) and pencils. Review the instructions at the top of the page. Then give group members a few minutes to complete the test.

Afterward, go through the questions as a group. Have kids raise their hands to indicate their responses to each question. Ask volunteers to explain why they chose certain answers.

Use the following information to supplement discussion of the sheet.

(1) What are some of the identifying features of a cult? (The correct answers are *a, b,* and *c.*) Point out that there are some exceptions, but most cults do have dominant leaders; they often follow extra-biblical writings; and they also isolate their members from society. However, many cult members seem perfectly normal.

(2) Which of the following is true about Mormonism? (The correct answers are *a* and *d.*) Emphasize that many Mormons are fine people. They even claim to accept the Bible. However, as we'll see later in the session, their beliefs are clearly unbiblical. For that reason, they can be considered a cult. We may "accept" Mormon people as friends, but we *cannot* accept their beliefs as being Christian or biblical.

(3) Which of the following are cults that exist today? (The correct answers are *a* and *b.*) Point out that Mormonism, Jehovah's Witnesses, and Christian Science are all "established" religions; but because their beliefs differ from traditional, biblical Christianity, they can all be considered cults. Scientology, the Unification Church, and Christadelphians are more modern cults. Gnosticism, Donatism, and Pelagianism were ancient heresies in the early church. While Madonna wannabees, sports fans, and youth groups (those with strong leaders and questionable teaching) might be considered cult-like, they can't be strictly defined as cults. Cults are generally well organized and claim some sort of religious truth.

(4) What's the difference between "a cult" and "the occult"? (The correct answers are *b* and *d,* though *d* is rather simplistic.) Explain that occult activities generally seek power from mysterious forces, and may or may not be religious in nature. Cults generally have some sort of religious organization and belief structure.

(5) If someone says to you, "Only Reverend Elmer knows the true meaning of Scripture," what should you do? (The best answers probably are *b* and *c.*) Emphasize that arguing does little good with cult followers. They are usually prepared with their answers, and they will

probably confuse you. It would be better to avoid the confrontation entirely, compare the teachings with the Bible, or ask the opinion of one or more Christians you respect.

It's important to recognize that *d* is far from the right answer, though some cultists may accuse us of this approach. If we were saying, "Everyone who does not agree with our teaching is in a dangerous cult," we would be guilty of the same isolation we accuse the cults of. But we are not following just some private interpretation. We are promoting (a) the clear meaning of Scripture, when it is clear; and (b) the historical tradition of the Church that fits with the clear meaning of Scripture. And we are not quibbling with cults over "minor" details. The cults differ on the basic tenets of Christian faith: Jesus' identity, the Trinity, sin, salvation, human nature, etc.

(6) *What should you do if someone gives you a book that claims to be the "revealed truth of God"—but is not the Bible?* (The best answer probably is *a,* though it may be a bit strong.) Point out that we shouldn't waste our time with cult material. If someone *were* to read the book to check out its claims, he or she should keep comparing those claims to Scripture.

(7) *Why are people attracted to cults?* (The correct answers are *a, b,* and *c.*) Explain that cults can be simple and complex at the same time. Many of them offer intricate philosophies but package it all in some easy answers. If you trust them for the heavy stuff, their simple truths seem to make sense of everything. But watch out for any teaching that asks you to shut down your mind. Many cults also offer great love and acceptance. People who crave love and acceptance are the most vulnerable, so this is a good conversion tactic. Also, many people are constantly looking for something new. Some have rejected the churches of their youth and want something different. Cults give them a chance to rebel, an opportunity to play with some radically different teachings.

(8) *What is the most important question you should ask of any cult?* (The correct answer is *a.*) Point out that most cults veer from traditional Christian teaching on the matter of Jesus' identity. Is He both divine and human? How does He relate to us? What is His place in our lives? How does He achieve our salvation? These are the crucial questions. Questions about the founder of a cult may be interesting, but they don't necessarily prove anything. And some very respectable people might be drawn into cults, so asking what kind of people are drawn to the cult doesn't prove much either.

STEP 3

That Was Then...

(Needed: Copies of Repro Resource 2)

Have someone read aloud Colossians 2:8. Then ask: **How might this verse apply to the way we deal with cults?** (We should beware of their hollowness and deception.) Suggest that *hollow* is a great description, since cults often have great appearances, but little substance. This verse urges us to base our beliefs on Christ, rather than on other philosophies or principles.

Explain: **The Colossians had a cult problem. There were people teaching philosophies there that were very similar to some modern cults. Through the miracle of drama, let's take a closer look at their situation.**

Ask for two volunteers to perform a brief skit. Give each a copy of "Colossian Cult-Watch" (Repro Resource 2). (You can use males or females for the sketch—Moe and Joe could be Mo and Jo.) Let the actors read through the skit once; then have them perform it.

Afterward, ask: **What was the attraction of this cult group? How did Moe try to "sell" Joe on this group?** (Moe suggested that Joe might be dissatisfied with his present church. He puffed Joe up as being "special." He promised an experience of "fullness" beyond anything Joe could imagine. He promised a group who would offer understanding and support.)

Have someone read aloud Colossians 2:1-3. Then ask: **Who is writing this?** (Paul.)

What is his "purpose"? (He wants the Colossians to be encouraged, united, and to know Christ deeply.)

Say: **On the surface, this doesn't seem to have much to do with cults. But think about what Moe was saying in the skit we just saw. There were teachers in Colosse who were promising a fuller, more enlightened experience of God. They said that the mysteries of the divine were revealed only to a few. And so on. Not unlike many modern cults.**

With this background in mind, do you see any new significance to Paul's words? (He is praying that the Colossian Christians will find their fullness in Christ. He is telling them that the mysteries of the divine are all wrapped up in Jesus Christ.)

Have someone read aloud Colossians 2:4-7. Then ask: **Why is Paul writing this?** (So that the Colossians wouldn't be deceived by "fine-sounding arguments.")

[handwritten note: Important to develop our own sound maturity through prayer, study & fellowship →]

Why does he think they might be swayed by such arguments? (Probably because he isn't around to help them oppose those arguments. Paul was the one who introduced the Colossians to Christianity.)

According to these verses, how does Paul want the Colossians to live? (In Christ—rooted, growing, strengthened, and overflowing with thankfulness.)

How would this type of life keep a person from falling into a cult? (It's focusing on Christ, the true Lord. If Christ is satisfying our spiritual needs, we don't need to look elsewhere.)

Have someone read aloud Colossians 2:8-10. Then ask: **How does Paul describe "cult" philosophies?** (Hollow and deceptive, based on human tradition and worldly principles.)

How does he describe Christ? (The fullness of the Deity, who gives fullness to His people; the head over all powers and authorities.)

Explain that some cults of that time acknowledged Christ as *a* son of God, or as one angel among many, who brought enlightened humans along a pathway to God. Jesus was, in their view, maybe the first rung of the ladder. Paul addresses that here by saying that, if there is a "ladder" to God, Jesus is the ladder Himself. Jesus is ultimately in charge of all angels and spiritual forces.

Summarize: **It's interesting that Paul does not say a lot about arguing with these cultists. He keeps turning the spotlight on Christ. We don't need to out-argue people in cults— we just need to stay close to Christ. What we have in Christ is better than anything cults can promise.**

STEP 4

...This Is Now

(Needed: Copies of Repro Resource 3, pencils)

Ask: **Have any of you ever had an experience with cult groups? Have any of your friends ever been involved with cults? If so, what did you or your friends think of the experience?** Encourage volunteers to share. Even if no one in your group has had any personal experience with cults, point out that it's still important to know what cults are like—to be prepared in case you or someone you know is confronted by a "questionable" group.

Distribute copies of "A Guide to Recognizing Cults" (Repro Resource 3) and pencils. Give group members a few minutes to unscramble the words on the sheet. Then go through the sheet as a group.

Use the following information to supplement your discussion of the sheet. (The words in capital letters are the unscrambled words.)

What to Watch For

(1) A LEADER or GURU who claims to have unique authority

Explain: **We should beware of anyone who claims to have had a special revelation from God. We are not to worship other people. If someone is exalting himself or herself, that person is not showing the way to God.**

(2) Claims that truth can be found in a BOOK or some "SCRIP-TURE" that is not the Bible

Explain: **A number of cults claim to believe the Bible, but they add another book, perhaps written by their founder, which tells the "real" truth. This book might "explain" the Bible or somehow "update" it. But these extra "Scriptures" often disagree with the Bible.**

(3) The ISOLATION of its members from society

Explain: **A person who feels misunderstood or lonely is a prime candidate for cults. After all, think of how great it would be for that person to find a place where people understand and accept him or her. But cults often reinforce this idea, emphasizing that "the world out there" doesn't understand you, and that you need to stay within the group. Some cults even offer communal living, so you never have to leave the group. The problem is, this keeps you from getting an outside perspective on what the cult teaches.**

(4) Group members who are not allowed to QUESTION their leader or the group's teachings

Explain: **The approach of many cults is to convey to their members, "Just accept what we tell you." They encourage their members to have faith in the leader or in the group. Those who don't have faith are told they're not spiritual enough. They are not encouraged to think for themselves.**

(5) Differences from Christianity concerning key DOCTRINES like the NATURE of CHRIST, the TRINITY, HUMAN NATURE, and SALVATION

Explain: **This is, of course, the most serious point. But in some cases, it takes a long time to get to what the cults really believe. As one salesman said, they "sell the sizzle, not the steak." They "sell" you on the wisdom they seem to have, on the love they seem to have. But what do they teach? You're well inside before you can find out.**

Point out that several of the items mentioned can apply to some Christian churches too. Some churches have dominant pastors, who

OPTIONS

EXTRA ACTION

SMALL GROUP

LARGE GROUP

HEARD IT ALL BEFORE

LITTLE BIBLE BACKGROUND

FELLOWSHIP & WORSHIP

MOSTLY GIRLS

MOSTLY GUYS

EXTRA FUN

MEDIA

EXTRA CHALLENGE

write books that "explain" the Scriptures correctly; they isolate their flocks from "the world" and they discourage questions. This is all cult-like behavior, and it is dangerous. But a cult becomes a cult when it denies biblical teaching on major issues of the faith.

Ask: **Do all Christians agree about every issue in Christianity?** (No.)

What are some issues Christians disagree on? (Predestination, eternal security, the gifts of the Holy Spirit and the baptism of the Spirit, baptism, the meaning of the Lord's Supper, etc.)

Because Christian denominations have different ideas about these issues, does that make some denominations cults? (Not necessarily. These may be important issues, but they are areas in which the Bible leaves us some room for opinion.)

Point out that the four doctrines on the list are matters that the Bible speaks *strongly* about and the Christian church—even in its many forms—has found general agreement on.

• *The nature of Christ*—He is fully God *and* fully human. Cults usually emphasize only one part of His nature.

• *The Trinity (Father, Son, and Holy Spirit)*—The Bible presents one God manifested in three unique persons. It's hard to explain, but it's important. All three are fully divine, fully united with one another, one God, yet three distinct personalities. Cults often underemphasize Jesus' part in the Trinity.

• *Human nature*—The Bible teaches that human beings share a "sinful nature"—that is, we have a tendency to displease God. We need God to provide salvation for us—which He has done in Christ. Cults often emphasize the goodness of humanity or some sort of untapped God-like nature within us.

• *Salvation*—Christ died to save us from our sin, to pay our penalty, to bring us together with God. The Bible speaks of salvation in many different ways, but it is always Christ's activity on our behalf. Cults often present salvation as a "oneness" with the divine, but it's something that is achieved through our efforts or through the uncovering of our internal divine nature.

Say: **We need to respond to cults with our minds in action. Cult members may try to baffle us or get us to turn off our thinking, but we need to keep focusing on central questions.**

Questions to Consider

(1) What does this group believe about JESUS?

Explain: **Christ is the center of our faith. We must insist on a biblically accurate portrayal of our Lord.**

(2) Do the beliefs of this group agree with the BIBLE?

Explain: **The Bible is God's Word to us. If cult beliefs differ from Scripture's teachings, we should stay with the Bible.**

(3) Do these beliefs make any sense to other CHRISTIANS I know and respect?

Say: **Check things out with other believers. Cults try to isolate members, so that they talk only with other cult members. Be sure to avoid this type of "closed society."**

(4) Does this group encourage me to THINK for myself?

Say: **Christianity makes sense. Many cults don't. If you keep "loving God with . . . all your mind," you'll be all right.**

(5) Do these teachings try to STRENGTHEN me as an individual?

Explain: **Christianity is not just a self-help method, but it does help people to be "all they can be." Beware of cults that tear you down, that weaken your individuality. God loves us as unique individuals.**

In closing, read aloud Colossians 2:16-19. Say: **We talked before about the "cults" in Colosse. Paul warns here that they will make their beliefs sound great. They will get all "puffed up." But they've lost connection with the Head—that is, Christ.**

Read aloud Colossians 3:1. Then ask: **Where should our focus be?** (On Christ.)

Close the session in prayer, asking God for wisdom in dealing with the beliefs of others around us.

THE **CULT** TEST

Some of these questions have more than one "right" answer. Some are matters of opinion. Circle any and every letter that seems good to you.

1. What are some of the identifying features of a cult?
(a) It has a dominant leader.
(b) It follows "holy" writings in addition to the Bible.
(c) It isolates its members from society.
(d) Its members have the letter "C" tattooed on their foreheads.

2. Which of the following is true about Mormonism?
(a) It should be considered a cult because it has unbiblical teachings about Jesus.
(b) It should be considered a Christian denomination because its members believe the Bible.
(c) It should be accepted because its members are nice people.
(d) It has a great tabernacle choir.

3. Which of the following are cults that exist today?
(a) Mormonism, Jehovah's Witnesses, Christian Science
(b) Scientology, the Unification Church, Christadelphians
(c) Gnosticism, Donatism, Pelagianism
(d) Madonna wannabees, sports fans, youth groups

4. What's the difference between "a cult" and "the occult"?
(a) A few letters of the alphabet
(b) A cult is a group that strays from Christian teaching, while the occult is the pursuit of mysterious power, often from Satan.
(c) The differences are very minor, except that the occult is worse.
(d) Cults usually claim to worship God in some form, while the occult focuses on the devil.

5. If someone says to you, "Only Reverend Elmer knows the true meaning of Scripture," what should you do?
(a) Argue
(b) Run away
(c) Check his teachings out with the Bible and with Christians you know
(d) Insist that only *your* pastor knows the true meaning of Scripture

6. What should you do if someone gives you a book that claims to be the "revealed truth of God"—but is not the Bible?
(a) Get rid of the book without reading it
(b) Take the book, but punch the person who gives it to you
(c) Read the book to check out its claims
(d) Send it to Reverend Elmer

7. Why are people attracted to cults?
(a) Cults offer easy answers to modern problems.
(b) Cults provide an atmosphere of love and acceptance.
(c) People are tired of traditional religion.
(d) Many cults often give you a free mug with your first visit.

8. What is the most important question you should you ask of any cult?
(a) "What do you believe about Jesus?"
(b) "Who started this group and what is their history?"
(c) "What kind of people follow this teaching?"
(d) "Where's my free mug?"

Colossian Cult-Watch

MOE: Hey, Joe! What's up?

JOE: Not much, Moe. Good to see you.

MOE: Hey, are you still going to that Christian church in Colosse?

JOE: I sure am.

MOE: Has that apostle—Paul—been around lately?

JOE: Not for a while. But I hear he's planning another mission trip. Can't wait to see him. Still, our leaders do a good job.

MOE: But do you ever get the feeling that you just don't belong there?

JOE: What do you mean?

MOE: Well, is there ever a time when you see things that others don't? Maybe the preacher is talking about the Scriptures, and you have an insight that he's totally missing?

JOE: Well, yes. Now that you mention it…

MOE: I thought so. Joe, I think you're special.

JOE: Well, thank you. You're pretty swell too.

MOE: No, I mean you are one of the enlightened.

JOE: Oh, I don't know about that.

MOE: I mean it! God reveals special things to special people. You and I are among those special people. Have you seen… (looks around) angels?

JOE: (Looks around) No.

MOE: Don't worry. You will. You do believe in angels, don't you?

JOE: Yes, of course, but—

MOE: I knew it. They're all around. And they want to lift you to a higher knowledge of God. Look for the angels, Joe. You will feel all the fullness of God. It's a great experience.

JOE: You've had this experience?

MOE: Yes! And it's great. It's everything that I was missing at the church I was going to. I have such enlightenment now. I understand things now that were so murky before. You can have this understanding too.

JOE: How?

MOE: I'm glad you asked. We have a group that meets each month at the new moon. We meditate and discuss philosophy—that sort of thing. It's so comforting to meet with others who really understand you. I really feel at home there. You have to come.

JOE: I'll let you know.

MOE: Just remember, Joe, you're special. You're enlightened. We would understand you.

A Guide to
RECOGNIZING CULTS

Unscramble the following words to discover some principles for spotting and guarding yourself against cults.

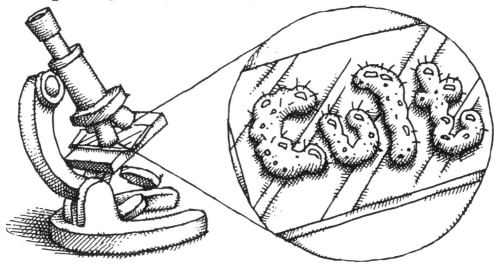

WHAT TO WATCH FOR

1. A **dealer** or **ruug** who claims to have unique authority

2. Claims that truth can be found in a **okob** or some **"ripercuts"** that is not the Bible

3. The **soiltanio** of its members from society

4. Group members who are not allowed to **stenqiou** their leader or the group's teachings

5. Differences from Christianity concerning key **codsniter** like the **retaun** of **cshirt**, the **nittyri**, **nuham treanu**, and **voalsatin**

QUESTIONS TO CONSIDER

1. What does this group believe about **essuj**?

2. Do the beliefs of this group agree with the **lebbi**?

3. Do these beliefs make any sense to other **snitshirac** I know and respect?

4. Does this group encourage me to **kihnt** for myself?

5. Do these teachings try to **eeghnnrstt** me as an individual?

NOTES

EXTRA ACTION

STEP 1

Replace the marketing plan with "Fingertip Twister." Give kids washable markers. Each person should number his or her fingernails from 1 to 10, writing the appropriate numeral on each nail (starting with a 1 on the left pinkie and ending with a 10 on the right pinkie). Form pairs. Partners sit facing each other. Call out two numbers from 1 to 10; partners must touch those fingertips together and hold them there. (Example: If you call out **Two and five,** Person A touches fingertip 2 to Person B's fingertip 5.) Then call out a different pair of numbers between 1 and 10; without separating the first pair of fingertips, partners must press the second pair together according to the numbers you called. Then repeat the process. Anyone who can hold three pairs of fingertips together stays in the game; the rest are out. Play as many rounds as you have time for. Then note that just as this game twisted fingers, cults usually twist the meaning of Scripture.

STEP 4

Wear grubbies. Bring at least ten "pies" (paper plates with a blob of whipped cream or shaving cream on each). After each guideline is unscrambled, make a statement that kids must decide is either cult-like or not. (Example: After the first guideline, you might say, **God has sent me to correct some of the things you heard in Sunday school when you were growing up** [a cult-like statement]. After the third guideline, you might say, **Let's get together with another church's youth group next month** [not a cult-like statement].) If it's the kind of thing a cult leader might say, the first kid up to the front gets to pelt you in the face with a "pie." Anyone unjustly pelting you gets a pie in return.

SMALL GROUP

STEP 1

The marketing project may take too long for a group that's too small to divide up tasks. Instead, start the meeting by asking kids to move their chairs as close together as they can. Put any empty chairs away, saying that you're glad no one else is at the meeting. Ham it up as you rant and rave about the "evils" of large youth groups (they can't fit in one car, they eat too much, they make too much noise when they turn the pages of their Bibles, etc.). Declare that your group is the only one in your town that's true to the Lord. Encourage kids to help you brainstorm five ways to keep others *out* of your group. Then drop the act and explain that what you've just done is typical of many cults; they claim that only their tiny group is right and the whole rest of the world is wrong.

STEP 4

Lecturing to a small group can be awkward, and the explanations you're supposed to deliver after each of the "What to Watch For" and "Questions to Consider" guidelines may feel like lecturing. Try a different approach. Before the meeting, photocopy Step 4. Cut out the aforementioned boldface explanations and put them in an envelope. At this time in the session, give one or more of these slips to each person. After you read each unscrambled guideline aloud, pause to let kids guess which explanation goes with the guideline you just read. Whoever reads the correct explanation gets a point; anyone reading the wrong explanation—or failing to read the right one—loses a point. The person with the most points at the end of the step wins a prize.

LARGE GROUP

STEP 1

Completing and sharing results of the marketing project might take too long in a large group. Try this instead. As kids enter, whisper to each one a color that he or she is supposedly allergic to—and a symptom of that allergy (sneezing, coughing, scratching, moaning, etc.). Let kids mill around the room. Each person should act out his or her symptom when within a few feet of someone who's wearing the "problem" color, then move on and repeat the process. After a few minutes of milling around, have kids try to guess what color each person's allergic to. Tie this into the fact that many cults don't want to show their "true colors" by revealing to outsiders and newcomers the strange doctrines they actually believe.

STEP 4

You may need to make this step more personally involving to avoid losing the attention of a large group. Have teams work together on the unscrambling activity. Add this rule: The first team to unscramble a guideline gets a small prize—if it tells the rest of the group (1) a concrete example of the cult behavior described in the guideline, or (2) one real-life action a person could take to follow the guideline.

STEP 3

Kids may see no need to listen, feeling invulnerable to cults. Before the Bible study, give kids this test. Have them number index cards from 1 to 9 and answer yes or no to these statements: **(1) I am considered bright in most things. (2) I am curious about the world around me. (3) I have been a leader among my friends at school. (4) I have been a member of a group and consider myself a follower. (5) I have times when I doubt myself and my abilities. (6) I am afraid of the future sometimes. (7) I am considered idealistic by people who know me. (8) I enjoy being liked and receiving compliments. (9) I sometimes like taking risks.** Note that Judy Israel, a contributor to the book *Cults and Consequences* (Jewish Federation Council of Los Angeles) created this test. She believes that if you say yes to even three of these, you're a prime candidate for a cult. Whether or not she's right, cults contain all kinds of people—including those who thought they'd never join a cult.

STEP 4

Kids may think these warnings about cults are exaggerated. After all, what's so bad about a little error? To illustrate, set two glasses of water on a table. Into the first one dump several spoonfuls of dirt, a piece of used chewing gum, and any dandruff or belly button lint kids will volunteer. Ask whether anyone wants to drink the water. When you get no takers, put just a pinch of dirt into the other glass. Offer it to the group. When kids don't want it either, act puzzled and offended. After all, it's only a *little* dirt. As needed, tie this into the fact that even a few lies in a "cup" of truth make it unfit for human consumption.

STEP 3

As needed, explain the following terms from Colossians 2:1-10. *The mystery of God*—Some false religions in Paul's day talked a lot about mysteries, meaning "secret" information only they knew. Paul uses mystery to mean "purpose" here; God has revealed His purposes through Christ. *Present with you in spirit*—This doesn't mean some out-of-body experience, but refers to Paul's interest in the Colossians. *Rooted and built up in him*—Basing your life on your relationship with Christ, growing closer to Him and more like Him. *Fullness of the Deity*—Christ is really God, not just godly or godlike or good. *Fullness in Christ*—Having everything you need for eternal life, contrary to the Gnostic [NAHS-tick] cult, which claimed knowledge was the path to salvation and taught that Christians weren't complete because they didn't have the Gnostics' special knowledge.

STEP 4

Be sure to include the basic session plan's explanation of the four key doctrines (the nature of Christ, the Trinity, etc.) rather than just naming the doctrines. If you read Colossians 2:16-19 in closing, you may need to explain that Paul is listing issues that cults of his day were making a big deal of—foods, special days, worshiping angels. He's assuring the Colossians that Christ is the one who matters, and if they have Him they have everything.

STEP 1

Form groups of two to four kids each. Each person should give his or her group an answer to the following questions: **What's your idea of the perfect youth group? If you started such a group, how would you get kids to join? How would you keep kids from changing it into something you didn't like?** Then bring the whole group together. Point out that many cults start as efforts to "perfect" the church. Many end up deceiving people into joining, then demand unquestioning loyalty to keep the group the way the leader wants it. Ask: **What would be the difference, if any, between your "perfect" youth group and a cult?**

STEP 4

Wrap up the meeting with worship. Point out the importance of the Bible in figuring out what's true and what isn't—which groups are cults and which aren't. On poster board, make two columns—one headed "Songs about Scripture" and the other headed "Scripture Songs." See how many songs kids can name in each category in a total of two minutes. Then spend some time singing songs about God's Word ("The B-I-B-L-E," "Wonderful Words of Life," etc.) and from it ("Therefore the Redeemed of the Lord Shall Return," "Surely Goodness and Mercy," etc.). Ask a few volunteers to close in prayer, thanking God for His book.

STEP 2

Liven up the discussion of the answers for "The Cult Test" (Repro Resource 1). Have each group member make four large letter cards, using 9" × 12" pieces of construction paper. The letters A, B, C, and D should be drawn on separate pieces of paper. Just before you discuss each question and its answer, each group member should hold up the appropriate letter card(s) to show how she responded to that question. After group members have responded, have all the "A" card holders move to one area of the room; have the "B" card holders move to another area; etc. (You might have those with multiple answers move to a fifth area of the room.) Have the members in each group decide why they answered as they did; then give them a few minutes to explain their position.

STEP 4

After discussing "A Guide to Recognizing Cults" (Repro Resource 3), focus on four of the key doctrines of Christianity. Have group members form four teams. Assign each team one of the following subjects: the nature of Christ, the Trinity, sin and human nature, and salvation. Ask each team to decide on a way to present its subject as if it were a completely new and unknown topic. The teams may use a skit, a debate, question and answer, or some other method.

STEP 1

Guys may appreciate a more down-to-earth, less cerebral project. Form teams. Assign each team a different geometric shape (square, triangle, octagon, etc.). Pass out paper and markers. Each team must design a new automobile tire that's made in the shape it was assigned. Each team will try to convince the others that its design is an improvement on the old-fashioned round tire. After giving teams a few minutes to come up with their presentations, have them share the results. Award a prize for the most convincing (or least convincing) argument if you like. Then point out that many cults try to do the same thing: convince people that they've improved on Christianity.

STEP 4

After going over the Repro Resource, make the ideas more concrete by using an analogy many guys can relate to. Ask:
How is being on a school football or basketball team like—and unlike—being in a cult? How is a coach like—and unlike—a cult leader? What attitude are players urged to have toward "outsiders"? Why is being in a cult dangerous when being on a team usually isn't?

STEP 1

Before the session, use a VCR to video-tape a TV commercial or 30-second portion of a sitcom scene. Start the meeting by playing the tape for the group. Announce that you're going to have a lip-syncing contest—not to music, but to the commercial or scene. Form teams (the size of each team depends on the number of actors required). Play the ad or scene several times, giving teams a chance to practice. Then let each team perform for the group, lip-syncing the dialogue and mimicking the TV actors' expressions and movements. Give a prize for the best imitation if you like. Note that most cults have their own form of "lip-syncing" in which all members must use the same terms and take the same positions as the cult leaders.

STEP 4

Form teams. Give each team a deflated balloon, a trash bag, and an apple (or any other three items of your choice). Say:
Your team is stranded on a desert island that's surrounded by sharks. Using only the three items you've been given, you must make it across shark-infested waters to another island 50 yards away, where an empty boat has washed ashore. You have two minutes to figure it out. After two minutes, see whether anyone came up with a solution. (If there is one, we don't know what it is—unless the three items you chose were a rubber raft, an oar, and a harpoon.) Discuss how it felt to be trapped. Then make the point: Cult members are often warned that people "out there" are dangerous, and the only way to be safe is to stay on the cult's "island." After hearing that time after time, it's hard to leave—even if the "sharks" out there are as imaginary as ours were.

STEP 1

Rent one of the following movies on video. Each contains a subplot about a cult of children that's awaiting a sort of messiah. After previewing for appropriateness, show the segment in which the film's hero discovers the cult, learns how it began, and what it wants from him.

• *Hook.* The Lost Boys have been waiting for Peter Pan (Robin Williams) to return and lead them in a fight against Captain Hook. In the meantime, one of the older boys has been ruling the group through intimidation.

• *Mad Max Beyond Thunderdome.* Most of the movie concerns the cruel, post-nuclear-war society of Bartertown. But further in the desert a ragtag bunch of kids is waiting in vain for a pilot to rescue them and take them home. A cult with myths and rituals has grown up around the messiah-pilot.

After watching, ask: **How did this "cult" begin? What do its members believe? How does its leadership keep the group in line? Is the cult like any real-life groups you've heard of? If so, how?**

STEP 4

Play a recording of George Harrison's old song, "My Sweet Lord." Ask: **What "Lord" is the singer referring to? What did you think the song was about in the beginning? At the end?** Note that discovering the beliefs of some cults is like listening to this song; in the beginning you hear a lot that makes you think it's about Jesus, but as you go along you hear more and more about other beliefs and "lords."

STEP 1

Save time by combining Steps 1 and 2 in a new opener. As kids enter, have them line up outside the door of your meeting place. Announce that they can't enter unless they correctly answer a question from your "cult quiz." Ask each person one of the questions from Repro Resource 1 (if you have more than eight kids, just start over after using the eight questions). No matter how kids answer, say, "That's right!" Praise each person for his or her great knowledge and insight. When everybody's inside, go over the real answers. Explain that some cults gain members by flattering them as you did—for having special knowledge or abilities.

STEP 3

Skip the skit. In Step 4, either skip the unscrambling and just talk through the Repro Resource guidelines, or simply hand out the sheet and let kids unscramble and read it on their own later.

STEP 1

In conjunction with the opening activity, discuss some of the dangerous or harmful products (like cigarettes or malt liquor) that target inner-city residents as their primary consumers. Ask your group members to name some billboards or advertisements they've seen in their neighborhoods promoting these products. Lead into a discussion of another dangerous "product" being peddled in the inner city: cults.

STEP 2

The city is a cauldron of cultic influences (which are usually promoted as Christian). Familiarize your young people with the following steps in responding to religious groups that may or may not be cults. Read aloud Galatians 1:6-10. Then give the following instructions:

1. Never accept membership into a religious group immediately, even if you're pressured to do so. Tell the "recruiter" you'll get back to him or her if and when you make a decision.

2. Gather as much information about the group as possible. Get brochures, pamphlets, tracts, and the address and phone number of the group's headquarters if possible.

3. Ask the following questions and pay close attention to the responses.

(a) Is the Christian Bible all that is needed to understand God?

(b) Is the Trinity real? Explain.

(c) Describe the purpose and nature of Jesus Christ.

(d) What happens when a person dies?

(e) Have there been any great prophets since Jesus' time?

4. Take the information you've gathered to a trusted adult—perhaps a parent, a pastor, or a youth worker. Have him or her determine if the group is a cult or not, and give you advice as to how to respond.

STEP 1

Replace the complex project with this opener. Bring the following, each sealed in its own opaque bag: a lump of Play-Doh; a cotton ball soaked with rubbing alcohol; an open container of cocoa mix. Pass around the bags, one at a time. Each person should open each bag, take a whiff, and say in one or two words what experience or place the smell reminds him or her of (not what the substance is). Chances are that most kids will associate the Play-Doh smell with childhood or making things; rubbing alcohol may make them think of a doctor's office; cocoa may bring back memories of winter or family. Ask: **How long did you have to think before you connected the smell with something?** (Kids probably didn't have to think at all.) Explain that automatic, unthinking reponses may be fine when it comes to smells—but not when it comes to accepting what we're taught. Many cult leaders want their members to follow commands without thinking or questioning.

STEP 3

Instead of using the skit on the Repro Resource, have teams try to outdo each other in "welcoming" a new person (played by you or a volunteer) to the group. Explain that cults often go out of their way to seem friendly and loving. Use the "Short Meeting Time" option for the Bible study. In Step 4, try to give a concrete example of each point. For instance, an example for #1 might be a leader who claims to know the year when Jesus will return; for #5 it might be a claim that people are saved by giving their money to the cult.

STEP 2

At the end of the step, read the following quote from Tom Wolfe: **"A cult is a religion with no political power."** Discuss this, using questions like these: **What does this quote mean?** (That the only difference between cults and religions is that cults don't have the power to keep people from calling them cults. Cults are just as good [or bad] as religions.) **Do you agree or not? Why?** Note that Christianity was thought of as a cult when it began. **Why is Christianity not called a cult anymore? Should we avoid calling other beliefs cults, since our faith was once seen as a cult? Should we just accept all beliefs as equal? Why or why not?**

STEP 4

Pass out a few phone books from your city or the nearest metropolitan area. Have kids look in the yellow pages under "Churches" to locate the nearest gatherings of Latter-Day Saints (Mormons), Jehovah's Witnesses, Christian Science adherents, Scientologists, Spiritualists, Theosophists, Eckankar followers, or similar groups. Pray for the people who go to these groups—with genuine concern that they'll come to know Jesus.

DATE USED:

Approx. Time

STEP 1: *Selling Out* _____
- ❏ Extra Action
- ❏ Small Group
- ❏ Large Group
- ❏ Fellowship & Worship
- ❏ Mostly Guys
- ❏ Extra Fun
- ❏ Media
- ❏ Short Meeting Time
- ❏ Urban
- ❏ Combined Junior High/High School

Things needed:

STEP 2: *Test Case* _____
- ❏ Mostly Girls
- ❏ Urban
- ❏ Extra Challenge

Things needed:

STEP 3: *That Was Then...* _____
- ❏ Heard It All Before
- ❏ Little Bible Background
- ❏ Short Meeting Time
- ❏ Combined Junior High/High School

Things needed:

STEP 4: *...This Is Now* _____
- ❏ Extra Action
- ❏ Small Group
- ❏ Large Group
- ❏ Heard It All Before
- ❏ Little Bible Background
- ❏ Fellowship & Worship
- ❏ Mostly Girls
- ❏ Mostly Guys
- ❏ Extra Fun
- ❏ Media
- ❏ Extra Challenge

Things needed:

Mormons and Jehovah's Witnesses

YOUR GOALS FOR THIS SESSION:
Choose one or more

☐ To help kids recognize how the teachings of Mormons and Jehovah's Witnesses differ from Christian teachings.

☐ To help kids understand some of the distinctive characteristics of these two cults.

☐ To help kids equip themselves to uphold the truth of Christianity in any conversations with members of these groups.

☐ Other:_____
_____

Your Bible Base:

Galatians 1:6-9

Simon Says Tag

Introduce your opening activity as "Simon Says"—with a twist. One person (of your choosing) will stand in front of the group and say, "Simon says, _____" ('bark like a dog,' 'take a bow,' etc.). The rest of the group members then have to do what the person says. If the person does not say "Simon says" before a command, group members should not follow the command. You may want to run through the basic game for a minute, before introducing the variation.

The variation is that you will "tag" a person to be the next leader. But, in giving commands, that person will have to use the name of the previous leader, plus "Simon." So let's say Arnold is your first leader. He says, "Simon says, 'Bark like a dog.'" Then you tag Betty to be next. She must say, "Arnold says Simon says, 'Pat your head.'" Then you tag Charles. He must say, "Betty says Arnold says Simon says, 'Jump up and down.'"

Again, though, if the person does not say "Simon says" directly before the command, group members should not obey it. Those who do are out. Likewise, if a leader forgets to mention a previous leader in his or her command, he or she is out.

Play two or three rounds of the game, depending on how well your group members do.

The Cult Connection

(Needed: Copies of Repro Resource 4)

Explain: **Cults sometimes start out like this "Simon Says" game. Some leader stands up and says, "The Bible says, 'Do this!'" But before long, people are saying, "The leader says the Bible says, 'Do this!'" And then it's "The leader's son says the leader says the Bible says, 'Do this!'" And so on. Then it** gets pretty easy to forget what the Bible says and to focus on the leader's teachings, all the while thinking the Bible really says those things.

Today we're going to focus on two groups that claim to believe the Bible. But both groups translate the Bible according to their own teachings, which they got from their founders. As a result, the clear meaning of Scripture has been twisted.

Hand out copies of "Cults Galore" (Repro Resource 4). This sheet will serve as a general introduction to some of the cults in our society today. Give group members a chance to look it over.

Then ask: **How would you define a "cult"?** (A religious group that differs from established religion in key areas.)

Ask several group members to share their ideas about what a cult is like. What do the members look like? How do they act? What kinds of things do they do? Their comments should be interesting. Some may have images of cults as being exclusively satanic. Others may think of cult members as long-haired, plant-eating holdovers from hippie days. Point out that the primary issue that makes a group a cult is what it believes, not how its members look. Most are quite normal people.

Refer to the list on Repro Resource 4. Ask: **Do you think it's an insult to call one of these groups a "cult"? Do you think the members of any of these groups would be offended?** Emphasize that you're not saying that "cult members" are bad people. You're merely saying that their beliefs are different from what the Bible teaches. If your group members have, say, Mormon friends who would be offended at being called "cult members," then your group members shouldn't use the term. The word cult is not as important as the realization of what those groups teach.

Go through the resource sheet quickly. There are numerous variations that have some roots that split off from historic Christianity, and may claim to be Christian, but go dangerously astray. There are also numerous Eastern cults, some of which have been specially packaged for American audiences. The "secular self-help" cults try to deny their "religious" nature, presenting themselves as scientific methods for unleashing the power within people. But that is still a religious pursuit.

The "culture/earth cults" combine a number of similar movements. These are attempts to find ultimate meaning in one's racial heritage or in the earth itself. "Occult groups" deal with satanic power, whether knowingly or not. "Channeling" and some other elements of what has become known as the New Age movement are viewed as possibly demonic. Aspects of the New Age movement actually fit within several categories.

[NOTE: Although Islam, Judaism, Buddhism, and Hinduism obviously differ from Christianity, they are "established religions" in their own right, and therefore not called cults. Mormons, Jehovah's Witnesses, and Christian Science may be rather "established" as well, but they have their

own versions of the Christian Bible and its doctrines, differing with historic Christianity on essential issues. Thus, we are calling them "cults."]

You will be addressing most of the cults listed in future sessions, so you don't need to get into deep discussions about them now.

Say something like: **Let's focus now on two of the "established" cults on this list.**

True or False

(Needed: Chalkboard and chalk or newsprint and marker)

Explain that you'll be giving a true-false test to see how much your group members know about Mormons and Jehovah's Witnesses. After you read each statement, have group members vote (by raising their hands) as to whether they think it's true or false. Insist that all group members vote on each statement, even if they're just guessing. Write the results for each statement on the board. Then reveal the answers.

1. Mormons and Jehovah's Witnesses believe that the Bible is true. (True, but with one major provision—"as long as it is translated properly.")

2. Mormons believe that God used to be a man. (True. They believe that humans progress toward godhood, and that we are now what God once was.)

3. Both Mormonism and Jehovah's Witnesses were started by teenagers. (True, sort of. Joseph Smith's first vision occurred when he was 14, though the church was not launched until he was 24. Charles Taze Russell began teaching his Bible classes at the age of 18, though his magazines were not published for another nine years.)

4. Mormons allow men to marry several wives. (False. At one time they did, but they stopped the practice in 1890.)

5. Mormons do not allow African Americans to be priests. (False. In 1978, they lifted their ban on African Americans becoming priests.)

6. Jehovah's Witnesses believe that Jesus is the Son of God. (True. But they don't believe He is God. He is viewed as a secondary being.)

7. Jehovah's Witnesses believe that Jesus is the angel Michael. (True. They believe Jesus appeared as Michael in Old Testament times.)

8. Both Mormons and Jehovah's Witnesses uphold high standards of holy living. (True. Often, that's what makes them seem so appealing and "harmless." Yet their teachings defy Christian truth.)

9. Mormons believe that the Garden of Eden was in Missouri. (True.)

10. Jehovah's Witnesses believe that only 144,000 people will share in God's kingdom. (True. But they believe that others may live forever in an earthly kingdom.)

Try not to get involved in a detailed discussion of these statements now. You'll be looking at the specific beliefs of these cults in the next section.

STEP 4

Fact-finding

(Needed: Copies of Repro Resource 5, copies of Repro Resource 6, pencils)

Have group members form teams of three or four. Distribute copies of "Fact Sheet: Mormons" (Repro Resource 5) and pencils to each team. Instruct the teams to read the information on the sheet. Then have them go through and circle any ideas or beliefs that seem unbiblical (or perhaps just questionable) to them.

Give the teams a few minutes to work. When they're finished, have volunteers share their responses. Use the following information to supplement the teams' responses.

Among the traditional, biblical Christian beliefs disputed by Mormonism are

- the sovereignty of God (by claiming that He was once human, like us);
- the nature of God's presence (by claiming that He has a physical body);
- the nature of Jesus (by claiming that He attained godhood through His actions);
- the authority of Scripture (by claiming that other writings have equal or greater authority);
- the creaturehood and sinful nature of humans (by claiming that we can become gods);
- the nature of salvation (by claiming that Christ has guaranteed eternal life to all beings—as opposed to only those who put their trust in Him).

OPTIONS

EXTRA ACTION

LITTLE BIBLE BACKGROUND

MOSTLY GUYS

SHORT MEETING TIME

JR. HIGH / HIGH SCHOOL COMBINED

Ask volunteers to explain which beliefs of Mormonism surprised them most and why.

Then ask: **Why might people be drawn to Mormonism?** (The idea of eventually becoming a god may appeal to some people. The fact that many Mormons are clean-cut, self-assured, and attractive may appeal to some.)

Point out that this is, of course, a quick rundown of a complex religion. Mormons might complain that we're not being fair to them. Yet these are the basic facts, the basic differences between Christianity and Mormonism.

Have group members reassemble into different teams of three or four. Distribute copies of "Fact Sheet: Jehovah's Witnesses" (Repro Resource 6) to each team. As before, the teams should read through the information on the sheet and circle any ideas or beliefs that seem unbiblical or questionable.

Give the teams a few minutes to work. When they're finished, have volunteers share their responses. Use the following information to supplement the teams' responses.

Among the traditional, biblical Christian beliefs disputed by Jehovah's Witnesses are

- the complete trustworthiness of Scripture (by claiming that Russell's interpretation of Scripture was the correct interpretation);
- the eternal nature of Christ (by claiming that God created Jesus);
- the Trinity (by claiming that Jesus is "second-greatest" to God);
- the deity of Christ (by claiming that He was an archangel);
- the bodily resurrection of Christ (by claiming that He was resurrected in a "spiritual" sense);
- the eternal nature of human souls (by claiming that our souls are inseparably linked to our bodies);
- salvation by grace (by claiming that they must "prove" their faithfulness by witnessing).

Ask volunteers to explain which beliefs of Jehovah's Witnesses surprised them most and why.

Then ask: **Why might people be drawn to Jehovah's Witnesses?** (Some may be fooled into thinking that Jehovah's Witnesses are just another Christian denomination, like Baptists or Methodists. As with Mormons, the fact that many Jehovah's Witnesses are clean-cut, self-assured, and attractive may appeal to some.)

Again emphasize that this is just a quick overview of a complex religion. But it's enough to show the differences between Jehovah's Witnesses and traditional Christianity.

Encourage group members to keep these resource sheets in their Bibles for future reference.

STEP 5

What Do You Say?

Explain: **Both Mormons and Jehovah's Witnesses have aggressive missionary programs. Chances are, at some time in your life, you will be confronted by someone from one of these faiths, trying to get you to convert.**

Choose someone you can put on the spot. Ask that person: **What would you say if someone who goes to a Mormon church came up to you and said, "Hi, I'm from a great church and I'd like to share some things that can change your life"?** The person may respond with anything from "Get lost!" to "How will it change my life?" Pursue the question with other group members.

Then ask the following questions one at a time, giving several group members an opportunity to respond to each question.

How can we show Christian love toward these people, yet avoid their persuasive tactics?

Do you think it's a good idea for us to try to share our faith with them?

What if a Mormon said to you, "Our religions are really very much alike. We believe the Bible too. We just have some additional beliefs that make a lot of sense for today"? What would you say?

What if a pair of Jehovah's Witnesses were at your door saying, "Have you thought much about the end of the world? Are you ready to stand before Jehovah?" What would you say?

What would you say if a Jehovah's Witness started quoting Scripture to you—from his Bible?

Pay attention to your group members' responses. When appropriate, supplement their answer with the following principles:

- Show love at all times. Try not to be rude. Don't make fun of the person's beliefs. As much as possible, show genuine concern for the person behind those words.

- It's OK to avoid the conversation. Mormons and Jehovah's Witnesses have prepared for confrontation with people of other beliefs; you probably haven't. They may thoroughly confuse you—especially if you're not well-grounded in the Bible or if you're a new Christian. It's fine to say, "Sorry, I'd rather not talk about this right now."

- If you are in a conversation, stay with what you know—what Jesus Christ has done in your life. No one can deny the reality of what you've experienced. It's your strongest argument.
- Do not accept other versions of the Bible. Check every verse cited by Mormons or Jehovah's Witnesses in your own Bible. They may talk about the "original Greek meaning" of this or that—but don't buy it! Virtually all modern English translations are based on the Greek and Hebrew originals. Obviously there are differences in wording among the New International Version, New American Standard Bible, New King James Version, Revised Standard Version, and other translations of the Bible—but they all agree on the substance of basic doctrines. If all of these translations—written at different times and with different strategies—can agree that "The Word was God" in John 1:1, how can Jehovah's Witnesses say that the New World translation ("The Word was a god") is the only proper translation?
- Get the whole context of any Scriptures quoted. Don't let Jehovah's Witnesses "cut and paste" phrases, verses, and words to come up with a blueprint for survival in the end times. God doesn't communicate in code. He has given us a Bible full of truth that's pretty easy to follow. Get the big picture.
- Rely on the Holy Spirit. He promises to give us words to say when we need them.

As you wrap up the session, read aloud Galatians 1:6-9. Affirm that we have the Gospel. It has been proven true in our lives. Not even an angel from heaven should convince us otherwise.

Close the session in prayer, asking God for strength and wisdom for your group members in dealing with Mormons and Jehovah's Witnesses.

CULTS GALORE

"Established" Variations That Split off from Christianity
- Mormons (The Church of the Latter-Day Saints)
- Jehovah's Witnesses (Watchtower)
- Christian Science

Other Variations That Split off from Christianity
- Children of God
- The Way International
- Unity

Eastern Variations
- Unification Church ("Moonies")
- Transcendental Meditation (TM)
- Hare Krishna (Krishna Consciousness, ISKCON)
- New Age

Secular Self-Help Cults
- Scientology
- est
- New Age

Culture/Earth Cults
- Black Muslims (Nation of Islam)
- Native American religions
- African religions
- Wicca
- Neo-paganism
- New Age

Occult groups
- Satanism
- Demon contact (seances, channeling, etc.)
- New Age

FACT SHEET:
MORMONS

In 1820, fourteen-year-old Joseph Smith had a vision of a "resurrected being" named Moroni, who revealed that the religions of that time all were on the wrong track. Throughout the next decade, Smith had several more visions, in which he claimed to receive some gold plates engraved in an ancient Egyptian language. He translated these plates into *The Book of Mormon.*

In 1830, the "church" was officially started in New York with six members. It grew and moved west ward, settling in Missouri for a time, then migrating to Utah.

Among the key doctrines in the Mormon reli gion is the belief that God has a physical body. In fact, Mormons believe that God was once human like us, but advanced to His state of God-ness.

Mormons believe that Jesus is the Son of God, born in the same way that angels or humans are born. Mormons also believe that Jesus died on the cross and was resur-rected. In fact, they believe that Jesus attained His Godhood because of His obedience in dying.

According to Mormons, the Bible is true, as long as it's translated correctly. However, Mormon writings, including *The Book of Mormon, Doctrine and Covenants,* and *The Pearl of Great Price* have greater authority than the Bible.

Mormons believe that humans can attain Godhood through obedience. In fact, they believe that Old Testament heroes like Abraham, Isaac, and Jacob have already become gods.

Another key doctrine of Mormonism is that Christ has guaranteed eternal life to *all* beings. Those who are obedient and have been baptized will spend eternity working toward Godhood in the heavenly kingdom of God. Others will spend eternity in an earthly kingdom, where they will have the presence of the Son, but not the Father.

The Mormon Church (also known as The Church of Jesus Christ of Latter-Day Saints) places great emphasis on marriage and children. According to the church, one of the most important commands of Scripture is to "multiply and fill the earth." Thus, Mormons originally encouraged men to have several wives. However, this practice was prohibited in 1890.

The Book of Mormon describes how some Israelites migrated to America around 2250 B.C. (and another group migrated around 600 B.C.). Moroni was supposedly the resurrected spirit of one of these immigrants. Mormon writings have placed the Garden of Eden in Jackson County, Missouri. Mormons also claim that blacks are descendants of the terrible sinners Cain and Ham. Therefore, Mormon writings barred blacks from the priesthood—until 1978, when that policy was overturned.

FACT SHEET:
JEHOVAH'S WITNESSES

In 1870, eighteen-year-old Charles Taze Russell began a Bible study. As he studied, he began to develop his own system of Bible interpretation. In the process, he discarded a lot of traditional Christian doctrine. In 1879, he began publishing *Zion's Watchtower* to publicize his Bible interpretations. In 1884, the Watchtower Society was officially incorporated. The Watchtower Society changed its name to Jehovah's Witnesses in 1931.

Jehovah's Witnesses believe that Jehovah God is sovereign over all. He created everything, including Jesus. Jesus, then, is the second greatest person in the universe. He is not God, but could be considered "a god." He is the Son of God, a secondary, created being. In the Old Testament, He was known as the archangel Michael. Born fully human, He submitted to God at His baptism and was anointed as the Messiah. He died on a stake, not a cross, to ransom humanity, and He was resurrected in a spiritual sense.

Jehovah's Witnesses believe that the Bible is true *as translated by the Jehovah's Witnesses.* Their writings (including the New World translation of the Bible) regularly alter Bible verses to fit their theories. For example, John 1:1 says, "The Word was God" in our Bibles; but the New World translation says, "The Word was a god."

According to Jehovah's Witnesses, our souls are inseparably linked to our bodies. So when we die, we stop being. They believe that there will be 144,000 faithful people who will share in God's heavenly glory. They will reign with Christ in immortal spirit-bodies. Other faithful ones will be raised in their physical bodies to live forever on earth at the end times.

Jehovah's Witnesses prove their faithfulness by "witnessing" to Jehovah's sovereignty. They do this by living pure lives and spreading the word of Jehovah (often door to door).

Jehovah's Witnesses are fascinated by the end times. They believe these end times began in 1914 and that we are hurtling toward a massive, final battle of Armageddon.

EXTRA ACTION

STEP 2

Instead of handing out the Repro Resource, have a "Cult Fair." Before the session, make (or get volunteers to help you make) poster board signs bearing the names of the groups from the Repro Resource. Post the signs around the room. As kids enter, give each person a pen and some cotton candy or popcorn. Kids should wander around and look at the signs, each person writing three words on each sign to show what he or she knows about that group. If a person knows nothing about a group, he or she should put a question mark on the sign. After several minutes, walk the group around the *fair*, reading and discussing what's on the signs.

STEP 4

Form two teams. Give Repro Resource 5 to one team and Repro Resource 6 to the other. Provide paper and markers. Have each team draw a storyboard (a series of drawings that tell a story) based on its fact sheet. Each team should prepare one drawing per paragraph from its sheet. (Give the "Mormon team" extra people, since that sheet has more paragraphs.) Have teams show their storyboards and try to guess the meaning of each other's drawings. Then each team explains the meaning of each picture to the other team. In Step 5, write the three statements from cultists ("Hi, I'm from a great church," etc.) on index cards and put them in one stack. Write the six principles on another set of cards. Pairs of kids take turns knocking on each other's "doors"; the "cultist" chooses a statement card and the Christian chooses a principle card. The cultist reads his or her card and the Christian responds in a way that shows the principle at work. Mix up the cards in each stack before giving the next pair a turn.

SMALL GROUP

STEP 1

Don't have enough kids for "Simon Says"? Try this instead. Pose the following trick questions. Each question must be answered with a yes or no within five seconds. Here are the questions: **(1) Have you stopped kicking your neighbor's dog? (2) If I gave you some money, would you do what I wanted you to? (3) Do you like my favorite TV show? (4) Will you give me that car radio you stole? (5) Did you drink any orange juice exactly five years ago today? (6) Will you know the answer to the next question I ask?** Discuss how it felt to try to answer the questions (frustrating, irritating, confusing, etc.). Use this to illustrate the things some cult members ask when they come to the door, like "I believe in the Bible—don't you?" The *trick* is getting you to agree with them before they reveal their strange interpretations of the Bible.

STEP 5

Telling kids the six principles and accompanying explanations may sound like lecturing. If you find that awkward with a small group, try this instead. Write the six principles on index cards, one principle per card. Give one or more cards to each person. Read one of the cultist statements from the session plan (**"Hi, I'm from a great church,"** etc.) and have each person respond in a way that violates the principle(s) on his or her card(s). See whether other kids can guess the principle that's being violated. Then collect the cards, mix them up, and pass them out again. Read another cultist statement (**"Our religions are really very much alike,"** etc.). Each person should answer in a way that follows the principle(s) on his or her card(s). See whether other kids can guess the principle that's being followed.

LARGE GROUP

STEP 1

Will it be hard to monitor whether kids follow only "Simon Says" commands? Here's an alternative. Form teams for a relay race. Each runner must go to the other side of the room and do one of the following before returning: (1) recite the Pledge of Allegiance; (2) drink a small paper cup full of instant coffee that has only half the right amount of water in it; or (3) spin around seven times while quacking like a duck. The team whose members complete the race first wins. Then ask: **Do you know of any religious groups that would have trouble with doing any of the things you did at the other side of the room?** (Jehovah's Witnesses aren't supposed to recite the Pledge of Allegiance; Mormons are supposed to avoid coffee and other caffeinated beverages; a lot of people would find acting like a duck undignified, but probably not on religious grounds.) **What else do you know about Mormons and Jehovah's Witnesses?** Adapt or delete the first paragraph of Step 2.

STEP 5

Add action to keep a large group's attention. Before going through the six principles, form two teams and have them stand on opposite sides of the room. Team members stand next to each other, arm's length apart. Give each person a paper cup to balance upside down on his or her head. Teams try to get from one side of the room to the other while balancing the cups. The first time each team tries to knock off the other's cups; the second time they don't. Note how much easier it was to stay balanced when kids weren't *knocking* each other. Use this as a reminder that, like us, people from cult groups have strongly held beliefs that mean a lot to them. Attacking them won't change their minds.

HEARD IT ALL BEFORE

LITTLE BIBLE BACKGROUND

FELLOWSHIP & WORSHIP

STEP 2

Cults misinterpret the Bible—but how is Scripture supposed to be interpreted? Share these four principles of **normal** interpretation—from Charles C. Ryrie's *Basic Theology* (Victor Books): *(1) Interpret grammatically.* Make sure you understand the meaning of the words and their relationships in sentences. *(2) Interpret contextually.* Study what precedes and follows a passage to understand how it fits in. *(3) Compare Scripture with Scripture.* Try to see what God means in a passage by comparing it to the rest of His book. *(4) Recognize the progressiveness of revelation.* In the process of revealing His message, God added to and even changed some things He'd said previously—like dietary rules in the Old Testament. That doesn't mean we can claim to have "new revelations" that disagree with the Bible; it means we can't ignore changes God already made between earlier and later parts of His Word. Many cults break all four of these rules.

STEP 5

Challenge complacent kids to consider why they believe the Bible rather than other "holy" books. Read this from the introduction to *The Book of Mormon*: **"We invite all men everywhere to read the Book of Mormon, to ponder in their hearts the message it contains, and then to ask God, the Eternal Father, in the name of Christ if the book is true. Those who pursue this course and ask in faith will gain a testimony of its truth and divinity by the power of the Holy Ghost."** Ask: **Is this a good test of whether a book is true? Do you believe the Bible is true simply because you believe it's true? If so, how can you argue with cults who believe their books are true? What objective evidence can you give for the Bible's accuracy?** Don't expect to resolve this now; recommend books like Josh McDowell's *Don't Check Your Brains at the Door* (Word) for further study.

STEP 4

Do kids understand the biblical beliefs that Mormons and Jehovah's Witnesses dispute? Try these explanations. *Sovereignty of God*—Only He is supreme, and He's always been that way (Ps. 90:2; Mal. 3:6). *Nature of God's presence*—Though the Bible sometimes symbolically describes God as having physical parts like hands (Ps. 139:10), He is not limited by a physical body (Ps. 139:7-10; John 4:24). *Nature of Jesus*—Christ did not become God, but was already God (John 1:1). *Authority of Scripture*—God's Word has His "weight" behind it (2 Tim. 3:16), so anything that contradicts it (as does **The Book of Mormon**) can't be from Him. *Sinful nature*—No human is even always good, let alone a potential god (Matt. 19:17; Rom. 3:10-12). *Nature of salvation*—Eternal life is given only to those who put their faith in Christ (John 3:16). *The Trinity*—No human understands exactly how this works, but even though God is one (Eph. 4:4-6), God is also Father (John 6:27), Son (John 1:1), and Spirit (Acts 5:3-4). *Deity of Christ*—See *nature of Jesus. Salvation by grace*—Salvation is God's free and undeserved gift, not something we can earn (Eph. 2:8-9).

STEP 5

As needed, explain the following phrases from the six principles. *Do not accept other versions of the Bible*—This refers specifically to the Mormons' and Jehovah's Witnesses' versions, which insert their own interpretations. *Get the whole context*—Read the paragraphs before and after a passage. Sometimes you even have to read the whole chapter or book. Check against related passages (found in a concordance) in other books of the Bible too. *Rely on the Holy Spirit*—See John 14:26-27.

STEP 1

Try starting the meeting with worship. Focus on Christ as Lord and eternal King, using songs like "He Is Lord," "Joy to the World," and "Jesus, Name above All Names." Later, contrast your worship with the fact that Mormons and Jehovah's Witnesses reject the biblical idea of Christ's deity.

STEP 5

Wrap up with application that builds openness in the group. In small groups, have kids discuss which of the following "cultish" things they tend to do: (1) trusting other information sources more than they trust the Bible; (2) counting on leaders to predigest Scripture for them instead of reading it themselves; (3) trying to earn their salvation by doing good things; (4) wishing they could get out of the church instead of improving it from within. You may want to write the four choices on chalkboard or poster board. Remind kids that we aren't immune to making the same mistakes cults make, even if we don't join them.

MOSTLY GIRLS

MOSTLY GUYS

EXTRA FUN

STEP 2

After you go through "Cults Galore" (Repro Resource 4), bring up the topic of respect for others. Ask: **How can you show your respect for a person without supporting his or her beliefs? What can you do to let others know that they, like you, were created by God and are loved by Him, so they won't think you have a "holier than thou" attitude?**

Then ask: **Should you avoid close friendships with people who are members of a cult? Why or why not? What if the cult emphasizes a lot of Christian values, and you share the same moral standards as the person in the cult?**

STEP 5

Before the session, you'll need to write out the five questions from Step 5 on separate pieces of paper. Have group members form five teams. Assign each team one of the questions to answer. Give the teams a few minutes to discuss; then have each one present its response.

STEP 2

Some guys' sole reaction to other beliefs is "Weird!" or "How could those people be so dumb?" Help guys to be more considerate of other people's points of view. Say: **Let's pretend you have a girlfriend who isn't into sports or any of your hobbies. How would you explain to her what's so great or necessary about football or basketball? About growing a mustache? About riding a motorcycle? About weight lifting?** After letting a few volunteers try to answer, ask: **How would you feel if your girlfriend reacted to your explanation by saying, "You must really be stupid to think that"?** Suggest that such a judgment would be unfair—just as it would be unfair to judge the motives or intelligence of people who join cults.

STEP 4

Instead of just reading the Repro Resources, try this if you have two guys who like to act. During the week before the session, give each guy one of the Repro Resources. One guy should prepare to play the role of Joseph Smith, the other Charles Taze Russell. At this point in the session, have your actors come to the front. Introduce them by reading the first paragraph on each sheet. Then let the rest of the group ask your actors questions about their religions and how they were developed. Follow with a discussion of the beliefs that group members found questionable.

STEP 1

Form teams. Seat them in different parts of the room. Announce that you're going to have a knock-knock joke contest. You'll call out a name, and teams will have one minute to work it into the best knock-knock joke they can create. You'll choose the best joke from that round, then go on to the next round by calling out a new name. Here are some names you might use: Howie; Dwayne; Dawn; Will; Imelda; Frank. (Example: "Knock, knock." "Who's there?" "Dwayne." "Dwayne who?" "Dwayne the bathtub, I'm dwowning.") After giving a prize to the team that wins the most rounds, introduce the subject of cult members who knock on doors. Point out that what they're trying to do is no joke.

STEP 5

After wrapping up the discussion, serve finger food. But next to the foods include bowls of *dip* that are bizarre as well as unnecessary (doughnuts with a bowl of relish, cookies next to onion dip, brownies with a side of guacamole, etc.) Use this to illustrate the strange and unneeded additions cults make to God's Word.

STEP 3

Through a local Christian bookstore, rent the video *The God Makers* (Jeremiah Films). This production takes a critical look at Mormonism, including "secret temple rituals" that are dramatized. You won't have time to show the whole 52-minute video during the meeting; preview it and play a segment that you feel is informative as well as attention-getting (or show the whole video at another session).

STEP 5

Before the session, get three volunteers (preferably not group members) to pose as the cultists who make the three statements ("Hi, I'm from a great church," etc.). Use a video camera to capture each "cultist" knocking on a door and speaking directly to the camera. When you play the video at this point in the meeting, freeze the picture or stop the tape after the first actor speaks; give kids a chance to respond. Do the same with the other two actors.

STEP 2

Skip Step 2, except for the first two paragraphs (assuming you used the Step 1 game) and the question **How would you define a cult?** If you want kids to have the cult list on Repro Resource 4, you could distribute it without discussion; encourage kids to talk with you later if they have questions. In Step 3, use only questions 1, 3, and 8. Most of the rest will be covered in Step 4.

STEP 4

Hand out the Repro Resources, but read just paragraphs 3-6 from Repro Resource 5 and paragraphs 2-5 from Repro Resource 6. Instead of having kids read silently and circle questionable doctrines, try this time-saver. As you read the sheets aloud, kids should "buzz" when they hear something questionable. Ask a buzzer or two to explain before you continue reading. In Step 5, prepare by writing the six principles on chalkboard or poster board. Read just one of the statements from cultists ("Hi, I'm from the Mormon church," etc.); point to a principle and ask what kind of response would fit that principle. Repeat the process with the other five principles.

STEP 3

For an activity that will impact your group members' understanding of cults, have your young people make a case for cults. Divide your group members into three teams: the attorneys for Jehovah's Witnesses, the attorneys for Mormons, and the jury. Instruct the attorneys to study their respective Repro Resources and construct a winning argument for their cult to present to the jury. Explain that this case is crucial because your state has decided to endorse only one religion. Give the attorneys a few minutes to prepare; then have them present their cases. The jury will decide which team presented the best case.

Afterward, as a group, construct a case for why Christianity is preferable to (or more believable than) Jehovah's Witnesses and Mormonism.

STEP 5

Some of your group members may know people who are involved in Jehovah's Witnesses or Mormonism. As you wrap up the session, offer your group members the following tips for sharing the Gospel with these people.

1. See the cult member as a person, not as a "religious freak" or an enemy. It's very difficult to convert an enemy.

2. Seek to understand (but not accept) the person's beliefs and point of view.

3. Emphasize Christ's deity. Jesus is God.

4. Recognize the Spirit's ability to minister. Don't feel like you have the responsibility to "do it all yourself."

STEP 2

Skip the Repro Resource, which could cause more confusion than enlightenment at this point. Most younger kids won't be prepared to absorb concepts like "Eastern Variations," "Culture/Earth Cults," and neo-paganism. Paraphrasing information in the session plan, concentrate on (1) what a cult is, (2) not offending cult members by calling them such, and (3) the fact that established non-Christian religions aren't called cults.

STEP 4

Younger kids may find it hard to spot heresies on the Repro Resources without help. Start by reading each of the biblical beliefs from the basic session plan—the ones disputed by each cult (six are listed for Mormons, seven for Jehovah's Witnesses). Pause after reading each biblical belief to let kids search for conflicting statements on the sheets. In Step 5, place less emphasis on how to answer cultists (since most younger kids aren't about to try), and more on showing love to cult-member friends without accepting false teachings. Ask volunteers to respond to the six guidelines by telling the group one thing Jesus has done in their lives. Wrap up by reading and explaining Galatians 1:6-9.

STEP 1

More "mature" kids may not want to play "Simon Says." Try this instead. Give one person a King James Bible. Give everyone a slip of paper and a pencil. The person with the Bible looks up an obscure, one-sentence verse (like Judg. 1:31) and writes it down without telling anyone what it is. The other players write on their slips sentences that *sound* like King James Bible verses but aren't. After a couple of minutes, players pass their fake verses to the person who has the Bible. That person adds the real verse, mixes the slips up, and reads them one at a time. Players vote on which verse is the real one; if the person with the Bible fools the whole group, he or she gets a prize. Play as many rounds as you have time for, passing the Bible to someone else each time. Then explain that some cults, notably Mormonism, have their own "scriptures" that try to sound like the Bible. Even though **The** *Book of Mormon* was "translated" centuries after King James English was spoken, it uses language like that of the King James Bible.

STEP 5

From your local Christian bookstore get a couple of copies of one of the following books: *Answers to the Cultists at Your Door* by Robert and Gretchen Passantino (Harvest House); *So What's the Difference?* by Fritz Ridenour (Regal Books). Offer an incentive (prize, lunch with you on a Saturday, etc.) to anyone who'll read the sections on Mormonism and the Jehovah's Witnesses and summarize them for the group at your next meeting. (Note: *Answers to the Cultists* concentrates on responding; *So What's the Difference?* is more of an overview of each cult, but may be easier for kids to read.)

DATE USED:

Approx. Time

STEP 1: *Simon Says Tag* _____
- ❏ Small Group
- ❏ Large Group
- ❏ Fellowship & Worship
- ❏ Extra Fun
- ❏ Extra Challenge
Things needed:

STEP 2: *The Cult…* _____
- ❏ Extra Action
- ❏ Heard It All Before
- ❏ Mostly Girls
- ❏ Mostly Guys
- ❏ Short Meeting Time
- ❏ Combined Junior High/High School
Things needed:

STEP 3: *True or False* _____
- ❏ Media
- ❏ Urban
Things needed:

STEP 4: *Fact-finding* _____
- ❏ Extra Action
- ❏ Little Bible Background
- ❏ Mostly Guys
- ❏ Short Meeting Time
- ❏ Combined Junior High/High School
Things needed:

STEP 5: *What Do You Say?* _____
- ❏ Small Group
- ❏ Large Group
- ❏ Heard It All Before
- ❏ Little Bible Background
- ❏ Fellowship & Worship
- ❏ Mostly Girls
- ❏ Extra Fun
- ❏ Media
- ❏ Urban
- ❏ Extra Challenge
Things needed:

Christian Science
and Scientology

☐ To help kids recognize how the teachings of Christian Science and Scientology differ from Christian teachings.

☐ To help kids understand some of the distinctive characteristics of these two cults.

☐ To help kids equip themselves to uphold the truth of Christianity in any conversations with members of these groups.

☐ Other:_____
_____

Your Bible Base:

Genesis 1:26-31
Romans 12:1-2
Ephesians 4:14-15
1 John 1:1; 4:2-3

The Shadow Knows

(Needed: Projector, screen or sheet, prize)

Set up a projector of some kind—movie, slide, or overhead—and a screen or sheet on which you can project shadows. Explain to your group members that they will be competing in a shadow-making contest. (Before the session, you may want to practice making your own shadow figures so that you can demonstrate to your group members what they'll be doing.)

Give group members a minute or two to think about what they'll do; then have everyone perform. Afterward, vote as a group on which shadow was best. Award a prize to that person.

Afterward, explain: **This activity is an illustration of some of the beliefs of the cults we'll be talking about today. According to them, our physical lives are just projections— like the shadows on the screen. Sin, sickness, and death are just illusions. The only thing that matters is our spirit. This may seem like a really interesting idea, but it goes completely against our Christian beliefs.**

Mrs. Eddy's Science

(Needed: Copies of Repro Resource 7, pencils)

Ask: **Do you know any people who go to a Christian Science church? If so, what do you know of these people and their beliefs?** Chances are, if any of your group members know some Christian Scientists, they probably consider them to be fine, upstanding Christians. After all, Christian Scientists go to church each Sunday and seem to live by Christian ethics. They tend to be devout, intelligent people. However, some of their beliefs may come as a surprise to your group members.

Have group members form teams of three or four. Distribute copies of "Fact Sheet: Christian Science" (Repro Resource 7) and pencils to each team. Instruct the teams to read the information on the sheet. Then have them go through and circle any ideas or beliefs that seem unbiblical (or perhaps just questionable) to them.

Give the teams a few minutes to work. When they're finished, have volunteers share their responses. Use the following information to supplement the teams' responses.

Among the traditional, biblical Christian beliefs disputed by Christian Science are

- the existence of the Trinity;
- God's creation of the universe (by claiming that matter does not exist);
- Jesus' deity (by claiming that Jesus is not God, but the Son of God);
- the nature of Jesus' virgin birth (by claiming that Jesus' birth came about through Mary's "spiritual thoughts of life and its manifestations");
- Jesus' death;
- the nature of Jesus' resurrection (by claiming that Jesus' resurrection showed how the spirit could triumph over the illusion of matter);
- the complete trustworthiness of the Bible (by claiming that a "material sense" has crept into it);
- the sinfulness of humans (by claiming that we are naturally holy);
- the nature of Christ's sacrifice for our sin (by claiming that we learn from Christ that sin and death have no power).

Ask volunteers to explain which beliefs of Christian Science surprised them most and why.

Then ask: **Why might intelligent people be drawn to a religion like this?** (Its emphasis on overcoming the material world through sheer mental power would seem to favor intelligent people.)

Remind group members that this is just a brief look at a complex philosophy. They are not experts on Christian Science after reading one "fact sheet." So they should be humble when talking to others about this religion. But at least they have a general idea of what it's about and what some of its problems are.

O P T I O N S

EXTRA ACTION

LITTLE BIBLE BACKGROUND

MOSTLY GIRLS

MEDIA

SHORT MEETING TIME

URBAN

JR. HIGH HIGH SCHOOL COMBINED

Mr. Hubbard's Principles

(Needed: Copies of Repro Resource 8, pencils)

OPTIONS

MEDIA

Ask: **How many of you have seen commercials for the book *Dianetics*?** Probably at least some of your group members have seen them.

Explain: **The ads ask questions that many of us ask ourselves: "How can I develop better relationships?" "How can I get the most out of my efforts at work?" "Why can't I accomplish what I set out to do?" The book supposedly gives the answers to these questions.**

How many of you know that this book is connected with a cult called Scientology? Because the commercials don't mention Scientology, chances are that most of your group members aren't aware of the connection.

Have group members form teams of three or four. If possible, make sure group members don't team up with the same people they were teamed with earlier. Distribute copies of "Fact Sheet: Scientology" (Repro Resource 8) to each team. As before, the teams should read through the information on the sheet and circle any ideas or beliefs that seem unbiblical or questionable.

Give the teams a few minutes to work. When they're finished, have volunteers share their responses. Use the following information to supplement the teams' responses.

Among the traditional, biblical Christian beliefs disputed by Scientology are
- perhaps the very existence of God;
- the role of God in our lives (by claiming that humans must deal with their own problems and "unleash" their own potential);
- the role of prayer (by claiming that the use of the E-meter is the way to be free from engrams, or sin);
- the helpless nature of humans apart from God (by claiming that our spirits have control over matter, energy, space, and time).

Ask: **Do any of these Scientology beliefs or ideas sound interesting to you? Do any of them sound reasonable or believable to you? Why or why not?** Get a few responses.

Why do you suppose Scientology is such a popular cult? (Probably a major part of its appeal is the fact that it relies solely on personal effort. There's no need to rely on a higher power for salvation [or a better life]; everyone can do it for himself or herself.)

Again emphasize that this was just a brief summary of a very complicated belief system.

Encourage group members to keep these resource sheets in their Bibles for future reference.

Let's Get Physical

Both Christian Science and Scientology emphasize the mind over the body. Christian Science goes so far as to say that material things don't really exist. But the Bible is full of physical things. It is rich with touch. Let's take a quick tour through Scripture to get a feel for this.

Have someone read aloud Genesis 1:26-31. Then ask: **What do Christian Scientists and Scientologists think of this idea of humans being made in God's image?** (They believe it means we are completely, or primarily, spiritual beings.)

Point out that we don't really know all of what the "image of God" means. Certainly this context gives us a sense of leadership over the earth's creatures—we are "lords" of the earth, in a way.

Say: **Look at the description of all that God had made— fish, birds, plants, and beasts. These are all material things. What grade does God give Himself on these physical things He's made?** (He says they are very good.)

Point out that many cults—and some churches—teach that physical creation—including humans—is bad. Because it's "unspiritual," it's viewed as a negative thing. But here God calls His creation very good. Who are we to argue?

Have someone read aloud Romans 12:1-2. Then ask: **Which of these verses do you think Christian Scientists and Scientologists would like better?** (Verse 2, with its emphasis on renewing your mind.)

But what does verse 1 say about our bodies? (We should present them as living sacrifices to God.)

Explain: **Once again, the cults have it half right. Yes, we do need to renew our minds. But Paul also says first we should present our bodies to God. This, along with the renewing of our minds, will allow us to discover God's will.**

Have someone read aloud I John 1:1. Then ask: **Who is the "Word of life" referred to in this passage?** (Jesus.)

What evidence does John give in this verse for "the Word of Life"? (John and others have heard Him, seen Him, and touched Him.)

Explain: **Even at that time there were cults who were saying that Jesus was not real, that He was just a spirit who looked real. John debunks this by saying that he knows better—he touched the Lord.**

Have someone read aloud I John 4:2-3. Then ask: **What "test" does John propose to see whether a spirit, or teacher, is "from God"?** (He or she [or it] must acknowledge that Jesus Christ has come in the flesh.)

Explain: **This is where most of the cults we'll encounter have gone wrong. Some cults say Jesus is God, but was not human. Some say He was human, but not God. This is the crucial test of any teaching.**

STEP 5

Word of Wisdom

Ask group members to turn to Ephesians 4:14-15. Explain that the previous verses talk about how God has set up church leadership to help Christians grow. Now have someone read the passage.

Ask: **How does Paul describe the situation of "infants"?** (Tossed by every wind of teaching—in other words, susceptible to the doctrines of cults.)

How can we avoid being tossed about like that? (Grow in Christ.)

Explain: **These cults may seem confusing or perhaps even convincing to you. Don't panic. We have a good thing going in this group, in this church. Stay with it. As you grow in Christ, you'll be more anchored.**

Also notice the phrase "speaking the truth in love" in verse 15. That's how we should behave with each other and with those we meet who belong to these cults or are looking into them.

If you have a friend who belongs to, say, a Christian Science church, how could you "speak the truth in love"? Get specific ideas from group members about how to do this. Can they show concern for such friends and still hold to the truth?

If you have time, set up the following roleplay situations and have volunteers demonstrate their ideas for speaking the truth in love.

- A Christian Scientist friend is coming down with a bad cold, but insists it's nothing—her religion says sickness is all in the mind.
- A friend saw an ad on TV and bought the *Dianetics* book. He's now saying how wonderful these principles are. They're changing his life!
- A Mormon friend invites you to his youth group.
- A couple of Jehovah's Witnesses stop at your door and ask if they can talk with you awhile.

Close the session in prayer, thanking God for His truth, His daily guidance, and His love. Thank Him especially for taking on human flesh and giving Himself for us.

FACT SHEET:
CHRISTIAN SCIENCE

In 1866, a middle-aged woman named Mary Baker (who later married and became Mary Baker Eddy) "discovered" the principles of Christian Science after a serious fall threatened to cripple her. She credits these principles with her own healing. In 1875, she published these ideas in a book called *Science and Health.* Four years later, she had established a group of followers.

According to Christian Science, all that truly exists is spirit. Matter does not exist. We just have a "material sense"—that is, we *imagine* that matter exists. In order to let our spirits live, we need to put this material sense away.

Among the key doctrines in Christian Science is the belief that God is "All-in-All." He is "the great I Am; all-knowing, all-seeing, all-acting, all-wise, all-loving, and eternal; Principle; Mind; Soul; Spirit; Life; Truth; Love; all Substance; Intelligence." In her writings, Eddy dismissed the idea of the Trinity as being three gods. And, according to Christian Science, God cannot be the Creator of a material universe, since matter does not exist.

Eddy also wrote, "Jesus Christ is not God … but the Son of God." She divides Him into Jesus (the material man) and Christ (the divine spirit). According to Eddy, Jesus' virgin birth came about through Mary's "spiritual thoughts of life and its manifestations." Jesus did not really die, according to Eddy, but His resurrection showed how the spirit could triumph over the illusion of matter.

Christian Scientists believe that the Bible is true, but that there are many problems in its translation. They believe that a "material sense" has crept into it. They believe that Eddy's *Science and Health* was inspired by God, and is the proper way to understand the Scriptures. Christian Science churches today use the King James Version of the Bible, alongside Eddy's writings, which are viewed as "keys" to unlocking the meaning of the Bible.

According to Christian Science, humans are made in God's image; therefore, we are spiritual—not physical. Sin, sickness, and death are all illusions. We are naturally holy.

The idea of Christ shedding His blood as a sacrifice for our sins is seen as primitive by Christian Scientists. According to them, Christ's suffering showed us the way to a truly spiritual life. Therefore, salvation, like everything else in Christian Science, is mental. We *learn* from Christ that sin and death have no power.

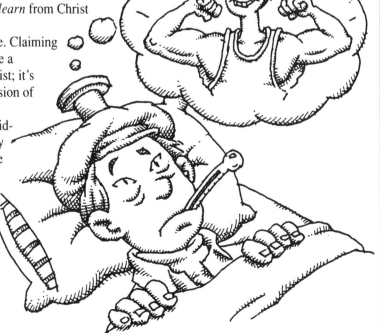

Healing is a major concern of Christian Science. Claiming to follow Jesus' pattern of healing, its followers take a "mind-over-matter" approach. Sickness does not exist; it's an illusion. Discipline your mind to dismiss the illusion of illness, and you'll be fine. Or so the theory goes.

Christian Scientists want very much to be considered just another denomination of Christianity. They do not like to be called a "cult." But their beliefs are clearly outside the realm of traditional Christianity. And they have an unhealthy reliance on the writings of Mary Baker Eddy. Some of her writings sound very Christian, even devotional, and Christian Scientists love to quote these passages to prove that they are legitimate. But other quotes from Eddy reveal a philosophy that is clearly unbiblical and un-Christian.

FACT SHEET: Scientology

L. Ron Hubbard led an amazing life. He was an explorer in Central America, a Navy officer, and a writer of science fiction stories. He claims that he was twice pronounced clinically dead, but his "dianetic" principles helped him regain his health. In 1950, he published *Dianetics*, the book that launched his new movement.

Scientology doesn't deal much with God. It's all about humanity dealing with its problems and "unleashing its potential." According to Scientology, our minds have two parts, the *analytic* and the *reactive* (sort of like the conscious and subconscious). Our reactive minds have received shocks throughout our lives, even in the womb. These shocks have produced *engrams* or impressions that continue to mess us up in various ways.

By meeting with an *auditor*, and paying the proper fee, people can get hooked up to an *E-meter*—sort of a lie-detector device—which, according to Scientology, helps them discover their engrams. Once people have discovered their engrams, they can confess them and be rid of them. The person then *goes Clear*, and is free from his or her problems.

According to Scientology, we humans are dualities—we have bodies and spirits. We need to get in touch with the *thetan*, that is, our spirit, and free it from our bodies and minds. The thetan supposedly has control over matter, energy, space, and time.

Though Scientology doesn't focus on the divine, it often gives the appearance of being a church. In some areas, Scientologists hold Sunday services. Leaders often wear clerical collars and use religious symbols and rituals.

Scientology costs money—perhaps a thousand dollars or more for enough "auditing" sessions to get rid of one's engrams. So the organization is very well-funded.

The principles of Scientology may seem hard to understand, but that's part of the cult's appeal. The system *seems* brilliant, whether it is or not. And as long as it promises answers to people's everyday problems, people will believe it.

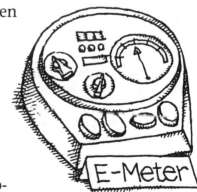
E-Meter

EXTRA ACTION

STEP 2

Bring two packs of assorted sandpaper sheets. The sheets in each set should vary slightly in "grit" (roughness). Using a marker or tape, hide the printing on the back of the sheets that indicates the grit of each sheet. Form two teams. See which team can arrange its set of sheets in order of roughness, judging by touch. Allow one minute; the team coming closest to the correct order wins. Then say: **Based on this contest, would you say your senses can always be trusted? Why or why not?** Explain that Christian Science asks that question, but reaches unusual conclusions. To start Step 3, try another contest with the same teams. Give each team a pie plate, pipe cleaners, and tape—with the challenge to make something in two minutes that will "benefit humankind." The most "beneficial" invention (let teams try to convince you of this) wins. Use this to introduce Scientology's E-meter, which supposedly helps people realize their potential.

STEP 4

Have the group move to different corners of the room to read each passage. In the first corner (Gen. 1:26-31) pass around a created object with an interesting texture (rose petals, sea sponge, etc.); in the second (Rom. 12:1-2), pass around a stick or cone of incense (reminiscent of a sacrifice) to smell; in the third (I John 1:1), pass around a nail (a reminder of the physical reality of the crucifixion) to touch; in the fourth (I John 4:2-3), pass around bread for kids to taste (a reminder of the fact that Jesus was so real He ate food as we do). Then ask: **Which senses did you use as part of this Bible study? Which of your senses do you rely on most to learn about God? Why?**

SMALL GROUP

STEP 1

A shadow contest might not be very interesting with just a few kids. If you'd like an alternative, here's one. Bring a plate of brownies or some other treat. Give some of the food to half the group, and no food to the other half. Kids with food should eat it, describing in detail to the others how delicious it is. Then ask the foodless half: **Wasn't that great? Isn't it satisfying just to think about that food? The mind is a wonderful thing, isn't it?** After kids reply, explain that you'll be discussing two groups—Christian Science and Scientology—that emphasize a separation between mental and physical, and tend to favor mind over body. Finally, just to be fair, let the foodless kids have a real taste of the leftover treats.

STEP 5

Take advantage of your group's size by making more personal application. Expand your reading of the Ephesians passage to 4:11-16. Ask: **What people in our church might be able to build you up so that you aren't a victim of every "wind of teaching"?** Brainstorm a list of names—not just those in official positions, but any adults or college/career people who have kids' respect. Then have kids rate their involvement (on a scale of 1 to 5, 5 highest) with each person on the list. Encourage kids to get to know these people better; you might want to plan an event that would get group members together with some on the list.

LARGE GROUP

STEP 1

You may find it hard to let everyone participate in the shadow-making contest. Here's an alternative that can involve everyone. Provide two beach balls and a volleyball net. Let kids see how long they can keep both beach balls going back and forth simultaneously over the net. The catch: They can use only their heads. Afterward, congratulate kids on "using their heads." Use this to lead into a discussion of "mind power" versus "body power." Ask: **Which is more powerful—the body or the mind? Why?** Note that Christian Science and Scientology talk a lot about the power of the mind.

STEP 5

Read the Ephesians passage, adding verse 16. Demonstrate the need to help each other become grounded in the truth in order to keep from being "tossed back and forth." Have one person lie on a large, strong blanket; others hold the blanket, toss the person into the air, and lower him or her gently to the floor. Then have two others lie on the blanket with the first person. Have the rest of the group try to toss the three who are lying down; chances are the blanket will be too heavy. Ask: **How can we be "anchors" for each other in this group?**

HEARD IT ALL BEFORE

LITTLE BIBLE BACKGROUND

FELLOWSHIP & WORSHIP

STEP 4

Kids may tune out as soon as you go to Scripture. The whole mind-versus-body debate may sound far removed from their lives. Make the concept more concrete by declaring a "new revelation" you have received: As long as kids' bodies are visible, they aren't worthy to read the Bible or have it read to them. Give them trash bags to wear over their torsos (cut out holes for head and arms) during this step to hide their "evil" bodies. At the end of the step, ask: **How did you feel about the idea that your body was evil? Do our bodies ever cause problems that make us feel unworthy to be close to God? On a scale of 1 to 10 (10 highest), how easy is it for you to believe that the physical part of you is really "good"?**

STEP 5

Kids raised in church may think they've heard so much about the Bible that they couldn't be "tossed" by cult teachings. Have them list their top five gripes about the church. It's likely that somewhere on that list will be styles of worship, hypocrisy of other Christians, boredom, lack of loving relationships, failure to make a difference in the world, etc. Note that cults appeal through these avenues too—offering different forms of worship, criticism of "lesser" Christians, lots of work to keep people busy, a "loving" atmosphere, and lofty goals. A surprising number of cult members grew up in Christian churches, but wanted something more. Many cult leaders grew up in church too.

STEP 2

In Steps 2 and 3, make sure kids understand the biblical beliefs that the two cults dispute. Refer to these notes as needed. *The Trinity*—No human fully understands this, but even though God is one (Eph. 4:4-6), He is also Father (John 6:27), Son (John 1:1), and Spirit (Acts 5:3-4). *Jesus' deity*—Christ is fully God, not a watered-down or miniature version of God (Phil. 2:5-7). *The virgin birth*—The Holy Spirit caused Mary to be pregnant (Luke 1:34-35); Jesus wasn't a product of Mary's thoughts. *Nature of Jesus' resurrection*—Christ's after-resurrection body wasn't the same as ours (Luke 24:31), but He went out of His way to show that He wasn't a ghost (Luke 24:37-43). *Sinfulness of humans*—without being changed through Christ, people tend to do the wrong thing, not the right thing (Matt. 19:17; Rom. 3:10-12). *Nature of Christ's sacrifice*—Jesus died for us because of the power of sin and death, not because they had no power (Romans 6:6-10). *Helpless nature of humans*—God is not impressed by our "powers" (Job 40:9-14).

STEP 4

As needed, explain these phrases from Romans 12:1-2. *Living sacrifices*—In the Old Testament, God's people "paid" for their sins by offering their best animals as *dead* sacrifices that were burned on an altar. Paul wants believers to surrender their bodies—in prime condition, not wrecked by disobedience—to God. He wants them, not as dead sacrifices or to pay for sin (Christ has done that), but for His continuing use. *Renewing of your mind*—Someone who becomes a Christian is a new person (2 Corinthians 5:17). Paul wants us to think like new people, a process of change that takes time.

STEP 1

For a relational opener, try this. Form small groups. Say: **I'm going to start some sentences. After I start one, each person in your small group should finish it in his or her own way.** Use these sentence starters, pausing after each to let kids finish them and to briefly discuss results. **(1) When I hear the words science fiction, I think of . . . (2) The best science fiction movie I ever saw was . . . (3) If people can go to other planets for vacations 20 years from now, I will . . . (4) Between science and science fiction, the one I like better is . . .** After letting kids talk about their answers, point out that the two cults you're about to discuss may seem scientific on the surface—but they're definitely based on fiction.

STEP 5

Close with worship by emphasizing the "living sacrifice" idea. Tape a paper target (draw several concentric circles around a bull's-eye) on a wall. Put an ink pad (preferably washable ink) on a table next to the target. Have kids sing a song of commitment ("I Have Decided to Follow Jesus," "Take My Life and Let It Be," etc.). As they do, invite individuals to go to the target and put their thumbprints (using the ink pad) on it to show how willing they are to let God use their bodies for His purposes. The more willing they are, the closer to the bull's-eye their thumbprints should be.

STEP 2

Have group members form two teams. Distribute copies of "Fact Sheet: Christian Science" (Repro Resource 7) to the members of Team 1. (In Step 3, you will distribute copies of Repro Resource 8 to the members of Team 2 for a similar exercise.) Instruct the members of Team 1 to read through the sheet once. Then they should choose one person to play the role of Mary Baker Eddy. She will explain to the Team 2 "her" book and organization. Each of the rest of Team 1's members will then take turns reading aloud a paragraph from the sheet. As the members of Team 1 are sharing information from Repro Resource 7, Team 2 should be writing down principles and beliefs of Christian Science that aren't supported by the Bible. Afterward, have the members of Team 2 share their list.

STEP 5

As you discuss the principle of "speaking the truth in love," ask for some examples of *not* speaking the truth in love. Ask: **What are some things we do and say that are *not* appropriate? Is avoiding someone, for any reason, ever the right thing to do? Why or why not?**

STEP 4

Some guys may not care that the Bible is "rich with touch," but they can appreciate that it's "full of physical things." Get physical to reinforce your Bible exploration. While each volunteer is looking up his Bible passage to read, the rest of the group must do (or at least try to do) 10 repetitions of an exercise (push-ups, toe touches, etc.) chosen by the reader.

STEP 5

Not-so-verbal guys may have trouble with roleplays. If that's the case with your group, try this instead. You take the role of the Christian in each of the four situations. Instead of setting a shining example, say all the wrong things (like telling the Mormon friend that you'd rather kill yourself than go to his weirdo cult youth group). The rest of the group should stop you when you say something that's either untruthful or unloving, and suggest something better.

STEP 1

Form teams. Give each team a pocket calculator. At your signal, the first person on each team punches in a one-digit number, hits the "plus" sign, and passes it to the next person. He or she enters another one-digit number, hits "plus," and passes it on. Kids keep adding numbers and passing the calculator until you suddenly call out **Clear!** Whoever has the calculator at that point must hit the "clear" button, starting the process over. Call out **Clear!** whenever you like. When you call out **Total!,** however, each person holding a calculator hits the "equals" button and tells you what the team total is. The highest total wins. Later in the session, use this to illustrate the Scientology theory of using an E-meter to "clear" the effects of past traumas.

STEP 5

Wrap up with a game that echoes Romans 12:1-2. Form teams. Each team chooses someone to serve as its "living sacrifice." Give each team markers and a big package of stick-on labels. At your signal, team members write "For God's Use Only" on their stickers and plaster the stickers on the head, arms, hands, legs, and feet of their "sacrifice." The team to cover its sacrifice most completely with labels in five minutes is the winner. Ask: **Other than labeling parts of your body, how can you remind yourself who owns you?**

STEP 2

Do one of the following: (1) Watch part of an exercise video. Have kids do the exercises as well as they can—as long as they remain seated. (2) Pass around body building ads you've cut from magazines like *Muscle and Fitness*; encourage kids to call out words that come to mind as they look at the ads. Whichever activity you choose, follow up by asking: **Do you think our physical bodies are overemphasized these days? Is Christian Science the right response to thinking too much about physical things? Why or why not?**

STEP 3

Rent three movies on video. Each should feature one of these actors: Tom Cruise (*Rain Man, Far and Away, The Color of Money*); John Travolta (*Look Who's Talking, Saturday Night Fever*); and Priscilla Presley (the *Naked Gun* films). Show any appropriate scene featuring the actor (preview it yourself) from each film. Then ask: **What do these people have in common?** (They've all been involved with Scientology.) **How might Scientology benefit from being associated with people like these? Does the involvement of these people with Scientology make it more believable to you? Why or why not?**

STEP 2

Save time by reading aloud condensed versions of the Repro Resources and letting kids react as you go along. Read just paragraphs 2-6 of Repro Resource 7. Have kids call out "Whoa!" when they hear something that sounds questionable. In Step 3, read just paragraphs 2-6 of Repro Resource 7 and follow the same procedure.

STEP 4

Have volunteers look up all the verses at the same time; call on them to read when you need them. In Step 5, skip the Ephesians passage and use just the first two roleplay situations.

STEP 2

Focus on the Christian Science belief that pain and sickness are illusions and that "mind over matter" is the solution. Ask for a volunteer who can take pain without flinching. Have this person sit in front of the group. Explain that if he or she can focus hard enough and express no pain for 20 seconds while being pinched, he or she will receive a prize. Then ask for a volunteer pincher. (Don't let the pinching get brutal or out of hand.) As the first volunteer is being pinched, watch his or her face carefully for signs of pain. When time is up, award the prize (if necessary). Then discuss how the person looked and felt while trying to repress pain. Ask: **Do you think mind over matter is a realistic way of dealing with pain and sickness? Why or why not?** [NOTE: If pinching seems too violent, try tickling with a feather.]

STEP 5

As you wrap up the session, point out that it's difficult to remain untarnished by cults or false doctrine in the city. However, there is such a thing as a godly "cult protector." Just as computer "surge protectors" protect data from being lost in an unexpected surge of voltage, so can your group protect young people from unexpected surges of cult activity. Explain that one of the best "cult protectors" throughout the ages has been Christian fellowship. If time allows, have your group members brainstorm ways they can work together in protecting each other from cults.

STEP 2

Instead of expecting younger kids to read and understand the Repro Resources in Steps 2 and 3, call on older students to paraphrase the handouts a paragraph at a time. Pause after each paragraph for questions. If none of your students can handle paraphrasing, do this yourself. Pause for questions after explaining the biblical beliefs these cults dispute, too. Younger kids may not understand the details, but help them grasp the key conflicts between the Bible and the teachings of these cults.

STEP 4

You may want to use the "Extra Action" and "Little Bible Background" options in Step 4. In Step 5, younger kids may find the roleplays (and the idea of confronting friends who are cult members) too threatening. With that in mind, change the emphasis as you wrap up the meeting. Call kids' attention again to the biblical principles the two cults dispute (see the basic session plan for Steps 2 and 3). Have kids practice "speaking the truth in love" by thinking of ways to say these biblical principles in their own words—words non-Christians probably would understand and might not be offended by. For example, "Jesus' deity" might be rephrased like this: "I believe what Jesus said about Himself—that He's God. I don't understand how He can be God and the Son of God, but I believe He knew what He was talking about."

STEP 1

Is your group too "sophisticated" for shadows? Let teams try to solve these "mind games" in two minutes: **(1) How can you multiply one times one and get twelve?** (When "one" is "one dozen." The total is 144, or twelve dozen.) **(2) What's in your mouth, looks the same backward and forward, and comes in a set of five?** (Each letter in the word "mouth." When printed as a capital letter, each looks the same backward and forward.) Note that you're going to look at two cults that believe the mind is more real and powerful than the body.

STEP 5

Read this from *Science and Health with Key to the Scriptures* by Christian Science founder Mary Baker Eddy: "The divine Principle of healing is proved in the personal experience of any sincere seeker of Truth…. The unbiased Christian thought is soonest touched by Truth, and convinced of it. Only those quarrel with her method who do not understand her meaning, or discerning the truth, come not to the light lest their works be reproved. No intellectual proficiency is requisite in the learner, but sound morals are most desirable." Ask: **What does this mean?** (If you don't agree with Christian Science, you're insincere, biased, immoral, or lack understanding.) **How is this different from Christ's invitation in Revelation 3:20?** Then read this disclaimer from L. Ron Hubbard's *Dianetics:* "The Hubbard Electrometer [E-meter] is a religious artifact used in the Church confessional. It in itself does nothing, and is used by Ministers only, to assist parishioners in locating areas of spiritual distress or travail." **Why do you think this is in the book?** (Perhaps because an examination of the E-meter would show that it doesn't do anything.) **How do these quotes make you feel about Christian Science and Scientology?**

DATE USED:

Approx. Time

STEP 1: *The Shadow Knows* _____
❏ Small Group
❏ Large Group
❏ Fellowship & Worship
❏ Extra Fun
❏ Extra Challenge
Things needed:

STEP 2: *Mrs. Eddy's Science* _____
❏ Extra Action
❏ Little Bible Background
❏ Mostly Girls
❏ Media
❏ Short Meeting Time
❏ Urban
❏ Combined Junior High/High School
Things needed:

STEP 3: *Mr. Hubbard's Principles* _____
❏ Media
Things needed:

STEP 4: *Let's Get Physical* _____
❏ Extra Action
❏ Heard It All Before
❏ Little Bible Background
❏ Mostly Guys
❏ Short Meeting Time
❏ Combined Junior High/High School
Things needed:

STEP 5: *Word of Wisdom* _____
❏ Small Group
❏ Large Group
❏ Heard It All Before
❏ Fellowship & Worship
❏ Mostly Girls
❏ Mostly Guys
❏ Extra Fun
❏ Urban
❏ Extra Challenge
Things needed:

The New Age Movement and the Unification Church

Your Bible Base:

Romans 8:16
2 Timothy 1:11-14;
    3:14-17
1 Peter 3:14-15

The Non-Game

(Needed: Play money, an "assistant" prepared to make up rules)

OPTIONS

You'll need to be on your toes for this opening activity. The idea is this: You're going to have your group members play a game that has no rules.

Start by saying something like this: **We're going to play a game. The red team starts.** Group members probably will ask who's on the red team.

Respond: **Anyone who wants to be.**

Distribute play money to some group members. Say: **OK, the red team needs to ask a question of the blue team.** The "red team" should ask a question and get an answer from someone who's decided that he or she is on the "blue team." Give that person some play money.

Now the green team gets to do a charade for the red team. This is just like charades, except there are no rules. Win or lose, award points and money to the players.

Continue this chaos for a few minutes until group members get totally frustrated. Then you'll need the help of an assistant from the group.

Say something like: **Rules? You want rules? OK, _____ here will make up rules.** The assistant should be prepared to make up rules that benefit him or her. He or she will then win every game, and get all the points and money.

Afterward, explain: **We're going to talk about two cults today that function a little like the "game" we just played. The first is not really a specific cult, but a general movement known as the New Age movement. Being a part of the New Age movement is like playing with no rules. There's no right or wrong. There doesn't even need to be a God. Jesus could be anything you want Him to be. Just make it up as you go along.**

The second cult is the Unification Church of Sun Myung Moon—otherwise known as the "Moonies." In this cult, the Reverend Moon has made up the rules. He has established himself as the supreme object of devotion for his followers. We're going to take a look at both of these cults today.

**STEP
2**

The Dawn of a New Age

(Needed: Copies of Repro Resource 9, pencils)

Ask: **When I say "New Age movement," what do you think of?** Group members may or may not have impressions of it. Some may mention New Age music; others may talk about crystals or channeling. Still others may see it as an anti-Christian conspiracy.

Explain: **As I mentioned before, the New Age movement is not an organized cult. But a number of different New Age groups have common beliefs—and we need to be careful about them.**

Have group members form teams of three or four. Distribute copies of "Fact Sheet: New Age Movement" (Repro Resource 9) and pencils to each team. Instruct the teams to read the information on the sheet. Then have them go through and circle any ideas or beliefs that seem unbiblical (or perhaps just questionable) to them.

Give the teams a few minutes to work. When they're finished, have volunteers share their responses. Use the following information to supplement the teams' responses.

Among the traditional, biblical Christian beliefs disputed by the New Age movement are

- the nature of God (by claiming that everything is God);
- the deity of Jesus (by claiming that He is a prophet or "way-shower");
- the complete authority of the Bible (by putting other books on an equal plane with Scripture);
- the sinfulness of humans (by claiming that people should recognize the "God that is in them");
- Jesus' role in salvation (by claiming that people can "merge" with God through meditation, yoga, and other methods);
- the role of the Holy Spirit (by claiming that "spirit guides" show the way to God).

Ask volunteers to explain which beliefs of the New Age movement surprised them most and why.

Then ask: **Why might people be drawn to the New Age movement?** (Its nonjudgmental, "do whatever is right for you" emphasis might appeal to people who are tired of "dos and don'ts" in religion. Its emphasis on the "God that is in each of us" might appeal to people

O P T I O N S

EXTRA
ACTION

HEARD IT ALL
BEFORE

LITTLE
BIBLE
BACKGROUND

MOSTLY
GIRLS

MOSTLY
GUYS

MEDIA

JR.HIGH
HIGH
SCHOOL
COMBINED

looking for self-esteem boosts. Its popularity among celebrities like Shirley MacLaine might appeal to some people.)

Based on what we've just discussed, do you think it's wrong for Christians to listen to New Age music? Get a few responses. If no one mentions it, point out that New Age music has very little to do with the New Age movement. Music is music. But as with any music, if you think it's having a negative effect on you, you shouldn't listen to it.

Do you think it's wrong for Christians to do yoga? Get a few responses. If no one mentions it, suggest that if someone were doing yoga in order to "merge with God," it would be wrong. If someone were doing relaxation exercises merely as a stretching/relaxing technique, it might be OK.

Do you think it's wrong for Christians to wear crystals? Get a few responses. Point out that some people wear crystals simply because they think crystals look cool. There's probably nothing wrong with that, as long as they know that crystals have no special powers and as long as they aren't offending someone else by wearing them.

Do you think it's wrong for Christians to have the attitude "If it works for you, do it"? Again get a few responses. Then emphasize that this philosophy is perhaps the most dangerous and seductive part of the New Age movement. Often we're so afraid of being thought of as closed-minded and intolerant that we fail to point out false teachings or ideas.

Emphasize that this is just a brief overview of a complex and diverse set of beliefs. But it's enough to show the differences between the New Age movement and traditional Christianity.

STEP 3

A.k.a. "Moonies"

(Needed: Copies of Repro Resource 10, pencils)

Ask: **When I say the word *Moonies*, what do you think of?** Because Moonies aren't as prevalent in our society today as they were several years ago, your group members may not know much about them. Some might mention the mass weddings performed by Sun Myung Moon. Others might mention the group's fund-raising efforts through flower selling.

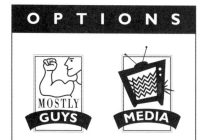

OPTIONS

MOSTLY GUYS

MEDIA

Have group members form teams of three or four. If possible, make sure group members don't team up with the same people they were teamed with earlier. Distribute copies of "Fact Sheet: The Unification Church" (Repro Resource 10) to each team. As before, the teams should read through the information on the sheet and circle any ideas or beliefs that seem unbiblical or questionable.

Give the teams a few minutes to work. When they're finished, have volunteers share their responses. Use the following information to supplement the teams' responses.

Among the traditional, biblical Christian beliefs disputed by the Unification Church are

- the complete trustworthiness of the Bible (by claiming that Moon's interpretation of Scripture is the correct version);
- the nature of Jesus' work on earth (by claiming that Jesus failed at His task on earth);
- the sovereignty of God (by claiming that God needs humanity in order to be complete);
- the deity of Jesus (by claiming that Jesus was not God);
- the nature of salvation (by claiming that Jesus' death and resurrection did not achieve complete salvation for us);
- Jesus' position as the only way to salvation (by claiming that people can receive rebirth through obedience to Reverend Moon).

Ask volunteers to explain which beliefs of the Unification Church surprised them most and why.

Then ask: **Why might people be drawn to the Unification Church?** (Some people may find it easier to obey the commands of Reverend Moon, who they physically can see and hear, rather than God, who cannot be physically seen or heard. The idea of undoing the original sin of Lucifer and Eve through marriage may appeal to some.)

Explain: **One of the disarming things about the Unification Church is its Christian language. Moon has used his own Christian background to develop a spin-off of Christianity that sounds very biblical—to a point. Unification churches even sing Christian hymns in their gatherings.**

Again emphasize that this was just a brief summary of a very complicated belief system.

Encourage group members to keep these resource sheets in their Bibles for future reference.

STEP
4

Word Wise

OPTIONS

EXTRA
ACTION

SMALL
GROUP

LARGE
GROUP

HEARD IT ALL
BEFORE

LITTLE
BIBLE
BACKGROUND

FELLOWSHIP &
WORSHIP

MOSTLY
GIRLS

EXTRA
FUN

SHORT MEETING
TIME

URBAN

JR.HIGH
HIGH
SCHOOL
COMBINED

EXTRA
CHALLENGE

(Needed: Chalkboard and chalk or newsprint and marker)

Write the following question on the board: "How Should We React to Cults?" Below the question, write the numbers 1-4.

Explain: **There are four principles for us to keep in mind if and when we encounter New Age philosophies or teachings from the Unification Church or any other cult.**

The first principle is "Know what you believe." Write this on the board next to #1.

Have someone read aloud 2 Timothy 1:11-14. Then ask: **Why is Paul "not ashamed" even though he's suffering?** (He knows Christ, and he's confident in Christ's faithfulness.)

Comment: **Perhaps this first principle should read "Know who you believe." Christ is where our faith rests. But what does Paul ask Timothy to do?** (Keep the pattern of sound teaching that he received; guard the Gospel.)

How do you think Timothy would "guard" the Gospel? (By making sure the church preached it properly, as it was received; by not allowing new ideas to creep in and twist it around.)

Write the second principle on the board: "Know why you believe."

Have someone read aloud 2 Timothy 3:14-17. Then ask: **According to this passage, why should Timothy be "convinced" of the Gospel he has learned?** (Because he knows the people from whom he learned it.)

Say: **Think about the people who have taught you about the Christian faith. What are they like? Of course they're not perfect—but do you see the reality of God in their lives? That's one testimony to the truth of the Gospel. We find another one in Romans 8:16.**

Ask someone to read the verse aloud. Then ask: **According to this verse, what additional testimony do we have concerning our faith? (The Spirit lets us know that we are God's children.)**

Explain: **There are many other reasons to believe in the Christian faith. The Bible gives us a historically reliable record of Jesus. Jesus' resurrection affirms that He is God. There are many external arguments; but unless we know internally that it's true, we might be swayed by a good arguer.**

Write the third principle on the board: "Don't be afraid."

Say: **There's a story in Isaiah in which the king of Israel is terrified about two dinky nations that are threatening to go to war against him. The Lord sends this message to the king: "Be careful, keep calm and don't be afraid. Do not lose heart because of these two smoldering stubs of firewood. . . . [Their threatened invasion] will not take place, it will not happen." And He adds, "If you do not stand firm in your faith, you will not stand at all** (Isa. 7:4-9)."

The message for us is that God is still in charge. These cults may seem to be taking over, especially something as huge as the New Age movement. But don't be afraid. Be careful, but keep calm.

Have someone read aloud I Peter 3:14-15. Then ask: **What should we do instead of being frightened?** (Set apart Christ as Lord; be prepared to explain our faith; be gentle and respectful.)

Explain: **If we know what we believe and why, we'll be able to explain our faith to those who ask. If we're not afraid, we'll behave with gentleness and respect.**

There's one final point. As you look through the various cults we've talked about, it seems that a lot of them grew out of a dissatisfaction with the church. People just weren't getting what they needed from organized Christianity, so they branched out and did their own thing. So here's the last point: "Get a good thing going." Write this on the board. **Don't be satisfied with a dull Christianity. Live in the joy of Christ. Face the adventure of being a Christian. Let His energy fill you day by day. Then you won't need to reach for some "higher consciousness," because your present consciousness will be all you could ever want.**

This may be an opportunity for you as a group leader to evaluate the quality of your group. Many kids are attracted to cults because of the love and caring they find there. How much caring does your group have? What can you do about it? If you have time, you may want to have group members offer their opinions and ideas.

Close the session in prayer, asking God for assurance, courage, and joy as we face the cults in our world.

FACT SHEET:
NEW AGE
MOVEMENT

The New Age Movement is nothing new. It's just a modern swell of interest in a very old Hindu philosophy. These teachings have been gaining ground in the Western world over the past century. But the recent momentum seems to have begun in the 1960's. The New Age Movement is a diverse collection of beliefs and practices. It's not an organized movement, but it is widespread.

According to New Age philosophy, God is everything and everything is God. There is just one reality, which is God. God is seen as a force, a power, the energy of the universe.

Jesus Christ plays a very little part in New Age philosophy. Some New Age followers may view Him as a prophet or "way-shower." Others may see Him as one of several incarnations (God appearing in human form) of the Deity. But He is not viewed as the uniquely divine Son of God.

Likewise, the Bible matters very little in New Age philosophy. The books preferred by many New Agers include the Hindu texts *The Upanishads* and *Bhagavad Gita*, Marilyn Ferguson's *The Aquarian Conspiracy*, and Shirley MacLaine's *Out on a Limb*.

According to New Age philosophy, humans are part of the oneness of God, the universe, and everything. Therefore, we are God. New Age teaching regularly challenges people to recognize the "God that is in you." We are part of each other, and part of everything that exists.

There is little need for salvation in New Age philosophy. Instead, the law of karma keeps a balance in the universe—basically, what goes around, comes around. And the idea of reincarnation keeps things "coming around" for thousands of years. According to New Age teachings, the best you can do is to free yourself from the illusion (maya) of daily life and merge your soul with the Everything, which is God. This can be done, supposedly, through meditation, communication with your "higher self," yoga, and other methods.

Channeling is another feature of the New Age Movement. Supposedly there are "spirit guides" who have been through the whole reincarnation circuit, and now speak through present-day humans, showing the way to the Everything God.

Another feature of the New Age Movement is the power of crystals. Many New Agers believe that certain things in nature, like crystals, contain special forces that give off healthful vibrations. Though medical science may not agree, many New Agers insist that crystals contribute to physical and spiritual well-being.

In summary, the one overriding feature of the New Age Movement is its acceptance. It's a very easy-going belief system. No one judges anyone else. The New Age attitude can be summarized by such phrases as "Whatever turns you on," "If it works for you, do it," and "We're just climbing different roads to the top of the mountain." In other words, there is no right or wrong. This is a popular attitude to have these days. Opponents of the movement who object to its teachings are often labeled "closed-minded" and "intolerant."

FACT SHEET:
THE UNIFICATION CHURCH

In 1936, in a Christian family in Korea, 16-year-old Sun Myung Moon had a vision. In this vision, Moon claims Jesus told him that God wanted a new relationship with humanity. He wanted Moon to complete the task that Jesus had failed at. Moon began developing his own unique interpretation of the Bible, calling it *The Divine Principle*. By 1944 he had a following in North Korea, but he ran afoul of the Communist authorities. In 1954 he established his Unification Church, which grew in Korea and was exported to the United States—with considerable fanfare—in the 1970's.

According to the Unification Church (whose members are often referred to as "Moonies"), "God is the Father and we are the children." But because of the dualist nature of things (every yang needs a yin), God *needs* humanity in order to be complete.

The Unification Church teaches that humans are made in God's image, and that we should exist within a "Four Base Relationship"—with God at the top, male and female coequal in the middle, and children at the bottom.

According to the Unification Church, Jesus was not God Himself, though He did "live God's ideal in fullest realization." As a "perfected man," He attained deity—just like we can. Jesus came as the Second Adam to set up God's perfect Kingdom—to become a True Father and to marry a True Mother who would give birth to sinless children. But Satan foiled things, and Jesus died, His mission unfulfilled.

The Unification Church teaches that Jesus' death did win *spiritual* salvation for those who believe, but not physical salvation. Physical salvation is left for the Third Adam, the Lord of the Second Advent. This person, Moon has said, would come from an Eastern country—say, Korea—and become the True Father, marrying the True Mother, and setting up God's kingdom on earth. People can receive rebirth by "loving" this Messiah, "and obeying and believing the Messiah more than my own life, and by doing what he requires with great faith." Moon was coy about it at first, but lately he has come right out with it—that Messiah, the Lord of the Second Advent, is Reverend Sun Myung Moon.

In their efforts to "obey and believe" Reverend Moon, his followers have sold millions of dollars worth of flowers and other things. The Unification Church has become a financial empire in Korea and the United States.

The Unification Church places great importance on marriage. According to Reverend Moon, marriage is the way we can right the original sin of Lucifer and Eve. That's why Moon has conducted mass weddings of his followers, many of whom had never met their new spouses.

STEP 2

Before the session, cut up one or two copies of Repro Resources 9 and 10 so that each paragraph is on a separate slip. Put each set of slips in its own envelope. Find the biblical beliefs disputed by the New Age movement (six are listed in the basic session's Step 2) and the Unification Church (six are listed in Step 3). Write each of these beliefs (without their parenthetical explanations) on a separate index card. Put the Step 2 and Step 3 cards in their own envelopes. When it's time for Step 2, give Resource 9 paragraphs to half the kids and corresponding biblical belief cards to the other half; let them mingle, read, and ask questions in an effort to match the biblical beliefs with the New Age teachings that dispute them. Do the same with the material on the Unification Church in Step 3.

STEP 4

Form teams. Give each team paper and markers. When you announce the first principle (**"Know what you believe"**), the first team to write the principle on paper (each word on a separate sheet), run to the front of the room, and hold up the words in the right order gets five points. As you ask follow-up questions (such as **Why is Paul "not ashamed" even though he's suffering?**), the team that won five points gets first crack at answering in the same way (coming up with a team answer and holding it up a word at a time). If that team doesn't come up with an acceptable answer in 20 seconds, give the other team a chance. A correct answer wins one point. Do the same with the other three principles (though the fourth principle has no follow-up questions). The team with the most points at the end of the step wins.

STEP 1

Hard to generate chaos with a few kids? Try Tongue Twister Twisters. You'll read "twisted" versions of well-known tongue twisters. The winner of each round is the first person who figures out what you're talking about, runs to the front, and quickly says the well-known version without making a mistake. Here are twisted and untwisted versions. Pause after reading each one to let players do their untwisting. (1) **Resilient infant conveyance pads.** (Rubber baby buggy bumpers.) (2) **The female person purveys mollusks at the edge of the Pacific.** (She sells seashells down by the seashore.) (3) **The grizzly hemorrhaged as a result of a puncture wound inflicted by a large, dark insect.** (The big black bug bit the big black bear and made the big black bear bleed blood.) (4) **A flute player named Petrus harvested a large number of preserved capsicums.** (Peter Piper picked a peck of pickled peppers.) (5) **If a marmot were able to throw sawn trees, in what amount might he or she do so?** (How much wood would a woodchuck chuck if a woodchuck could chuck wood?) After congratulating the best untwister, note that cults tend to twist Scripture—and we need to learn how to untwist their interpretations.

STEP 4

Want to avoid "preaching" to your small group? Let kids teach each other. Before the session, photocopy Step 4 in four sections. The first section begins with **"The first principle is . . ."** The second starts with **"Write the second principle on the board . . ."** The third section begins with **"Write the third principle on the board . . ."** The fourth section begins with **"There's one final point . . ."** Hand each section of the session plan to a different individual or pair. Kids should follow the directions as you would.

STEP 1

If you're concerned about the chaotic "non-game" getting out of hand, try this instead. Form two teams. Give each some masking tape and a large supply of newspaper. Each team's goal: to cover a wall with newspaper. One team has a strong leader (appoint him or her) whose followers must do only what he or she says. The other team has no leader, but each member believes strongly that the wall must be covered with paper. The team whose wall is covered more completely in three minutes wins. Use this as an illustration of the New Age movement (the team with no leader) and the Unification Church (the team with a strong leader). Note that the teams' performance may differ widely, but both are capable of reaching their goals.

STEP 4

Unless you're a riveting speaker, you may have trouble holding kids' attention with the mini-lecture. Before the session, enlist the help of two student actors to dramatize the four sections. In the first section, as you talk about guarding the Gospel, they should fight each other with fake swords. In the second section, as you talk about the teachers who have influenced group members, your actors should fawn over you and ask for your autograph. In the third section, when you tell the Isaiah story, they should make threatening noises and gestures until you call them "smoldering stubs of firewood"; then they should make chicken noises and run away. In the final section, as you talk about living in the joy of Christ, your actors should run through the group, tossing confetti everywhere. Bring your actors out for a "curtain call" when you're through.

STEP 2

With all the warnings Christians have sounded about the New Age movement, and the failure of the movement to "take over the world," kids may think it's time to move on to something else. After all, aren't New Agers harmless crystal-wearers? And aren't Moonies just irritating flower sellers? Tell this fable: **Once upon a time, there was a group of very nice people who wore crystals for good luck. There was another group of smiling people who sold flowers along the highway. Unfortunately for them, God hated crystals and flowers. He smote these nice people asunder, causing the earth to open and swallow them up, and they all died.** Ask: **Does that seem fair? What could God have against such nice people? Do you think Christians might be overreacting to New Agers and Moonies? Why or why not?** Note that some Christians may have gone overboard in their descriptions of these groups. But there's a lot more to these cults than crystals and flower selling; the real dangers lie under the surface.

STEP 4

Jaded kids may tune out a "sermon" on the four principles. Instead of lecturing, try this. Photocopy the basic session plan for Step 4, one copy per person. Use the copies as you have the "fact sheets" on cults; let kids read them and circle things they find questionable. Encourage kids to look up the Bible passages to see whether they teach what the session plan says they do. Then discuss anything kids have circled. Don't feel you have to defend the principles; just urge kids to think about them. Spend some time on the next to last paragraph of Step 4, letting kids talk about whether your group needs improvement in the caring department.

STEP 2

In Steps 2 and 3, explain as needed the biblical beliefs that the two cults dispute. *The nature of God*—God is greater than His creation, not identical with it (Rom. 1:25). *Jesus' deity*—Christ is God, not just a very wise human (Phil. 2:5-7). *Sinfulness of humans*—On their own, people aren't even always good, much less gods (Matt. 19:17; Rom. 3:10-12). *Jesus' role in salvation*—Faith in Christ is the only way to God (John 14:6). *The role of the Holy Spirit*—God's Spirit, not other spirits, shows us the truth (John 14:25-26; 1 John 4:1). The Bible forbids divination, which includes the practice of consulting spirits (Lev. 19:26; Acts 16:16-18). *Nature of Jesus' work*—His death was no failure. It was voluntary and necessary to complete His mission (Phil. 2:8-11). *Sovereignty of God*—God has always existed (Ps. 90:2). He created humans relatively recently. Why did He wait so long if He was incomplete without us? *Nature of salvation*—Christ's death has freed us from sin, period (Rev. 1:5-6).

STEP 4

The basic session assumes your group members are Christians. If that's not necessarily the case, change questions like **What additional testimony do we have concerning our faith?** to **What other proof do Christians have that they belong to God?** In discussing the fourth principle, invite kids to "get a good thing going" by beginning the adventure of being a Christian. Briefly describe how to receive Christ as Savior, or offer to meet later with anyone who wants to know how.

STEP 1

Try this getting-to-know-you activity. Form pairs; partners sit facing each other. You call out a word or phrase; partners tell each other the first word that pops into their head, then briefly explain to each other why they thought of that word (if they can). Then move to the next word. Here are the words and phrases: school; vacation; favorite; moon; Moonies; UFOs; crystals; reincarnation; New Age. Ask volunteers to share their reactions to "Moonies" and "New Age" with the whole group.

STEP 4

Finish the meeting with worship. Responding to the weakened New Age image of Jesus and the false messianic claims of Sun Myung Moon, listen to a recording of the "Hallelujah Chorus" from Handel's *Messiah*. Then encourage sentence prayers praising the King of kings and Lord of lords, Jesus Christ.

STEP 2

For a more in-depth discussion of the last question in Step 2, try a debate format. Have group members form two debate teams. The topic of your debate is the following statement: "If it works for you, do it." One team will argue for the statement; the other team will argue against it. Point out that, in a debate, you don't necessarily have to believe in a point of view to argue for it. Give the teams a few minutes to prepare their arguments. You may want to offer some help to both teams with their arguments, if necessary. For the debate, give each team two minutes to present its case and one minute for a rebuttal.

STEP 4

Have group members form teams of three or four. Instruct each team to make a list of things that would be included in an "ideal" religion. These things might include a nonjudgmental attitude, love and acceptance for all members, mutual financial support among members, fun worship services, etc. Give the teams a few minutes to work. When they're finished, have each team share its list. Write the teams' suggestions on the board as they are named.

Then ask: **Which of these things do cults like the New Age movement and the Moonies tend to focus on? Which of these things seem most attractive to you? Why is it more important to know and accept the truth of Christianity than to look for belief systems that are attractive to you?**

STEP 2

With all this talk of crystals and yoga, guys may wonder how the New Age movement could appeal to males. Start the step by giving a prize to the guy who can get in the most contorted yoga-like position. Then ask: **Do you think you'd like yoga? How about wearing crystals? Do you think these things appeal to guys, girls, or both? Do you think guys could get interested in a religion that does away with the Bible's rules? Which rules would a lot of guys like to get rid of?** (Having to go to church; rules limiting sexual activity; turning the other cheek; serving others instead of thinking of yourself, etc.) Note that the New Age movement's basic message is, "You can be like gods." Adam and Eve fell for that one. Guys continue to grab for power that belongs only to God, whether or not they become "official" New Agers.

STEP 3

Why would the Unification Church appeal to males? Start the step by giving each guy an artificial flower. Announce that anyone without a flower at the end of one minute will get a prize. No throwing flowers away or forcing others to take them; guys must somehow convince each other to take the flowers. Most guys will still be stuck with flowers at the end of a minute. Then ask: **Why would any guy want to sell flowers as a Moonie?** Explain that most people don't join the Unification Church in order to sell flowers. Many have joined because the group appears at first to offer friendly, committed relationships; some may be drawn by the chance to do something, to be part of a big movement that promises to change the world. Others might be impressed by the financial success of Moon's organization, or other reasons.

STEP 1

Form teams. Announce: **Your team's goal is to get me to bark like a dog. Each team will have one minute to try. You can try anything as long as you don't touch me—threats, hypnotism, brainwashing, promises, bribes, trickery, etc. Any team that gets me to bark wins a prize.** Let kids give it a shot. Whether you bark is up to you. After the contest, discuss: **Which methods did you think were best? Which methods might work best on you? What method did I use to get you to play this game?** (Promising a reward.) Tie this into the ways in which cults recruit and keep members. Promises (and sometimes trickery) are used to get people into cults; threats are sometimes used to get them to stay. Some groups, such as the Unification Church, have been accused of using brainwashing (keeping recruits tired, feeding them low-protein diets, repeating teachings over and over, etc.) to get and keep members.

STEP 4

Stage a relay race that requires teams to carry water in leaky containers. If you're outside, use very leaky buckets or plastic jugs to fill trash cans; if indoors, have each team race to transfer water from one mixing bowl to another using a spoon that's full of holes. After the contest, make the connection: Your buckets (or spoons), like cult teachings, just don't hold water.

STEP 2

Try either or both of the following: (1) Play some New Age music. (Look under "New Age" in a record store or tape some from a radio station that specializes in this style. Some stations refer to it as "smooth jazz.") Ask: **How does this music "feel" to you? What view of life do you think it's meant to reflect? Do you think it might influence you? If so, how?** (2) Rent the video of the movie *All of Me*, starring Steve Martin. Preview and show some opening scenes in which a dying woman (Lily Tomlin) follows the advice of a New Age guru who wants to store her soul in a bowl and transfer it to someone else's body. After watching, note that people are already making fun of New Age teachings. Ask: **Why might some people still take this movement seriously?** (For one thing, its practices take many forms. As soon as one fad like "channeling" is debunked or stops being trendy, another takes its place.)

STEP 3

Try either of these. (1) Rent and show scenes from the video of the film *Ticket to Heaven*. This film doesn't mention a cult by name, but is based on articles written about a former Unification Church member. The movie depicts recruiting methods said to be used by the Moonies. The film is rated R, so be sure to preview scenes you plan to show. (2) Rent videos of a few movies that depict Christ (*Jesus, The Greatest Story Ever Told, Jesus Christ Superstar, Godspell, King of Kings*, etc.). Show a scene from each. Discuss which portrayal of Christ seems most believable. Ask: **How would you expect Sun Myung Moon to act if he's a "messiah"? How would you compare him to Christ?**

STEP 1

Skip Step 1. Combine Steps 2 and 3 in this new opener. Before the session, set up chairs in two sections. As kids enter, you and a helper should act as ushers. Give half the entering kids Repro Resource 9 and tell them, **Welcome to the New Age movement.** Usher them to one section. Give the other half Repro Resource 10 and say, **Welcome to the Unification Church.** Seat them in the other section. Each group studies its own sheet. Then, as "members" of the two cults, groups explain their beliefs to each other. Each group gets to challenge the other group's beliefs for two minutes. Ask how it felt to be a "member" of each group. As needed, summarize how each cult is at odds with Scripture, using the lists in the basic Steps 2 and 3.

STEP 4

Write the first three principles on the board. Then assign the four Scripture references to four people (or pairs) in no particular order. Ask kids to read their passages, decide which passages go with which principles, and explain that to the rest of the group. Then write the fourth principle on the board, explaining it briefly. Skip as many of the other comments and discussion questions in the basic Step 4 as time requires.

STEP 1

To increase the chaos potential of the opening activity, don't have group members form teams. Instead, inform each group member that he or she must create his or her own game. Explain that group members may do anything they want (within reason). They can make up their own rules and choose their own means of having fun. No one can tell them their activities are "stupid" or "wrong" because what is "right" is relative to each individual. Give group members a few minutes to figure out what they will do. Just before they begin their games, inform them that they must not get in each other's way and that they must respect the needs of each other as they play. Then, without answering any questions, have them begin their games and let the confusion begin.

STEP 4

Include the following Scripture passages and questions in your discussion.

Romans 1:16-17. Ask: **Why do you think Paul said he was not ashamed of the Gospel? How can you be more like Paul in your attitude toward the Gospel?**

Romans 8:28-39. Ask: **What does this passage say about having a relationship with Jesus? How would you answer the question Paul raises in verse 31? If nothing can separate us from Christ, why do some people who were involved in Christian churches get involved with cults? After reading verse 37, what are some areas you want to "conquer" in your personal life, in your social life, and in your city?**

COMBINED

STEP 2

In addition to having teams circle questionable items on the Repro Resources used in Steps 2 and 3, have them underline things they don't quite understand—words and phrases as well as teachings. Have teams pass the sheets to you anonymously. Explain as many of the underlined items as you can; if something isn't clear to you either, feel free to say so. Then discuss the questionable items kids circled.

STEP 4

Younger kids may appreciate being told the simply worded principles more than older kids will. If you have mostly younger kids, keep things as straightforward as possible by skipping the Isaiah story and adapting the last section (starting with **There's one final point …**). Omit esoteric phrases like "live in the joy of Christ," "let His energy fill you," and "higher consciousness." Emphasize "the adventure of being a Christian" and give concrete examples of how being a Christian can be an adventure. For instance: You never know what good things God might suddenly give you; you can help change people's lives by introducing them to Jesus; God may call you to serve Him in a place where few Christians have gone; you can invent new ways to get God's work done on earth; you're going to live forever, so the adventure will continue; etc.

EXTRA CHALLENGE

STEP 1

If your kids feel too "mature" for the charades and play money of the "non-game," try the challenge of "Triple Meanings." You'll read three definitions, all of which apply to the same word. Kids try to guess what the word is. Here are some definitions and the words to which they apply.
(1) **Reddish brown; to cry out; an inlet of the sea.** (Bay) (2) **Prison; to write; a female swan.** (Pen)
(3) **Vertical edge of a square sail; to drain; a bloodsucking worm.** (Leech)
(4) **Plump; a specific number of plays in a game; a cut of beef.** (Round) (5) **Marked for measuring; received a diploma; slowly changed.** (Graduated.) (6) **Without motion; nevertheless; moonshine machine.** (Still) (7) **Portion of a year; to mature; to add spice.** (Season)

After noting that the same word can have several meanings, point out that cults often use words Christians use (messiah, salvation, born again, etc.)—but with very different meanings.

STEP 4

If possible, after the meeting or during the week take kids to look at New Age books in a nearby bookstore. Many cities have bookstores dedicated solely to New Age books; most towns have a Religion or Philosophy section in secular bookstores that includes at least a few New Age books. Then go out for a snack and discuss what you found. If you can't do that, offer an incentive to anyone who will either (1) go to such a store and report to the group; or (2) read and report on the book *Unmasking the New Age* by Douglas R. Groothuis (InterVarsity Press).

PLANNING CHECKLIST

DATE USED:

Approx. Time

STEP 1: *The Non-Game* _____
- ❏ Small Group
- ❏ Large Group
- ❏ Fellowship & Worship
- ❏ Extra Fun
- ❏ Short Meeting Time
- ❏ Urban
- ❏ Extra Challenge
Things needed:

STEP 2: *The Dawn of a New Age* _____
- ❏ Extra Action
- ❏ Heard It All Before
- ❏ Little Bible Background
- ❏ Mostly Girls
- ❏ Mostly Guys
- ❏ Media
- ❏ Combined Junior High/High School
Things needed:

STEP 3: *A.k.a. "Moonies"* _____
- ❏ Mostly Guys
- ❏ Media
Things needed:

STEP 4: *Word Wise* _____
- ❏ Extra Action
- ❏ Small Group
- ❏ Large Group
- ❏ Heard It All Before
- ❏ Little Bible Background
- ❏ Fellowship & Worship
- ❏ Mostly Girls
- ❏ Extra Fun
- ❏ Short Meeting Time
- ❏ Urban
- ❏ Combined Junior High/High School
- ❏ Extra Challenge
Things needed:

Astrology, Witchcraft, and Satanism

YOUR GOALS FOR THIS SESSION:

Choose one or more

☐ To help kids recognize that occult practices, even in "mild" forms, are extremely dangerous.

☐ To help kids understand what the Bible teaches about occult practices.

☐ To help kids guard themselves against the occult and to prepare them to help friends who may be involved in the occult.

☐ Other:_____

_____

Your Bible Base:

Deuteronomy 18:10-12
Isaiah 47:13-15
Matthew 4:8-10
Romans 1:25

Fright Attendants

To begin the session, ask: **What's the scariest thing that's ever happened to you? When were you most frightened?** Explain that you're not really looking for "serious" stuff here, like being scared about your parents' divorce or being frightened when you found out a loved one had cancer. Instead, you're looking for relatively harmless situations like investigating a "haunted" house or having your car stall on a deserted road at night. To give group members an idea of what you're looking for, share a story of your own.

If your group members are reluctant to talk about their personal experiences, ask volunteers to talk about the scariest movies they've ever seen or the scariest books they've ever read. Ask them to explain what it was that made the movies/books so frightening.

After several kids have responded, ask: **Do you ever like being scared? If so, why?** (For many people, being scared makes them feel more "alive." If their lives are boring, they may need the excitement of being scared. They may need to feel that things are a little out of control, especially if they can remind themselves, "It's only a movie/book." Some people like to live "on the edge," always in a little bit of danger.)

Do you think it's ever good to be frightened? If no one mentions it, point out that fear often prevents us from doing risky or foolhardy things. For instance, the fear of being attacked prevents some people from walking in dangerous areas of the city at night.

Explain: **Today we're going to be talking about some subjects that scare many people—satanism, witchcraft, and astrology. Then you'll decide for yourselves whether or not to be scared of these things.**

Testing the Spirits

(Needed: Copies of Repro Resource 11, pencils)

Distribute copies of "Quick Quiz" (Repro Resource 11) and pencils. Explain to your group members that the purpose of this quiz is to find out what their opinions and beliefs are concerning astrology, witchcraft, and the occult. Emphasize that they may circle more than one answer for each question. If none of the answers seem right, group members may write another response. Give group members a few minutes to complete the quiz.

When everyone is finished, go through questions 1-4. Have group members indicate their responses to each question by raising their hands. Instead of grading the quiz, use it as a tool to get kids talking and sharing their opinions.

Then ask: **How many of you know your astrological sign? For instance, are you a Taurus, a Capricorn, a Gemini, etc.?** Probably most of your group members know their astrological sign.

How many of you believe that your astrological sign affects your personality? For instance, because you're a Taurus, does that mean you have a good sense of humor? Encourage group members to respond honestly. Make sure no one is made fun of for his or her opinions.

How many of you read your horoscope regularly? If so, why? Some people may read it just for fun or to make fun of it. Others may seriously believe its predictions.

How many of you have had a horoscope prediction come true? Encourage volunteers to share predictions that have come true.

How do you explain that? Some people may say its just coincidence. Others may say that newspaper horoscopes are so vague and general that they can be applied to any one of a number of situations. Still others may believe that horoscopes have the power to predict the future.

Point out that most astrologers agree that newspaper horoscopes are necessarily vague and general. These astrologers say that if you really want to get specific, you need to "have your charts done," pinpointing the exact day and hour of your birth.

Ask: **Do you know anyone who's ever had his or her chart done by an astrologer? If so, what did the person find out?** If possible, get a few responses.

Would you say it's wrong for a person to make changes in his or her life based on astrology predictions? (It could be dangerous. Instead of relying on common sense or other decision-making abilities, the person is making decisions based on something that at best is a nonscientific parlor game, and at worst is a demon-controlled activity.)

Point out that if there is some supernatural force behind astrology, it must come from one of two places—God or Satan.

Have someone read aloud Isaiah 47:13-15. Then ask: **What is God's attitude in this passage toward astrologers?** (He seems to be mocking them, making fun of their supposed abilities.)

Explain that God's prophets in the Bible were held to a 100% success rate. If even one of their predictions didn't come true, they weren't approved by God. Even the most committed astrologers have to admit that astrology is wrong sometimes. Therefore, astrology cannot be sanctioned by God.

Dabbling in astrology seems harmless enough. Do you think there's a chance it could lead to other, more serious, occult involvement? If so, how? (The key is power. Power is addictive. If people sense that there is power in astrology, they will be drawn to deeper and deeper experiences of that power. This opens the door to more occult involvement.)

So where do you draw the line? How do you know when you're "in too deep" in astrology? Is reading your daily horoscope dangerous? What about having your charts done? Encourage several group members to offer their opinions. Supplement their responses with the following comments, as you see fit.

We've already concluded that astrology is either a meaningless game or that it has some supernatural power. If it's a meaningless game, then why play it? Why let it influence your life at all? That would only make sense if it had power.

If astrology "works" and there is supernatural power behind it, that power is not from God. Involvement in it could open the door to deeper occult activity. In other words, it's not a good thing to dabble in.

Which Witch Is Which?

(Needed: Copies of Repro Resource 11)

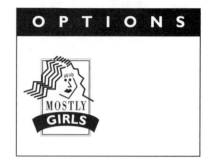

MOSTLY GIRLS

Go through questions 5-7 on Repro Resource 11. Have group members indicate their responses to each question by raising their hands.

Then quickly ask for three volunteers to stand in front of the group and do their best witch imitations. Some may choose to imitate the Wicked Witch of the West from *The Wizard of Oz*. Others may choose to imitate someone else. Give each contestant 15 seconds to perform. Then vote as a group on the winner. Give that person a round of applause.

Ask: **When you think of a witch, what images come to mind?** (An old woman dressed in black, wearing a pointy hat, riding a broomstick, etc.)

Do you know of anyone who is personally involved in witchcraft? If so, how would that person describe witchcraft? If no one mentions it, point out that witches tend to categorize themselves as either "black" or "white." Black witches intentionally call upon demons and dark forces in order to gain power for themselves. White witches, on the other hand, usually consider themselves nature worshipers and try to tap into the power of nature and the human mind.

Explain: **Witchcraft has a long-standing connection with supernatural forces. Most witches—black and white—perform precise rituals in their gatherings. They use candles, chants, and herbs in their spell-casting; and they use songs, prayers, and dances in their "worship times." So witchcraft is not simply "unleashing the power of the mind," as some witches claim. There are some supernatural aspects to it.**

What are the two possible sources of supernatural power? (God and Satan.)

Have someone read aloud Deuteronomy 18:10-12. Then ask: **According to this passage, how does God feel about witchcraft and "sorcery"?** (They are detestable to Him, and anyone who practices them is detestable to Him.) If you have time, look up Galatians 5:19-20 also.

So what does this tell you about the supernatural forces behind witchcraft? (They must come from Satan.)

It's obvious that black witches get their power from Satan. But what about white witches? They claim that their

power comes from nature and that they use their spells to help others. **Can that really be satanic?** Get a few opinions.

Then have someone read aloud Romans 1:25. Ask: **What is the problem described in this verse?** (People worshiping created things instead of the Creator.)

Explain: **That's what "white witches" are doing. They are worshiping nature, a created thing, instead of God, the Creator.**

So, are they really just as evil as "black witches"? We could give them the benefit of the doubt on their intentions. Maybe they really are trying to make the world a better place. Maybe they have no desire to get involved with the devil. But Scripture tells us that their activity displeases God. And the power that they have must come from somewhere. So it's logical to conclude that demons are behind even so-called white witchcraft. These white witches may have good intentions—but if so, they are dangerously naive.

How Serious Is Satanism?

(Needed: Copies of Repro Resource 11)

Go through questions 8-10 on Repro Resource 11. Have group members indicate their responses to each question by raising their hands.

Say: **We hear a lot of horror stories on the news about satanic cults and blood rituals. Do you really think satanism is a big problem in our society, or is it blown out of proportion?**

Do you think satanism is a big problem in this area? Why or why not? Encourage most of your group members to offer their opinions on these questions. Let them inform you of things they've heard from people they know. Is it happening in your community? You might be surprised.

When you think about satanism, what images come to mind? What kind of people get involved in satanism? Pay particular attention to group members' responses here. Probably many of your kids will think of blood sacrifices performed by drugged-out weirdos with pentagrams tattooed on their foreheads. Others, however, may think of relatively normal people worshiping in the religion of their choice, as Christians do.

What might cause someone to get involved in satanism?
(Friends who are involved may convince the person to try it. Certain types of movies or music might cause the person to be curious about it. The urge to rebel against traditional Christianity might cause the person to try satanism.)

Have someone read aloud Matthew 4:8-10. Explain that the setting of this passage is Satan's temptation of Jesus in the wilderness.

Ask: **What did Satan promise Jesus?** (All the kingdoms of the world and their splendor.)

What did he want in exchange? (Worship.)

How did Jesus respond? (By quoting Scripture—the Bible says, "Worship the Lord your God, and serve him only.")

Explain: **Jesus resisted Satan's temptation—but sometimes people don't. Satan promises power, pleasure, freedom from "silly" rules. To some people—especially young people who feel powerless, who don't know who they are, and who desperately want to be someone special—these promises sound awfully good.**

But Jesus called the devil "a liar and the father of lies." Peter described the devil as "a roaring lion looking for someone to devour." That's why satanic rituals are full of blood and death. The devil is into destruction. He promises fulfillment, but he will eat you up.

Refer to question 10 on Repro Resource 11. Ask: **Based on what we've talked about, what would you say is the best way to combat satanism?** Use the following information to supplement group members' responses.

- Ignoring it is probably not the best tactic. Satan thrives on secrecy and ignorance.

- Exposing the secrets of satanism—making public the names and practices of satanists—might be difficult to do from the "outside." And we must stay on the outside. On the other hand, advising friends to stay away from satanic activities is a very good way to combat satanism.

- Praying for wisdom to recognize satanic activities and strength to withstand satanic temptation is perhaps the most effective way to combat satanism.

- Scripture passages like Philippians 4:6-7 and 1 John 4:4 give us encouragement and hope, and let us know that committed Christians have nothing to worry about, because God is infinitely more powerful than Satan. He will protect those who obey Him from satanic activity.

STEP 5

Voices

(Needed: Copies of Repro Resource 12, pencils)

Hand out copies of "Voices in the Darkness" (Repro Resource 12) and pencils. Have group members form teams of three or four. Instruct team members to read through the six accounts on the sheet and decide how they would respond to each speaker. Give the teams a few minutes to work; then have them share their responses. Use the following information to supplement the teams' responses.

- *Joanne*—Your astrological sign has nothing to do with your personality. Not all Leos snap at their friends. Astrology may seem like just a way to have fun for you, but you should find other ways to have fun. It may seem harmless now, but it could get dangerous if you begin to rely on it too heavily.
- *Charlie*—Thank God you got out of the astrology scene in time. You should let people know how dabbling in astrology can lead to deeper occult involvement.
- *Serena*—You may not have "gone off the deep end," but you're playing with something that could turn ugly. You say there's a real power in witchcraft that you can't explain. That should make you uneasy. Rather than worshiping nature, a created thing, why not worship God, the Creator?
- *Tara*—Get out while you can. You're already feeling weird about it. There is a presence in your room when you cast spells—a demonic presence. Trust Christ to protect you and to give you the satisfaction you want.
- *Todd*—Stop what you're doing. The ideal solution would be to resolve your differences with your parents. But if that's not possible, find some less dangerous way of expressing yourself. You're playing with fire, whether you realize it or not.
- *Frank*—Get out of the group now! Talk to your parents, a youth leader, a pastor, a school guidance counselor, or a teacher about what you should do. Stop hanging out with those guys, and stay away from those rituals.

As you close the session in prayer, thank God for protecting us from satanic forces, and ask for wisdom in recognizing satanic/occult situations and strength for withstanding temptation to get involved with them.

OPTIONS

SMALL GROUP

HEARD IT ALL BEFORE

FELLOWSHIP & WORSHIP

MOSTLY GIRLS

MOSTLY GUYS

EXTRA FUN

MEDIA

SHORT MEETING TIME

URBAN

JR. HIGH HIGH SCHOOL COMBINED

EXTRA CHALLENGE

NOTES

Quick Quiz

Circle all the answers that you think are right.

1. Astrology is…
   (a) a scientific way to determine influences on a person's life.
   (b) a way for demons to control people's lives.
   (c) a game that's fun for those who believe in it.
   (d) silly.

2. Astrology's predictions are…
   (a) true all of the time.
   (b) true most of the time.
   (c) lucky guesses, when they come true.
   (d) so vague they're useless.

3. People who check their horoscopes every day…
   (a) usually just do it for fun.
   (b) make changes in their lives according to what's predicted.
   (c) sometimes get pulled into other occult activities.
   (d) need to "get a life."

4. If you get serious about astrology and "have your charts done"…
   (a) you allow demonic forces to gain more control of your life.
   (b) you are wasting your time.
   (c) you will learn a lot more about yourself.
   (d) you will be starting an expensive habit.

5. Witches are…
   (a) always women.
   (b) nature-lovers who commune with the powers of the earth.
   (c) demon-possessed.
   (d) often found teaching high school.

6. When a witch casts a spell…
   (a) usually nothing happens.
   (b) it's a lucky coincidence if it comes true.
   (c) there are psychic powers in the human mind that make it come true.
   (d) supernatural powers are unleashed.

7. "White witches"…
   (a) try to use their powers for the good of humanity.
   (b) believe that God exists in everything.
   (c) are really just as evil as "black witches."
   (d) try to act like Glenda in *The Wizard of Oz.*

8. Satanism…
   (a) is not as much of a problem as most people think.
   (b) is more of a problem than most people think.
   (c) isn't much of a problem around here.
   (d) only attracts weirdos.

9. Satanists…
   (a) are rebelling against traditional Christianity.
   (b) are under the control of Satan.
   (c) usually just want to shock their friends.
   (d) are greedy for supernatural power.

10. The best way to combat satanism is…
   (a) to ignore it.   (c) to pray.
   (b) to expose its secrets.   (d) to worry a lot about it.

VOICES IN THE DARKNESS

Joanne, 15

I don't see what all the problem is with astrology. It's just fun. I'm a Leo, and I'm just the way a Leo is supposed to be. I'll snap at my friends sometimes—"roaring," I call it—but then I'll apologize and say, "Hey, I'm a Leo. That's just the way I am." It's not a religion for me or anything. It's just something I do for fun. What's wrong with that?

Charlie, 42

I got into astrology when I was a teenager. I had a group of friends, and it was great to do each other's charts and try to figure out what would happen. When I was in college, some friends and I went to a professional astrologer to "do it right." This woman began to tell me things about my past that she could not have known. It was really spooky, but instead of scaring me away, it drew me in. I got my palm read, and did the tarot cards. And soon I was learning to do these things for my friends. As I progressed deeper into it, I began to realize that there were other spirits involved in this, and they wanted more and more of me. Thank God I had a Christian friend who invited me to a concert. In that Christian situation, I was able to see the mess I was in, and I got out.

Serena, 24

I learned about the Old Religion in college. You might call it witchcraft, but it's not like old hags in pointy hats. It's just a lot of neat women—and sometimes men, but our coven is just women—who try to get in touch with the powers of nature and use them for good purposes. It's such a good experience to be in that circle with the others, singing. There's a real power there, I just can't explain it. I've tried to do some minor spells with candles and herbs, with mild success. I'm still learning. But it's always good things. I wish luck for all my friends. I know you think I've gone off the deep end or something, but I really find meaning in it.

Tara, 15

I got this book from my friend Sherry. It's all about magic and witchcraft and stuff. I mean, it has, like, recipes for spells you can cast and stuff. At first I thought it was weird, but Sherry says she's tried some of them and they sometimes work. So I tried one. I got three different kinds of candles and put them all around me and I said this prayer thing. I was trying to get this cute guy at school to like me. And the next day—you know what happened? That guy still ignored me, but another guy—just as cute, and smart, too—asked me out. Isn't that so weird? I mean, it's not exactly what I asked for, but it's close. So I tried it again for good grades. But I have to say I get a weird feeling when I do the spell. It's like there's this presence in the room with me. Is that good or bad?

Todd, 17

I just like to keep my parents guessing. They've spent their whole lives controlling me, and now it's time for me to break loose. They're good Christians—at least they say they are. They're really big in church and all, but you should see them at home! Well, that's a different story. So anyway, it started when I got this poster for a new rock group, Satan's Slime, and I put it on my wall. Did they ever freak! I loved it! They made me take down the poster, but then I started getting patches and stuff with Satanic symbols. And late at night I sometimes chant in my room. Nothing special, I just want to bug Mom and Dad. I think it's working.

Frank, 15

My friend Joey and I started hanging with some guys at school who were, like, "I don't care" about everything. Long hair, torn clothes, and heavy, heavy metal. I didn't have to pretend with these guys. I could just be myself, do what I felt, you know? But then they invited us to this group. It was a Satan thing, but I didn't find that out until I was there. There were drugs and booze and music. Then they drew a star on the floor and started this "service." It was really weird. I just watched the first time, but then they made me join in. It was all right, I guess, until we started killing things. They said they needed blood. So we got animals and killed them. They made me kill a chicken last week. It was awful. But I had to do it to get into the group. It's getting weirder and I don't know what to do.

STEP 1

Play "Power Struggle." Form pairs, roughly matching kids by height, weight, and gender. Have partners face each other, one pair at a time, in a four-foot-square space that you've marked on the floor with tape. Partners should face each other like football players, but with a pillow between their opposing shoulders. The goal: Push the other person out of the square. But if the pillow falls down, both lose. If neither person pushes the other out within 30 seconds, both lose. Tie this into the quest for power—to tell the future, to control people, etc.— that astrology, witchcraft, and satanism appeal to.

STEP 2

Make the Repro Resource quiz more active by having four kids (representing answers a, b, c, and d) stand in the four corners of the room. Give only these kids a copy of the quiz. After you read a sentence starter (like **Astrology is...**), each "corner person" tries to convince group members to flock to his or her position. Kids must move to one position in 20 seconds or less. Then regroup and repeat the process for the rest of the quiz. Make discussions in Steps 2 through 4 more active by having kids "side" with or against the first person who answers each question (by standing next to him or her in agreement, or further away, depending on the degree of disagreement). In Step 5, give the Repro Resource to only four kids who'll play the parts of Joanne, Tara, Todd, and Frank (skip the other two). Other group members pretend they're at a party (provide refreshments if you like), when your four actors walk in. The four go from person to person telling their stories. Each person who hears a story must respond with advice.

STEP 2

Steps 2 through 4 include so many questions that a small group might wither under the bombardment. Try this to vary the pace. Call one person up to the front to sit with you and be "interviewed" for the opinion/experience questions (those asked before verses are looked up) at the beginnings of Steps 2 through 4. Choose a different interviewee for each step. Adapt questions to the interview format as needed (**How many of you know...?** becomes **Do you know...?**). Treat your interviewees with extra respect, as if they were movie stars or world leaders appearing on your talk show. If they can't answer all the questions, that's fine. At the end of each interview, lead applause for your "guest" and let other group members add their opinions and experiences if they wish. Address all Bible exploration questions to the whole group.

STEP 5

A large group could split up the six cases, but a small group might find that six is too many to cover. Skip the cases of Charlie and Serena. Give no more than two cases to each person. Have each group member write a short note of advice to the fictional person(s) he or she read about. Then each group member trades notes with another group member, who writes a P.S. to each note received. Read and discuss the notes.

STEP 1

For a more involving opener, try this. Group kids by the months in which they were born. Make sure you have at least two kids in each group, even if you have to combine months. Ask members of one group: **What kinds of food do you usually have for breakfast?** Ask another group: **What color are the buses at your school?** Ask another: **Which would you rather eat—pizza or liver?** Ask similarly obvious questions of the other groups. Then marvel at the "amazing" similarities in each group. Ask: **Does this prove that horoscopes are right—that people born under the same "sign" have the same personalities? Why or why not?**

STEP 2

Make Steps 2 through 5 more involving in order to keep the group on track. Turn your meeting place into a courtroom and put each kind of occult involvement "on trial" to see whether it's really a serious offense. You play the prosecutor. Choose a jury. Instead of just asking questions of the whole group, call a series of "expert witnesses" (group members) to the "witness stand" at the front of the room to answer one or two questions each from the basic session plan. Appoint a "public defender" who may cross-examine each witness with one question. Follow this procedure for Steps 2 through 4. At the end of each step, use the comments in the basic session plan as your "summation" to the jury; then let the jury vote on its verdict. In Step 5, let five "defendants" read the statements on the Repro Resource (skip Charlie). Let the jury decide whether each person is guilty of occult involvement.

STEP 2

Kids may have heard warnings about astrology, but think horoscopes are just dumb, not dangerous. Help them understand that God opposes *any* system that draws people away from Him (see Deut. 18:9-12). Use this analogy: **Alex just discovered that he has leukemia. His doctor wants him to start chemotherapy right away, saying the cure rate is high if treatment starts early. But Alex sees a story on TV about a clinic in Mexico that uses watermelon juice to treat leukemia. The clinic says it has no records of how many of its patients have been cured. Alex likes watermelon, so he tells the doctor he's going to Mexico. The doctor gets very angry. Why? Is he jealous of the Mexican clinic? What do you think Alex should do?** Point out that taking watermelon juice for leukemia wouldn't just be dumb, it would be dangerous. The juice might not hurt Alex, but he would lose valuable time that should be spent in better treatments. In the same way, astrology gives people the mistaken idea that they've found the truth, keeping them from a relationship with God.

STEP 5

Kids may be tired of hearing connections made between heavy metal music and satanism (as in the cases of Todd and Frank). Ask kids to comment on the following quotes. From a music therapist who works at a hospital in Texas: **"All heavy metal fans are not involved in satanism, but all kids who are involved in satanism are listening to heavy metal music."** From the song "Welcome to Hell" by the metal band Venom: **"We're possessed by all that is evil / The death of you, God, we demand / We spit at the virgin you worship / And sit at Lord Satan's left hand."**

STEP 2

Need background on who Satan is and how he's involved with the occult? Explain that Satan (also called Lucifer, the devil, etc.) was one of God's angels who decided that he wanted God's power for himself. Satan, along with other angels who joined his rebellion, were thrown out of heaven. Since then Satan has been trying to get people to rebel against God, offering them godlike power (Gen. 3:1-5; Matt. 4:8-10) among other things. The Bible doesn't detail how much occult power is real and from Satan, and how much is fake. But the Bible connects at least some fortune-telling with evil spirits (Acts 16:16-18), and bans all occult involvement (Deut. 18:10-12). Many Christians believe demons (who are led by Satan) are behind any displays of occult power that aren't faked. This could include uncovering "secret" knowledge (ouija boards, astrology, tarot cards), appearances of spirits (séances, channeling), and casting spells (witchcraft).

STEP 4

Kids need to know that there are limits to Satan's power and that he's already defeated by God. He is a created being, not God's equal. Unlike God, he's not all-knowing, all-powerful, or capable of being everywhere at once. God has already announced the ultimate destination of Satan and his demons—punishment in an ever-burning lake of fire (Rev. 20:10). Until then, God has given us effective weapons for fighting Satan (Eph. 6:10-18; Jas. 4:7).

STEP 1

Let kids mingle as you serve refreshments in "light and dark" pairs (a plate of white chocolate and dark chocolate; cups of cola and cups of lemon-lime pop; sugar cookies and chocolate brownies; banana slices and plums; light grapes and dark grapes; etc.). Have kids discuss these questions as they eat: **What do people mean when they talk about the "forces of light" and "forces of darkness"?** You may want to point out that connecting good with light and evil with dark has to do with the safety of daytime and the dangers that sometimes lurk at night. Some people have tried to add racial overtones, associating good with light-colored skin and evil with dark skin—which the Bible never does. **What "forces of light" and "forces of darkness" do you think are at work in the world today, and why?**

STEP 5

During worship, stress God's infinite superiority to the devil. Sing songs like "Our God Is an Awesome God," "He Is Able," "Nothing Is Impossible," and "Now unto the King Eternal." Have volunteers read Romans 8:31-39 a verse at a time, each one reading more loudly than the last. If you have enough copies of the same Bible version, have the group read the whole passage together, building from quiet voices to shouting.

MOSTLY GIRLS

STEP 3

In your discussion of witchcraft, focus on its relationship to gender. Ask: **How would you respond to people who say that all girls are born with the tendency or potential to be a witch? Do you think it's possible to have the power of witchcraft without knowing it? Why or why not?**

STEP 5

Ask for six volunteers to play the roles of the characters on "Voices in the Darkness" (Repro Resource 12). You'll need to change some of the names on the sheet: "Charlie" will become "Carol"; "Todd" will become "Terri"; and "Frank" will become "Fran." The volunteers will read their parts (in character) from the sheet. If possible, you might bring in some costumes and props for the volunteers to use. After each volunteer reads her part, have the rest of the group members suggest changes the character should make in her behavior.

MOSTLY GUYS

STEP 1

If you think your guys won't want to admit they've been scared, or that question-answering won't get their attention, try this opener. Assign each person the name of a movie monster—Dracula, the Mummy, Creature from the Black Lagoon, etc. Let kids come up with their own names if they like. Then pair kids up randomly—Frankenstein meets the Wolfman, Dracula meets the Mummy, etc. Have guys act out who would be stronger in each confrontation. Then ask: **Are these characters scary? Are any supposed to have supernatural powers? Are any linked with the devil?** Note that Dracula is identified with evil forces and reacts violently to the sight of a cross; the Wolfman supposedly has an evil curse on him. Then move into the last paragraph of the basic session's Step 1.

STEP 5

When using the Repro Resource, change Joanne to Jon; skip Charlie, Serena, and Tara; use Todd and Frank. Add the following case of "Greg, 16": **"I'm really into computers. And games. I've got some great computer games that just happen to have some occult-type stuff in them. Not Satan or anything. But one game takes you inside a haunted house, where you collect magic potions and figure out spells while you're trying to defeat an evil force that's in the house. Another game takes you on a quest with wizards, witches, and even a few demons. It's not like I can't tell the difference between the games and reality. I don't have to give this stuff up, do I?"**

EXTRA FUN

STEP 1

Have an "invisible man" contest. Form teams, three to six kids per team. Give each team a hat, coat, pair of pants, pair of gloves, and pair of shoes. Members of each team hold the clothes to form the shape of an "invisible" man and manipulate the clothes to make it look like the man is walking, bowling, and tap dancing. Give a prize to the team that creates the most believable effect. Mention that in this meeting you'll be talking about someone else who likes to manipulate things from behind the scenes. He's the one behind occult activities.

STEP 5

Try "Miniature Bungee Jumping." Form teams. Give each team a plastic action figure, a big handful of rubber bands, and a pair of scissors. Each team must cut its rubber bands and tie them together to form a long elastic cord. The cord will be tied to the action figure, which will then be dropped, bungee style, by a team member standing on the second step of a ladder and holding the other end of the cord. But each team must decide exactly how long its cord will be without testing it in any way (no tying it to the action figure yet). After all teams have decided on lengths, set up a step ladder. Let kids tie the cords to the figures and start dropping them from the ladder. The team with the longest cord that still keeps the figure from hitting the floor wins. Ask: **Would you take this "guess the cord length" approach to bungee jumping in real life? Why not?** Note that some kids don't seem to mind taking this approach with the occult—jumping in and seeing how far they can go without getting hurt. The risk just isn't worth it.

STEP 1

Watch a *scary* scene from a relatively tame horror movie on video (a classic like *Frankenstein* or *Dracula*, spoofs like *The Addams Family* or *Munster Go Home*, or part of a compilation of clips like *Terror in the Aisles*). Be sure to preview the segment you plan to show, to make sure it's appropriate. Let kids rate the scariness of what they saw by giving it one, two, or three screams (three being scariest). Discuss what makes a movie scary. Is a show that features supernatural evil (*Hellraiser, Witchcraft, Christine, The Exorcist*, etc.) scarier than one featuring aliens, monsters, or crazed killers (*Alien, Wolfen,* the *Friday the Thirteenth* movies, etc.)? Why or why not?

STEP 5

Try a Newspaper Scavenger Hunt. Form teams; give each a daily newspaper from the nearest metropolitan area. Teams will look for (1) the *Broomhilda* comic strip; (2) a movie ad or TV show listing that refers to supernatural power, evil, or the occult; (3) the word *devil* or *demon*; (4) a horoscope; (5) a reference to satanism; (6) a picture or title of a record album that contains a reference to evil, hell, or the devil; (7) the word *zodiac*; and (8) a prediction about the future. Have teams also look for other references to Satan or occult influences. Allow up to 10 minutes for the hunt. Then discuss: **Are astrology, witchcraft, and satanism "news"? Do most people seem to accept these things as harmless? What three reasons could you give this newspaper to do a story on the destructiveness of the occult?**

STEP 1

Skip Step 1; also delete the Step 2 quiz that uses the Repro Resource. As kids enter, direct their attention to two sign-up sheets on poster board. One should say at the top, "Sign up here if you'd like the power to predict the future. Put your name on the left side of the sheet; on the right side put the amount you'd be willing to pay for this power." The other sheet should say at the top, "Sign up here if you'd like the power to make people do what you want them to. Put your name on the left side of the sheet; on the right side put the amount you'd be willing to pay for this power." When everyone has arrived, discuss whether kids signed up, why, and what they'd be willing to pay. Tie this into the power promised by astrology, witchcraft, and satanism—all of which cost a lot spiritually and don't necessarily deliver.

STEP 5

Rather than having teams come up with advice for all six Repro Resource cases and share it with other teams, try this. Before the session, cut photocopies of the Repro Resource into six separate stories. You'll need one cut-up sheet per team. Have each team read the stories and arrange the slips on the floor in a line to show how "in trouble" each person is— from "safe" on the left to "point of no return" on the right. Share results. Emphasize that until a person dies, he or she can turn to Christ for help.

STEP 2

Emphasize to your group members that Satan has power. His power is much weaker than God's, but he can do things that seem miraculous. When it comes to astrology, witchcraft, palm readings, and tarot cards, it's possible that some predictions will come to pass. However, they are limited in power and scope. There is no omnipotence, omniscience, or omnipresence involved.

Make the following points:

• Many false prophets are at work in the world (I John 4:1).

• A miraculous sign is not necessarily of God (Deut. 13:1-5; Matt. 7:21-23; 2 Cor. 11:14-15; I Thess. 5:21-22; 2 Thess. 2:9).

STEP 5

Supplement or substitute the case studies on Repro Resource 12 with the following:

Juan, 16

Look, I know I've been doing ice and crack for two years, but after a while this stuff starts taking you over. I've tried rehab, but this stuff is better to me. It's like the devil gets in my veins or something. It's good.

Sue-Min, 14

Yes, I'm into the "black scene" (satanism) —but I'm not harming anyone. I like wearing black lipstick, black eyeliner, and black clothes because they express the hatred I have inside. I can't show love anymore. The Satanic Bible says to show "kindness to those who deserve it, instead of love wasted on ingrates." So you see, the darkness on the outside shows my darkness inside. It's a great way to live. You should try it.

STEP 2

In Step 2, explain the difference between astrology and astronomy: **Astrology is a set of beliefs about how the positions of stars and planets supposedly determine people's personalities and things that happen to them. Astronomy is the scientific study of stars, planets, and other bodies in space.** In Step 3, kids may wonder whether witches exist—since our culture mostly treats them as make-believe. Explain that in the Bible, a witch is one who casts spells and practices "magic." The Bible forbids this (Exod. 22:18). In medieval times and in early America people greatly feared witchcraft, sometimes accusing innocent people of being witches and burning them to death. Many have reacted to those "witch-hunts" by denying that witches exist. In Step 4, explain that satanism is the worship of the devil. Satanism is dangerous to those who practice it, and to those who might be abused or even killed as part of a satanic ritual. Assure kids that if they are committed to Christ, the devil can't wrestle them away from God (Rom. 8:31-39).

STEP 5

Use only the cases of Tara, Todd, and Frank. Add these: (1) **Kayla, 13, reads her horoscope every day in the newspaper. She says she's just curious, that she doesn't know whether to believe it or not. A couple of times she's done what her horoscope said to do—like avoiding a trip that might be dangerous.** (2) **Montel, 14, is a Christian guy who feels half scared, half fascinated by the occult. It's like he's looking over the edge of a canyon, afraid he might fall in, but with this weird urge to jump. He hasn't told anybody about this feeling.** Younger kids may need help coming up with advice; try asking them what they'd do if they had a friend in each situation.

STEP 1

If your kids would like an opener that's more mentally challenging, try this spelling bee. Form two teams. Call out a word and give the first person on one team a chance to spell it. If he or she can't, let the first person on the other team try. Keep alternating until the word is spelled correctly (or you run out of kids). Here are three sets of words: (1) **Pisces** (PIE-seez); **Gemini** (JEM-in-eye); **Sagittarius** (saj-ih-TARE-ee-us); **zodiacal** (zoe-DIE-ick-ul). (2) **Wicca** (WICK-uh); **Macbeth; Massachusetts; coven** (KUH-ven). (3) **Pentagram; Beelzebub** (bee-EL-zih-bub); **demoniac** (dih-MOE-nee-ack); **ritualistic.** After declaring a winning team, ask: **What do the words in each set have in common?** (Set 1 relates to astrology; set 2 to witches; set 3 to satanism.) Note that you'll be talking about all of these, and a different kind of "spelling"—casting spells.

STEP 5

Wrap up with a personal challenge. Ask kids to close their eyes. Say: **We may think we're great compared with astrologers, witches, and satanists. But sometimes we have the same attitudes that get them into trouble. I'm going to ask three questions and give you a few moments to think about each of them. Just answer them for yourself. (1) How willing are you to trust God about the future instead of doing everything possible to predict it? (2) Do you find yourself trying to manipulate and control other people instead of letting God be in charge? (3) Are you working from God's "to do" list, or are you spending too much time figuring out how to satisfy every physical appetite you have?** After letting kids consider these, close in prayer.

DATE USED:

Approxf. Time

STEP 1: *Fright Attendants* _____
- ❏ Extra Action
- ❏ Large Group
- ❏ Fellowship & Worship
- ❏ Mostly Guys
- ❏ Extra Fun
- ❏ Media
- ❏ Short Meeting Time
- ❏ Extra Challenge

Things needed:

STEP 2: *Testing the Spirits* _____
- ❏ Extra Action
- ❏ Small Group
- ❏ Large Group
- ❏ Heard It All Before
- ❏ Little Bible Background
- ❏ Urban
- ❏ Combined Junior High/High School

Things needed:

STEP 3: *Which Witch Is Which?* _____
- ❏ Mostly Girls

Things needed:

STEP 4: *How Serious Is Satanism?* _____
- ❏ Little Bible Background

Things needed:

STEP 5: *Voices* _____
- ❏ Small Group
- ❏ Heard It All Before
- ❏ Fellowship & Worship
- ❏ Mostly Girls
- ❏ Mostly Guys
- ❏ Extra Fun
- ❏ Media
- ❏ Short Meeting Time
- ❏ Urban
- ❏ Combined Junior High/High School
- ❏ Extra Challenge

Things needed:

Unit Two: "They're Not Like Us!"

Opportunity, Not Difficulty!

by Fran and Jill Sciacca

If you're honest with yourself, most likely you will confess that teaching on what different churches believe will be about as easy as pushing a chain! Many of us in youth ministry are very adept at "doctrine dodging" or "polite postponement" ("Let me answer that question near the end of the session"). We dodge questions because of the difficulty associated with subjects that tend to generate a lot of heat, but very little light. If you were to solicit a list of the top ten topics to avoid in a class or youth group meeting, right behind theology would be denominationalism. So how is it, in the sovereignty of God, that you have been called to teach a class that contains both?!

On the other hand, you may be experiencing a sense of exhilaration at the opportunity to finally point out the folly of the Christians whose cars don't happen to be parked in your church's lot each week. You may see this as your chance to teach the "truth" of *your* denomination amidst a host of misled saints! Obviously, neither of these extremes is true, nor is it productive. In fact, the quickest way to alienate any teenager is to attack or poke fun at what's dear to him or her—be it music, sports, his or her church, or a *friend's* church. Your goal should be to use this excellent curriculum to educate yourself. Then you can educate your group regarding major denominations, their differences and distinctives.

"They're Not Like Us!" is an excellent opportunity to teach student about the history of the family of God as it grew and established itself in different denominations, doctrines, traditions, and practices. Understanding what we believe and why provides a sense of belonging and purpose—two needs of today's teens. This unit will guide you and your group to a better appreciation and admiration of God's creative tapestry of reconciled sinners known as the Church. It will help cultivate a spirit of cooperation without compromise among the generation that constitutes the future of Christianity.

A Foundational Focus

In a classic passage on divisions within the church at Corinth, Paul lays out what must be understood as a crucial principle in denominationalism—namely, that the ultimate worth of any spiritual endeavor is only as good as its foundation.

"By the grace God has given me, I laid a foundation as an expert builder, and someone else is building on it. But each one should be careful how he builds. For no one can lay any foundation other than the one already laid, which is Jesus Christ. If any man builds on this foundation using gold, silver, costly stones, wood, hay, or straw, his work will be shown for what it is, because the Day will bring it to light. It will be revealed with fire, and the fire will test the quality of each man's work. If what he has built survives, he will receive his reward. If it is burned up, he will suffer loss; he himself will be saved, but only as one escaping through the flames" (I Cor. 3:10-15).

The Corinthian church had succumbed to the temptation of setting themselves apart from one another and were coming apart at the seams because they wanted to form factions based on whose teaching they agreed with! Sound familiar? Paul's exhortation to them is not merely cultural, because it is intrinsically bound to the evaluation of all believers at the end of the age. Quite simply, Paul advises the

Corinthians to focus on the foundation first, and the ministers second. He emphasizes the fact that only one foundation exists, a truth well worth building on as you prepare to teach this unit.

Your group members need to know that the crucial question of any denomination or body of believers is whether or not Jesus Christ is at the center. What or who is esteemed? If it is the teaching of some person rather than the Person of Jesus, then the foundation is faulty no matter how attractive the rest of the fellowship appears. It is significant that Paul never sought anything for himself along the lines of notoriety. In fact, he defined his mission by saying, "When I came to you, brothers, I did not come with eloquence or superior wisdom as I proclaimed to you the testimony about God. For I resolved to know nothing while I was with you except Jesus Christ and him crucified" (I Cor. 2:1-2).

Paul preached the foundation of Jesus Christ and built his ministry from there. A foundation holds up a structure. If the structure is doing its job, it will be holding forth the foundation. Help your group members develop this critical perspective for evaluating other denominations and variations of the faith that populate our planet. Teach them to ask questions and study other denominations rather than pronouncing quick and final judgments. Is Jesus Christ the focus and foundation of this church, or is someone or something else being exalted?

Organism More Than Organizations

A second principle that the Apostle Paul stood firmly upon and sought to perpetuate was that the church of Jesus Christ is *not* primarily an institution. It is a living, changing, growing organism. In fact, the one metaphor that Paul uses more than any other to describe the church is the "body of Christ." Look carefully at these statements in Scripture:

"Just as each of us has one body with many members, and these members do not all have the same function, so in Christ we who are many form one body, and each member belongs to all the others" (Rom. 12:4-5).

"The body is a unit, though it is made up of many parts; and though all its parts are many, they form one body. So it is with Christ. For we were all baptized by one Spirit into one body—whether Jews or Greeks, slave or free—and we were all given the one Spirit to drink" (I Cor. 12:12-13).

"Let the peace of Christ rule in your hearts, since as members of one body you were called to peace. And be thankful" (Col. 3:15).

The significance is obvious: we are related to one another on a level that transcends biology and pedigree. We are each *part* of Jesus Christ and therefore we are part of one another. This is not just sound theology; it is reality! The people down the street, across the country, or around the globe who genuinely confess Christ are a part of a larger whole to which we also belong. And we are not merely "connected," we are dependent upon one another. God has carefully and creatively arranged each part of His church to function together to accomplish His purposes in the world. Paul's use of the metaphor "body" is not merely an insightful concept. Together, we are Christ's voice, His hands, His heart, and His eyes. It is a sobering truth!

Help your kids see themselves as an integral part of this larger, living whole (I Cor. 12:14-26). Young people need to know that in spite of denominational distinctions, there exists just one essential body of believers in this world that is known in God's Word as "the body of Christ." Your kids must see that though we often mistakenly categorize and separate ourselves denominationally, we really do need one another. We are not merely on the same team; Paul says we are the same body! Fortunately, young people seem more accepting of this truth than many adults. Young people tend to be more devoted to a "vision" (the body of believers) than to details (who's "right" and "wrong").

More Than Good Intentions

In an era when polls are considered to be the arbiters of truth, your kids need to understand that although the body of Christ knows no boundary, any endeavor claiming to be in fellowship with God must be judged by more than the number of warm bodies or depth of sentiment. I repeatedly emphasize to my students that it is possible to be sincerely wrong!

While there is a tremendous need for tolerance on issues that are secondary and acceptance of those whose heritage and worship styles don't work for us, there is also the absolute necessity for a standard by which to judge religious experience. It was this commitment to the standard of God's Word that set the Jews in Berea apart from those who mocked Paul in Thessalonica: "Now the Bereans were of more noble character than the Thessalonians, for they received the message with great eagerness and examined the Scriptures every day to see if what Paul said was true" (Acts 17:11).

The measure of dedication one has to an idea cannot be a standard by which to judge its validity. Frequently, young people fail to distinguish between mere sentiment and commitment. Here is where balance belongs—in the need to look beyond the "vision" to details and distinctives, to discern right from wrong, heresy from truth. It is possible to have very strong feelings about something that is not true. Intensity of feelings never *makes* something true. This is important simply because in the midst of a discussion such as denominationalism, one has to remember that everyone can't be right about everything! "Everyone" includes me, you, and all of your group members.

The more serious truth is that God holds *me* responsible to make *my* judgments upon the basis of the best understanding I can muster of His Word. My feelings about an issue can never substitute for a thorough understanding of what God has said about it. This is as true of a mode of baptism as it is of the veneration of Mary and the saints. My standard must be the same as the Bereans—Scripture itself. Emphasize the importance of studying and regularly seeking to understand the Word of God above all things.

Don't Underestimate Your Audience

Very early in the twentieth century, a massive revival broke out in Wales. Thousands were turned to Christ in a span of just a few months. Taverns closed because they had no customers. Traveling theater groups stopped performing because people were too busy sharing the Gospel and worshiping to come to their shows. Some cities did not record a single arrest during this period. The most sobering fact about this intense movement of God was that the majority of those ministering were between the ages of 16 and 26!

In the midst of a challenging season for helping today's youth, Jill and I are seeing a growing number of people who work with high school students talk of strange rumblings among their groups. There appears to be a discontent with the status-quo Christianity that characterizes many of our churches. Increasing numbers of Christian young people are hungering for depth and devotion. They speak of sacrifice and authenticity rather than success and affluence. Is it possible that if such a movement of God is to come, it might come from among the likes of those who sit before you each Sunday?

If God does bring revival to our land, it will certainly not be constrained to the boundaries set by denominationalism. It will be a movement of the Spirit across the sinews of the body of Christ. Perhaps the part you will play by teaching *"They're Not Like Us!"* will be far more significant than you ever imagined!

Fran and Jill Sciacca have been involved with youth ministry for nearly two decades. Fran is a high school teacher. Jill has a degree in journalism and sociology and is a full-time homemaker and a free-lance writer/editor. She has written for Discipleship Journal *and* Decision *magazine, and has served on the editorial team for the* Youth Bible *(Word). Fran and Jill coauthored* Lifelines *(Zondervan), an award-winning Bible study series for high schoolers. Fran is the author of the best-selling Bible study,* To Walk and Not Grow Weary *(NavPress), as well as* Generation at Risk *(Moody), and* Wounded Saints *(Baker).*

Why Are There So Many Different Churches to Choose From?

The images on these two pages are designed to help you promote this course within your church and community. Feel free to photocopy anything here and adapt it to fit your publicity needs. The stuff on this page could be used as a flier that you send or hand out to kids— or as a bulletin insert. The stuff on the next page could be used to add visual interest to newsletters, calendars, bulletin boards, or other promotions. Be creative and have fun!

Shouldn't all Christians believe the same thing? What do Baptists believe that Lutherans disagree with? What's the difference between a Catholic church and a Greek Orthodox church? How should I treat people from other denominations? Is there anything that all Christians agree on?
Join us for a new series called *"They're Not Like Us!"* as we tackle these and other tough questions concerning what different churches believe.

Who:

When:

Where:

Questions? Call:

Unit Two: "They're Not Like Us!"

Ever wonder why
other churches worship
the way they do?

Hear ye, hear ye!

Which church is right?

A reformed church?

So Many Flavors
(Why Different Churches Believe Different Things)

BAPTIST
CHURCH OF GOD
PRESBYTERIAN
ASSEMBLY OF GOD
EPISCOPALIAN
EVANGELICAL FREE
METHODIST

SUE

YOUR GOALS FOR THIS SESSION:
Choose one or more

☐ To help kids become familiar with some basic beliefs of different Christian denominations.

☐ To help kids understand that there is a proper diversity among Christians in some religious practices and non-essential beliefs.

☐ To help kids accept believers of other denominations as Christian brothers and sisters.

☐ Other:_____
_____

Your Bible Base:

Acts 6:1-4; 11:1-3,
    19-21; 15:1-6, 36-41;
    18:24-28; 19:1-5
1 Corinthians 3:3-9
Philippians 1:14-18
3 John 9-10

What Do You Know?

(Needed: Copies of Repro Resource 1, pencils, prizes [optional])

Welcome your group members as they arrive. Explain that you're starting a series on denominations. Ask: **What is a denomination?** You're not necessarily looking for a "right" answer here; instead, you're looking for kids' impressions of what a denomination is. (Our best definition is "a subgroup of Christians that worships in a particular way or believes particular doctrines.")

Then ask: **How many different denominations can you name?** See how many examples your group members can come up with in one minute. Examples might include Baptist, Methodist, Catholic, Episcopalian, Presbyterian, and Evangelical Free.

Hand out copies of "This Is a Test" (Repro Resource 1) and pencils. Let kids work in pairs or small groups to complete the sheet. Emphasize that this quiz is just for fun; if group members don't know the answer to a question, they should guess. Give kids a few minutes to complete the sheet. When everyone is finished, go through the answers as a group. You might want to award prizes to the pair or group that came up with the most correct answers. Use the following information to supplement your discussion of the sheet.

1. *What is the method of baptism favored by Baptists?* (b—Dunking.) The fancy term is *immersion*, which involves dunking a person underwater as a symbol of Christ's burial and resurrection. Many other churches use sprinkling. If there were any churches that used drowning, they've died out by now.

2. *Where does the name "Presbyterian" come from?* (b—The Greek word presbuteroi, for the elders who govern the church.)

3. *What does the "method" of the Methodist denomination refer to?* (a—John Wesley's system of spiritual development.) John Wesley, the supposed founder of the Methodist group, tried to get Anglicans to be more serious about their faith, so he developed a "method" of personal devotion and small group fellowship. The term "Methodists" was first used by others, in derision.

4. *Why are Lutherans named for Martin Luther?* (b—The Lutheran church follows Luther's approach to the Scriptures.) Martin Luther led the first major break from the Roman Catholic church in the 1500s.

5. *Which of the following statements is true?* (b—Episcopalians are pretty much the same as Anglicans.) *Episcopal* comes from the Greek

word for "bishop"; it refers to the denomination's system of church government. You might say that Episcopalians are "American Anglicans"—they do belong to the worldwide Anglican church. By the way, Plymouth Brethren are named for their origins in Plymouth, England. They may drive any car they want. The Evangelical Free church is free to attend. The name refers to its style of worship. The Reformed church goes back to the Reformation led by John Calvin in the 1500s.

6. *Where does the name "Mennonites" come from?* (d—A man named Menno.) Menno Simons was a Dutch church leader who inspired the founding of the Mennonite church.

7. *Which of the following denominations promotes speaking in tongues?* (c—Assemblies of God.) This is the largest of several Pentecostal denominations, which promote the use of tongues as an evidence of the Spirit's filling.

8. *Of Swedish Baptists, Roman Catholics, Greek Orthodox, and Dutch Reformed, which group has the tastiest fellowship dinners?* You're on your own here.

9. *What is the largest group in Christendom within the United States?* (a—The Roman Catholic church.) The Roman Catholic church has approximately 58.5 million members. The Southern Baptist Convention has about 15 million members (though Baptists of all kinds number about 31 million). The United Methodist church has about 8.9 million members.

10. *If you hear people talking about sprinkling babies, meetings of "the session," and the teachings of John Calvin, where are you most likely to be?* (a—A Presbyterian church.) Babies are baptized by sprinkling, "the session" is the ruling group of elders, and John Calvin is the Reformer whose teachings have informed most Presbyterian theology.

STEP
2

Where It All Began

(Needed: Bibles, chalkboard and chalk or newsprint and marker)

Say: **Sometimes these denominations seem ridiculous. I mean, why do we have so many divisions? Why can't all Christians agree? Why can't we have unity—like they had in the early church?**

OPTIONS

LARGE GROUP

LITTLE BIBLE BACKGROUND

MOSTLY GIRLS

SHORT MEETING TIME

JR. HIGH HIGH SCHOOL COMBINED

Unity? In the early church? Not exactly. Almost from the start, there were disagreements and divisions. And—surprise—not all of these divisions were bad.

Assign the following Scripture passages for kids to look up and have ready to read: Acts 6:1-4; Acts 11:1-3; Acts 11:19-21; Acts 15:1-6; Acts 15:36-41; Acts 18:24-28; Acts 19:1-5; 1 Corinthians 3:3-9; Philippians 1:14-18; 3 John 9-10.

Go through the passages quickly, not mulling over details, but simply getting a feel for the climate of the early church. Use the following questions and information to supplement your discussion of the passages.

Acts 6:1-4

Ask: **What was the problem here?** (Greek-speaking widows were complaining that they were being discriminated against.) This was probably a cultural division. At this time, all Christians were Jews. However, the Hebrew-speaking Jews would have been more conservative and local to Jerusalem. Greek-speaking Jews were probably more progressive; they may have been out-of-towners who stayed in Jerusalem after Pentecost, and thus had no family support.

Was the result of this division good or bad? (It was probably good. Deacons were appointed to handle the problem.)

Acts 11:1-3

Ask: **What was the problem here?** (Peter had preached to Gentiles, something the more conservative Jewish Christians had a problem with.) In order to understand the scandal here, you must remember that Gentiles were "unclean" according to their understanding of Old Testament law.

Acts 11:19-21

Ask: **Who was "speak[ing] to Greeks"—that is, to Gentiles?** ("Men from Cyprus and Cyrene.")

Why weren't men from Jerusalem doing this? Wasn't Jerusalem the center of the church? (Yes, but people had scattered as a result of persecution. In addition, the Jerusalem believers seemed to be hesitant about opening up to Gentiles.) A very important point to remember here is that geography matters. Write "Geography" on the board. First, persecution scattered Christians out of Jerusalem. Was this good or bad? Bad in one way, but the scattering meant that the Gospel was going to new places like Cyprus and Cyrene. The new Jewish believers from Cyprus and Cyrene then had no problem going to Antioch to preach to non-Jews. Cypriot Jews were doing what Jerusalem Jews would not do.

Today there are many geographically based groups or denominations (Swedish Baptist, Greek Orthodox, African Methodist Episcopal, etc.). It's likely that they can reach their particular cultures in ways that other churches cannot.

Acts 15:1-6

Ask: **What was the problem?** (Some people were saying that Gentile converts had to "become Jews" in order to become Christians.

Paul insisted that this was not necessary.) This was a major dispute that plagued Paul throughout his ministry. The "Judaizers," who insisted that Gentile Christians convert to Judaism and follow Jewish law, were believers in Christ. But they had a major disagreement with Paul over the nature of Christianity. Paul seems to have "won" in the long run.

Acts 15:36-41

Ask: **What was the problem here?** (Barnabas wanted to give a second chance to John Mark, the deserter. Paul refused.)

Who was right? (Who knows? Maybe both.)

Was the result good or bad? (Perhaps it was good, since it resulted in two missionary teams being formed.)

Acts 18:24-28

Ask: **What was the problem with Apollos's teaching?** (He knew only the baptism of John—that is, he preached that people needed to repent, but he probably didn't have the full awareness of Jesus' sacrificial death. He emphasized a *part* of the truth.)

Why do you think Apollos had this problem? (Perhaps he was out of touch with recent events. He may have been studying in Alexandria while Jesus was fulfilling the preaching of John the Baptist.)

Acts 19:1-5

Ask: **What was the problem?** (The Ephesians had heard a partial gospel, based on John's baptism. As Priscilla and Aquila had done with Apollos, Paul explained the way of God more thoroughly.) Denominations develop at different paces in different places. There were three or four "Reformation" movements that broke from the Catholic church—Luther's took hold in Germany, Calvin's in France and Switzerland, while there were ongoing rustlings of Anglican Reformers in England and Anabaptists in Central Europe. Like Apollos and the Ephesians, these Reformers developed independently of others, though their teachings were parallel to the others. Many denominations are the result of *history*, how things developed at a particular time. Write "History" on the board.

I Corinthians 3:3-9

Ask: **What was the problem?** (Christians in Corinth were breaking into factions, following certain leaders.)

How did Paul respond to this problem? (He emphasized the teamwork of the various leaders.)

Do you think it was wrong for the Corinthians to admire the work of one leader more than that of another? (Probably not. The problem came in the division. When one group claimed superiority over another, that was a problem.)

Philippians 1:14-18

Ask: **Who was preaching while Paul was in prison?** (Apparently there were other preachers who didn't like Paul. They may have puffed up their own credentials and tried to "outpreach" Paul.)

What was Paul's response to them? (He was just pleased that the Gospel was being preached.)

How might Paul's attitude be a model for our attitude toward other denominations? (We may disagree with others' style, or even their motives, but we can support them if they preach the true Gospel of Christ.)

3 John 9-10

Ask: **What was the problem here?** (Diotrephes had an attitude problem. He was probably the leader of a house church, and he was shunning other Christians.)

How can we avoid this problem in our attitude toward other denominations? (We can remain humble, while still clinging to our understanding of the Truth. We can have fellowship with others and "agree to disagree" on points that are not essential matters of Christian faith.)

Ask: **Based on what we've read, what other reasons are there for Christians to have different groups, different beliefs, and different denominations? We have Geography and History written down. What else could we say?** Write the best of your group members' answers on the board. If no one mentions them, suggest these two reasons: "Disagreements" and "Personality Conflicts."

STEP
3

God Is.../We Are...

(Needed: Copies of Repro Resource 2, pencils)

Have kids form small groups. Ask each group to choose a number from 1 to 4 and a letter from A to D. The groups may duplicate a number or a letter, but you should not have two groups with the same letter-number combination. Based on the letters and numbers that the groups choose, you will assign each of them a statement about God and a statement about a church congregation. The groups will then make plans to form a denomination based on those statements.

The statements are as follows:

Statements about God

1. God is a shepherd.
2. God is a rock.
3. God is love.
4. God is holy.

Of course all of these statements are true, but each group should emphasize its own statement and forget about the others.

Statements about the congregation

A. We are shy.

B. We are loud.

C. We like to move.

D. We like to think deep thoughts.

Whether or not a statement is true of the kids in that group, they are to make their plans for a denomination as if it is true.

Hand out copies of "Invent Your Own!" (Repro Resource 2) to each group. Give the groups a few minutes to complete the sheet based on their assigned statements. When everyone is finished, go through the sheet one section at a time, asking each group to share and explain its responses for that section.

Add two more points to your list on the board: "Emphasis about God" and "Personal Style." Then ask: **How do these two issues affect some of the denominations you know of?** (For instance, Presbyterians and Reformed folks tend to emphasize the sovereignty and election of God, while Methodists emphasize human free will. Both groups believe in all of these issues, but choose to emphasize certain ones in certain ways. Many conservative churches emphasize God's holiness and judgment, while some other churches emphasize His love and forgiveness. Anglicans emphasize a God-given leadership structure, while Baptists and Brethren emphasize the personal priesthood of each believer. Charismatics and Pentecostals tend to have lively, emotion-filled worship. Some other denominations, by contrast, appear to them to be "God's frozen people." Some people enjoy a highly structured liturgical worship service; others prefer to "go with the flow." Some like having a leader to tell them what to do; others prize their independence.)

O P T I O N S

SMALL GROUP

HEARD IT ALL BEFORE

MOSTLY GIRLS

MOSTLY GUYS

EXTRA FUN

MEDIA

URBAN

JR. HIGH / HIGH SCHOOL COMBINED

STEP
4

Essentials

(Needed: Poster-making materials, tape)

Read aloud the following quote from Puritan teacher Richard Baxter: **"In essentials, unity. In non-essentials, liberty. In all things, charity."** Then ask group members to tell you what they think the quote means.

Ask: **What are the essentials of Christianity?** Suggest that group members look up passages like John 14:6; Acts 4:12; Ephesians 2:8-10; and Hebrews 11:6. These passages all point to one primary Christian essential: faith in Jesus Christ as the only way to God. Scripture is clear that there is no other path, other than Jesus, and that our good works cannot save us. Of course, this faith implies a belief in a caring God who wants to be found by those who seek Him (Hebrews 11:6).

Ask: **What are some non-essential matters that Christians care about?** [NOTE: It's not that these matters aren't important; it's just that they're not at the center of our faith.] (Non-essential matters might include mode of baptism, what happens at the Lord's Supper, forms of church leadership, style of singing, speaking in tongues, and beliefs about the end times.)

Have kids form groups of three. Hand out poster-making materials to each group. Instruct each group to make a poster that illustrates the Richard Baxter quote you read earlier. Group members may add any drawings or other words to their posters that they want. For instance, they might list some specific essentials and non-essentials of the Christian. Or they might write down some specific ways to show "charity" (or love). Give kids a few minutes to work. When everyone is finished, have each group display and explain its poster. Then display all of the posters around your meeting area.

Bridge-Building

As you wrap up the session, say: **You probably know some Christians who belong to other denominations—perhaps some kids at school. How might you reach out to one of these people this week? Not to get them to come to this church or anything, but just to say, "I'm a Christian too." You might get into an interesting discussion about what the other person believes. If so, that's great. Or you may just say, "Praise God!" and go on your way. Regardless, try to make a connection like that this week.**

Close the session in prayer, asking God for the wisdom to hold to the essentials, while living in charity toward people of other denominations.

This Is a test

1. What is the method of baptism favored by Baptists?
- a. Sprinkling
- c. Spitting
- b. Dunking
- d. Drowning

2. Where does the name "Presbyterian" come from?
- a. The Latin term *pressus butus*, for "pressing into service"
- b. The Greek word *presbuteroi*, for the elders who govern the church
- c. The English word *presby*, for the kind of hat often worn by church founder John Knox
- d. The computer term *pre-byte*, for the early calculators that were used to count the offering

3. What does the "method" of the Methodist denomination refer to?
- a. John Wesley's system of spiritual development
- b. Its form of collegial church government
- c. The acting technique used by nineteenth-century star Sarah Bernhardt, the denomination's most famous member
- d. A code name for Methuselah, because most Methodists are very old

4. Why are Lutherans named for Martin Luther?
- a. They worship him as a god.
- b. The Lutheran church follows Luther's approach to the Scriptures.
- c. The Lutheran church was started in a country where he was king.
- d. Early church leaders thought he had a cool name, but didn't want to call themselves Martinians.

5. Which of the following statements is true?
- a. Plymouth Brethren are forbidden to drive Fords.
- b. Episcopalians are pretty much the same as Anglicans.
- c. It actually costs $10 to join an Evangelical Free Church.
- d. To join the Reformed Church, you must have served time in prison.

6. Where does the name "Mennonites" come from?
- a. The denomination's practice of having women worship in the morning and "men at night"
- b. The teaching that men are superior to women
- c. From the Latin word *mens*, which indicates an emphasis on the mind
- d. A man named Menno

7. Which of the following denominations promotes speaking in tongues?
- a. Nazarenes
- c. Assemblies of God
- b. Conservative Baptists
- d. Berlitzians

8. Of Swedish Baptists, Roman Catholics, Greek Orthodox, and Dutch Reformed, which group has the tastiest fellowship dinners?

9. What is the largest group in Christendom within the United States?
- a. The Roman Catholic Church
- c. The United Methodist Church
- b. The Southern Baptist Convention
- d. The Multiplistic Offerings Church

10. If you hear people talking about sprinkling babies, meetings of "the session," and the teachings of John Calvin, where are you most likely to be?
- a. A Presbyterian church
- c. A child psychologist's office
- b. An Orthodox church
- d. Heaven

Invent Your Own!

Statement about God: _____

Statement about the Congregation: _____

Music
Will your worship services include singing? Why or why not?

If your worship service includes singing, what kind of songs will you sing? Why?

Are there any specific songs you would want to include in your hymnal? If so, what are they?

What will the members of your denomination do as they sing? (Stand? Sway? Dance? Pray? Jog?)

Preaching
Will your worship service include a sermon? Why or why not?

What kind of preaching or teaching would you prefer?

Organization
What sort of church leadership will your denomination have? (Ordained pastors? Elders? Deacons? Democracy? A pope?) *[Remember to answer the questions on the basis of the statements you've been given.]*

Other
What other activities will be included as part of your denomination? (Fellowship dinners? Outreach programs? A bowling team?) Explain.

How would a church in your denomination relate to the community around it? (Would it be heavily involved in community affairs? Would it separate itself from the community? Would it be evangelistic? Would it be judgmental? Would it get involved in local politics?) Explain.

What would a church youth group be like in your denomination? Explain.

STEP 1

Designate four areas of the room as *a, b, c,* and *d.* Rather than having kids fill out Repro Resource 1, read each of the questions on the sheet aloud. Have each group member indicate his or her response by moving to the appropriate area in the room. Ask volunteers to explain why they answered as they did.

STEP 5

Close the session with an ice cream-tasting contest. You'll need to bring in several containers of different flavors of ice cream. Cover the containers so that kids can't see the labels. Number each container. Hand out paper, pencils, and spoons. Have kids file past the containers one at a time, sampling each flavor of ice cream. Then have them write down their guesses as to what each flavor is. After everyone has had a chance to sample all flavors, reveal the correct answers. Close the session by letting kids finish the rest of the ice cream. Use this activity to serve as a reminder of the many different "flavors" of Christianity.

STEP 3

Rather than having kids form small groups to work on Repro Resource 2, let your group members pick several random letter-number combinations and work together to discuss each "denomination" option. You won't need to make copies of the Repro Resource. You can simply ask the questions from the sheet for each "denomination" you create. To keep this activity from becoming redundant, designate one person each time to be the decision-maker in case there are differences of opinion. Also be aware that throughout this series, kids are probably going to have questions about how their own church fits into the picture. During this first session, they may not be ready to ask bold questions, but their concerns are likely to come up as they design "new" kinds of churches. Listen for clues to unexpressed confusion or unasked questions.

STEP 5

Before you send the members of your small group out into the world in search of other "brands" of Christians, you may want to make sure that they know they have the support of each other. One thing you can do is create pins or buttons to wear, or perhaps provide them with matching articles of clothing (caps, T-shirts, etc.) that would help them identify with each other before they begin to try to identify with people they don't know as well. If other kids see a few people displaying the same kind of jewelry or clothing, they may feel they are missing out on something. (Perhaps they will discover they are, and will give church a chance.)

STEP 2

Have kids form teams. Assign each team one or more of the passages listed in Step 2. Also give each team the appropriate questions from the session to answer regarding its passage. After a few minutes, have each team explain its passage and answer its assigned questions for the rest of the group. If teams don't mention it, emphasize the role that geography and history played in the formation of denominations. Then pick up the session plan with the last paragraph in Step 2.

STEP 5

Have kids form small groups. Instruct each group to come up with two brief role-plays—one that demonstrates the wrong way to approach someone from a different denomination and then one that demonstrates the right way. The wrong-approach scenarios may be exaggerated and humorous, but the right-approach scenarios should be serious. After a few minutes, have each group perform its scenarios. Close the session in prayer, asking God to help your group members live in charity toward people of other denominations.

STEP 1

If your kids think they've heard it all before when it comes to denominations, add a little excitement to the quiz on Repro Resource 1. At the beginning of the quiz, give each person ten jelly beans (or some other kind of candy). Explain that for each question on the quiz, kids may risk any or all of their jelly beans. If they get the correct answer, they win the number of jelly beans that they risked; if they don't get the correct answer, they lose that number of jelly beans. Rather than having kids fill in Repro Resource 1, read each question aloud and let kids indicate their responses by raising their hands. See who has the most jelly beans at the end of the quiz.

STEP 3

Have kids form two teams. Give each team five minutes to list as many different denominations as it can think of. When time is up, have each team read its list. Award one point for each denomination, two points for each denomination not mentioned by the other team. Give prizes to the winning team, if you desire. Then move on to the "statements about God/statements about the congregation" activity.

STEP 1

Group members with little knowledge of the Bible probably have even less knowledge of church history and doctrinal differences between denominations. It will do little good to discuss all sorts of other churches if your kids know nothing about their own church. The quiz on Repro Resource 1 should be all right because of its light tone, but it should be followed immediately with a discussion of what your church believes. If it turns out that the plan of salvation is new to many of your members, matters such as baptism and history should be postponed. Spend your time focusing on what is most important.

STEP 2

The whirlwind tour through the Book of Acts is likely to be too "windy" for group members with little previous understanding of what is taking place. Rather than bouncing from passage to passage, it will be better for you to do a lot of summarizing as to what problems the early church faced. From time to time, have your group members get personally involved by looking up a passage; but you will probably need to scale back considerably on the amount of reading and responding that is required in the session as written.

STEP 1

As group members arrive, have soft instrumental music playing. Gather kids together for a short time of worship. Play a recording of (or have kids sing) "Jesus Loves Me." Ask group members to talk about what Jesus' love means to them. Close your worship time in prayer, praising God for His love. Then say: **There are many different ways in which people react and respond to the truth of God's love, and there are many different ways of worshiping Him. We're going to take a look at a few of those different worship styles in this series.**

STEP 4

After kids have completed their posters, take them to an area which you've prepared for them to make a "gutter banana split." You'll need a clean plastic gutter, several different kinds of ice cream and toppings, and spoons. Give kids an opportunity to make a giant banana split in the gutter; then let them dig in. As kids are flailing about in chocolate syrup and whipped cream, point out that they started with a wide variety of ingredients, and put them all together to form one pretty good whole. Similarly, there are many different types of worship, but all believers come together to form the whole body of Christ.

STEP 2

After your girls have read and discussed the Scripture passages listed, say: **Paul wrote many letters to churches that he had a relationship with. Now we're going to write some letters of our own.** Have each of your girls identify a "problem" they see in the church today, whether in your own church or the church universal. Instruct your girls to write a letter to the people who may be involved in the problem, addressing their concerns and fears; let them know that they don't have to come up with answers. After a few minutes, ask volunteers to read their letters.

STEP 3

For the opening activity in Step 3, replace Statement C about the congregation with the following: "We believe in equality of the sexes." After the activity, ask: **How do you think your church would feel about women having equal status as men? How do you think God feels about it?** This could be a hot topic for discussion. Field questions and comments as necessary.

STEP 3

When you get to Repro Resource 2, let your guys design an all-male church. The statement about God should be "God is male" and the statement about the congregation should be "No women allowed." Work through the questions on the sheet. Afterward, ask: **What would you think about having all-male and all-female churches? What would be the potential advantages? What would be the shortcomings?** After discussing the shortcomings, ask: **How do you think women feel when they try to worship in a place that seems to put more emphasis on guys than on girls? What can you do to help keep this from becoming a problem in our church?**

STEP 5

Try to be more specific about the challenge to identify and speak to other Christians at school. (Guys sometimes need incentives and challenges spelled out for them.) Rather than asking guys to find one church attender this week, designate Thursday (or any other school day) as "Fellow Christian Identification Day." Have the guys in your group compete to see who can compile the longest list of other Christians at school. In each case, your guys should find out what church (and denomination) the other person goes to. At your next meeting, see who has listed the most different Christian peers and how extensive a list of churches and denominations you can compile.

STEP 1

Before you begin the quiz on Repro Resource 1, create a quiz to see how much your group members know about their own church. Find a copy of the church constitution, information about its denominational ties, and so forth. Ask kids to identify the entire official name of the church, the name of the pastor, what kind of church government it has, what missions it supports, what it does to attract new people, and anything else that seems relevant. Although the subject is a bit dry, keep the quiz lighthearted by cheering correct answers and acting pained when kids don't know something they should about their own church. Food rewards (such as wrapped pieces of candy) for correct answers usually add to the fun level of any activity as well.

STEP 3

After kids complete Repro Resource 2, ask them to consider starting a church that's based almost exclusively on "personal style." Each group member should create "The First Church of [the person's name]." Give kids time to come up with ways that their churches will be different than any others that currently exist. For example, at what time will the meetings take place? Many churches have baptistries, but what special rooms might your kids' churches have? What will their churches offer to get new people to attend? Explain that this should be a fun activity—not an actual church-building plan.

STEP 1

Before the session, record ID clips (station identifications) from as many different TV channels as possible. Play the tape for your group members; see how many clips they recognize. Then ask kids to list as many other TV channels as they can think of. Use this activity to introduce the topic of different denominations.

STEP 3

Play recordings of several different hymns and Christian songs. Make sure that you include a variety of styles of music. Play some up-tempo songs that encourage kids to clap their hands or tap their feet. Then play some slow songs that encourage kids to silently reflect on God. Afterward, discuss the different styles of worship employed by different denominations.

STEP 1

Rather than using Repro Resource 1, try a shorter opener. Ask volunteers to share examples of times when they attended a worship service at a church of a different denomination from your church. Ask them to explain some of the differences between the two worship styles. Use group members' examples to lead in to the discussion in Step 2.

STEP 2

Use only the Acts 11:19-21 and Acts 19:1-5 passages, emphasizing the role that geography and history played in the formation of denominations. In Step 3, use only the "God is love" and "God is holy" statements about God and only the "We are shy" and "We are loud" statements about the congregation.

STEP 1

Rather than using Repro Resource 1, try a different opener. Ask volunteers to talk about some of the various ethnic cultures represented in their neighborhood. (If there are a variety of ethnic groups represented in your group, simply ask a few kids to talk about their cultures.) How does the Korean culture differ from the African-American culture? How does the Hispanic culture differ from the Polish (or German or Irish) culture? Use this discussion to introduce the topic of different denominations.

STEP 3

Spend a few minutes finding out what preconceived notions your kids have concerning various denominations and Christian groups. Ask group members to call out the first things that come to mind when you mention terms like "Baptist," "Roman Catholic," "Charismatic," "Pentecostal," and so forth. After listening to kids' responses, lead in to a discussion of Richard Baxter's quote in Step 4.

STEP 2

Pair up your junior highers with high schoolers. Assign each pair one of the passages in Step 2. Instruct each pair to translate the problem faced by the early church into a modern-day dilemma. (For example, the widows being discriminated against in Acts 6:1-4 might be changed to modern-day divorcées.) The pair should look at how the early church addressed the issue and then suggest a solution for the modern-day scenario. After a few minutes, have each pair share what it came up with. Afterward, point out that human nature is much the same today as it was in the first century—and that God's Word still addresses our problems.

STEP 3

Divide kids into two teams—a junior high team and a high school team. Assign each team the same letter-number combination; then let the teams make their plans to form a denomination. After a few minutes, have each team share what it came up with. Compare the junior highers' plan with the high schoolers' plan. Discuss any similarities and differences that you see. Point out that there are many things that affect our worship style, including age. If you have time, repeat the process, using a different letter-number combination.

STEP 4

After reading the Richard Baxter quote, ask: **What are some practices of our church that might be considered "nonessential"? How do they differ from the practices of other denominations? How should we feel about such practices? Why?** Encourage several group members to offer their thoughts.

STEP 5

As a group, brainstorm some ideas for bringing together young people from different churches (of various denominations) in your area. For example, you might plan a bowling party in which youth groups from different churches compete against each other. Whatever activity you plan, make sure that you include a time of fellowship to demonstrate to the kids that though they come from different denominations, they still have a common bond.

DATE USED:

Approx. Time

STEP 1: *What Do You Know?* _____
- ❏ Extra Action
- ❏ Heard It All Before
- ❏ Little Bible Background
- ❏ Fellowship & Worship
- ❏ Extra Fun
- ❏ Media
- ❏ Short Meeting Time
- ❏ Urban
- Things needed:

STEP 2: *Where It All Began* _____
- ❏ Large Group
- ❏ Little Bible Background
- ❏ Mostly Girls
- ❏ Short Meeting Time
- ❏ Combined Junior High/High School
- Things needed:

STEP 3: *God Is . . ./We Are . . .* _____
- ❏ Small Group
- ❏ Heard It All Before
- ❏ Mostly Girls
- ❏ Mostly Guys
- ❏ Extra Fun
- ❏ Media
- ❏ Urban
- ❏ Combined Junior High/High School
- Things needed:

STEP 4: *Essentials* _____
- ❏ Fellowship & Worship
- ❏ Extra Challenge
- Things needed:

STEP 5: *Bridge-Building* _____
- ❏ Extra Action
- ❏ Small Group
- ❏ Large Group
- ❏ Mostly Guys
- ❏ Extra Challenge
- Things needed:

The Big Three
(An Overview of Protestant, Catholic, and Orthodox Beliefs)

YOUR GOALS FOR THIS SESSION:

Choose one or more

☐ To help kids learn the basics of the history and distinctives of Protestantism, Catholicism, and Orthodoxy.

☐ To help kids understand some of the theological issues that brought these groups into being.

☐ To help kids determine the importance of those theological issues in their own lives.

☐ Other:_____
_____

Your Bible Base:

Ephesians 2:1-10

Pizza! Pizza!

(Needed: Chairs, pizzas [optional])

O P T I O N S

To begin the session, have kids form small groups. If possible, arrange the chairs in your meeting area to accommodate the small groups before the session. Pretend that your meeting room is a pizza parlor. Explain that each group is sitting at a "table," getting ready to order one pizza. The members of each group must decide what they want on their pizza—mushrooms, olives, sausage, anchovies, or whatever.

For one group, appoint a leader who will decide for the group what to order on the pizza. Instruct the members of another group to select a leader to decide what to order on their pizza. Make sure that at least one group is leaderless.

Give the groups a couple of minutes to decide; then take their orders. (If possible, go ahead and order real pizzas. If that's impossible, make it clear from the start that this is merely a game.)

Afterward, discuss the process of group decision making. Ask the leaderless group(s): **In your group, did one person take the lead or were all group members equally involved in the process?**

Did the majority rule or did your group seek the "lowest common denominator"—for instance, ordering a cheese pizza because one person doesn't like anything?

For those of you who ordered a half-and-half pizza, what does that indicate about your decision-making process?

After hearing all of the orders, do any of you wish that you were in a different group?

Ask the groups with leaders: **How did the appointed or elected leader affect the decision-making process?**

Then ask everyone: **What do you think this activity has to do with the topic of this series—denominations?** Field some of your kids' ideas. If no one mentions it, point out that churches are groups. In order to worship together, to conduct business together, to fellowship together, people need to decide certain things. In some cases, a leader—perhaps a pope or a bishop or a pastor—makes the key decisions for everyone else. In other cases, the church people decide for themselves.

New denominations are formed when a minority group says, "We hate mushrooms! We're going to order a separate pizza!" Sometimes those "mushrooms"—those disputed issues—are silly little *details*. But often they are major points of *doctrine*. Sometimes it's a *personality conflict* or a *leadership* question.

STEP 2

As Far As the East Is from the West

(Needed: Copies of Repro Resource 3, pencils)

OPTIONS

Ask: **How are people in California different from people in Illinois? How are Texans different from New Yorkers?** There are no right or wrong answers here. You'll probably get a lot of generalizations; encourage kids to keep them kindhearted. The point is that people from different places act in different ways.

Why do these differences exist? (There might be root causes like weather, population density, pace of life, and history; but after a while, it just *is*. Californians become laid-back because they see everyone else being laid-back.)

Explain: **The same thing is true in the history of Christianity. For the first thousand years, there was one large, comprehensive church—though splinter groups arose from time to time. But Eastern churches developed different customs and practices from the Western church. The two churches were *officially united*, but *practically different*. For example, if today you went to a Catholic church in Chicago and a Catholic church in Brazil, they'd be similar, but they'd also have differences based on their geographical location.**

The official split took place in 1054, when the leader of the Western church tried to get the leader of the Eastern church to submit to his authority. When he refused, the Western leader excommunicated the Eastern leader—threw him out of the church—and the Eastern leader excommunicated the Western leader. Suddenly there were two churches—the Roman Catholic and the Eastern Orthodox.

So the *official* split occurred because of a leadership dispute—a personality conflict. But it really just expressed

some basic geographical differences that had been causing friction for some time.

Hand out copies of "Different Strokes" (Repro Resource 3) and pencils. Encourage kids to take notes on the sheet while you talk (or at least try to dissuade them from turning the sheet into a paper airplane).

Explain: Two major differences in these denominations are probably the result of that initial "divorce." First is the issue of *leadership*. Catholics have a Pope and Eastern Orthodox churches do not. The Orthodox groups have a head patriarch who sort of runs the church, but he is considered "first among equals." He does not have the same amount of authority that the Pope has over Catholics. A second difference is that the Orthodox denomination seems to allow for geographical distinctions. Greek Orthodox, Russian Orthodox, Romanian Orthodox, and other local branches have been allowed to develop their own worship customs. These are all members of the larger Orthodox fellowship.

Other differences have occurred since the split. For instance, the Catholic church developed teachings regarding the celibacy of priests, the infallibility of the Pope, and purgatory, while Orthodox churches did not.

There are several other distinctives of Orthodox churches that should be noted. First, they have a strong tradition of mysticism. They emphasize the spirit more than the mind. How can a believer grow closer to the Lord? How can the church be united with God? How can we "pray without ceasing" as we live our lives? These are crucial questions for the Eastern Orthodox Church.

One element of this tradition is the practice of saying the "Jesus Prayer." Very simply, it's the repetition of the words, "Lord Jesus, be merciful to me a sinner," as you go through your day. If it truly comes from your heart, it's a way of grounding yourself in the love of God.

A second distinctive is the elaborate worship in Orthodox churches. In fact, the word *Orthodox* comes from the Greek for "proper worship." In Orthodox belief, Christianity is not just an individual thing; rather, each believer is part of the larger drama of salvation. That drama is played out in each worship service. To the uninformed, an Orthodox worship service may seem like a jumble of processions, incense, music, chants, and statues; but everything in the service means something. The whole service is intended to play out the Gospel.

One distinctive of Orthodox churches that Protestants find difficult to accept is their use of icons. Icons are basically statues or pictures of saints. They are used in public worship and personal devotion. As in Roman Catholic tradition, the saints are *venerated*, or shown respect, but they're not supposed to take the place of God as the object of worship. The idea is that their spirits can continue to help us grow closer to God. Just as you might ask a respected pastor for advice on a spiritual matter, or you might ask a fellow believer to pray for you, so we can ask great Christians of the past for spiritual help—at least, that's what Orthodox teachings hold. In the Orthodox faith, the saints, as depicted in their icons, testify to worshipers about Christ.

STEP
3

Nailed to the Door

(Needed: Copies of Repro Resource 4, various trinkets)

Say: **I've got a great idea. Here's how we can raise money for _____** (fill in the blank with some youth group or church project, either real or potential).

Hold up a small piece of wood. Say: **See what this is? It's no ordinary piece of wood. The man who gave it to me said it was a piece of Jesus' cross! How much do you think we could sell this for?** Get a couple of responses.

Hold up four or five other trinkets. Ask group members to come up with "biblical identities" for them. For instance, you might have a string from Simon Peter's fishing net, a strap from John the Baptist's sandal, one of the pebbles that David *didn't* sling at Goliath, and so on.

Continue: **Oh, but these aren't just collectibles. They have spiritual power that still resides in them. They can solve your problems.**

Ask: **What do you think about my idea? Would we succeed in making money? Would it be a good thing to do? Why or why not?** (Would it succeed? Probably. Perhaps people are less gullible now, but look at the recent craze regarding crystals. Would it be a good thing to do? No. Obviously it focuses worship on objects rather than on God. No matter how good the cause is, we shouldn't stoop to such methods.)

Explain: **There was a time in the Roman Catholic church when this kind of thing was going on. To be fair, many modern Catholics are rather embarrassed about this**

OPTIONS

LARGE GROUP

LITTLE BIBLE BACKGROUND

MOSTLY GIRLS

MOSTLY GUYS

MEDIA

URBAN

JR HIGH HIGH SCHOOL COMBINED

EXTRA CHALLENGE

time in their history. It was a period of great corruption. Later, the Catholic church took steps to clean up its act.

But at the time, the church was building a cathedral in Rome and needed money, so all sorts of items were sold. One Reformer joked that if all of the "pieces of the cross" were assembled, you could make a hundred crosses.

Not only that, but some priests were doing what amounted to selling *forgiveness*. If a loved one had died, you could pay money to get him or her to God faster. These were called "indulgences."

Ask: **Do you see a problem with this line of thinking? If so, what is it?** (The whole notion of paying for one's sins with money is outrageous. To Protestant ears, the whole notion of paying for one's sins at *all* is unbiblical. That is, we are saved by God's grace, not by our money or our deeds. God's forgiveness is granted freely.)

Say: **One Catholic priest during this time also had problems with the Church's actions. His name was Martin Luther. When an indulgence seller came to town, Luther wrote up a list of 95 complaints against these practices, and he nailed the list to the door of the church in Wittenberg, Germany. A number of Germans supported Luther, and the Protestant Reformation was born. Over the next century, the Reformation spread throughout Europe. It was a political revolution and a social revolution, but it was also a religious revolution.**

Ask for two volunteers to present a brief skit. Hand out copies of "MTV Meets ML" (Repro Resource 4) to your volunteers. ("Zap" could be either male or female. "Luther," of course, should be male.) After giving your actors a minute or two to read through the script, have them perform the skit.

Afterward, explain: **One key issue of the Protestant Reformation was the one made by Luther in this sketch: *salvation by faith, not by works*. The Reformers objected to the strong Catholic emphasis on doing religious deeds or giving money in order to gain favor with God. According to one story, Luther was in Rome and visited the staircase that Jesus had supposedly climbed to see Pilate. As was the custom, he was climbing it on his knees, saying a prayer at each step. But a Bible verse kept going through his mind, "The righteous will live by faith" (Rom. 1:17). As he neared the top, he began to realize that this ritual could never save him, but that he would receive eternal life only through faith in Jesus. As the story goes, he stopped, turned around, and went home.**

Another key issue was the *priesthood of the believer*. In the Catholic tradition, the priest was a necessary link between any individual Christian and God. The priest was

the only one who could interpret Scripture properly or handle the sacraments. The Reformation brought out the idea that every Christian can deal with God directly, cutting out the "middle man."

Along with this was the *availability* of Scripture. The Catholic church had blocked any effort to translate the Bible into the language of the people. At that time, the Bible was written in Latin, which almost no one except the priests spoke anymore. Luther translated it into modern German and, thanks to the newly invented printing press, people could suddenly read the Bible for themselves.

Ask: **How do Catholics and Protestants differ today?** Get as many responses as possible. Use the following information to supplement group members' responses.

- While the differences aren't as huge as they were at first, Catholics still tend to emphasize good *works* as essential to one's faith. Protestants emphasize the response of *faith* in making a personal decision to receive Christ. Both groups would agree that we are saved by God's grace, but they tend to differ on the human involvement and what that consists of.

- Catholics have the *unity* of one large worldwide organization, while Protestants have many splinter groups. This is a product of the Catholics' strong *central authority*, a superstructure of priests, bishops, and ultimately the Pope. Protestants, again, are more *individualistic*—basically, anyone with a strong opinion can start a denomination.

- Catholics also boast a *direct line of descent* from the New Testament church. (It should be noted that Orthodox churches make just as strong a claim to this.) But anyone would have to admit that there were some crazy twists and turns along the way. Most Protestants would say that *spiritual continuity* is more important. Does the church teach the authentic biblical Gospel?

Saved by Grace

(Needed: Bibles, paper, pencils, chalkboard and chalk or newsprint and marker)

OPTIONS

Have kids reassemble into the groups they formed in Step 1. Distribute paper and pencils to each group. Instruct the groups to read Ephesians 2:1-10. Explain that you will write some questions on the board for the groups to discuss (and jot down answers to).

Write the following questions on the board:

- *The "you" in this text refers to all believers. With that in mind, what is our situation? What have we done?*
- *Where is the turning point in this passage?*
- *What does this passage say about God? What is He like? What does He do?*
- *Based on verses 8-10, what is the role of good works in the Christian's life?*

After a few minutes, go through the questions on the board, asking each group to share its responses. Use the following information to supplement your discussion of the questions.

- *The "you" in this text refers to all believers. With that in mind, what is our situation? What have we done?* (Our situation is that we're dead in transgressions and sins, objects of wrath, made alive by God, saved, raised up, seated with Christ, prepared to do good works. We have lived in sin, followed the ways of this world, gratified cravings, and followed our desires. But later we've done good works.)
- *Where is the turning point in this passage?* (Verse 4: "But because of his great love for us, God . . .")
- *What does this passage say about God? What is He like? What does He do?* (He is rich in mercy. He has made us alive. He saves us by grace. He's raised us with Christ and seated us with Him. He shows us riches of grace. He's kind to us. He prepares us as His workmanship.)
- *Based on verses 8-10, what is the role of good works in the Christian's life?* (Works are not irrelevant, but they enter late in the story of salvation. We are not saved by the works that we do. However, we are God's "good work." God has created us to be good. Having received His grace, we can begin to live as He intended all along.)

You may wish to conclude this session with your denomination's particular slant on the "good works" issue. You might want to make reference to James 2:26: "faith without deeds is dead."

In this material, we are not trying to pick on any particular religious tradition. The fact is that *many* churches and believers have forgotten the simple message of Ephesians 2 from time to time. Baptists, Catholics, Lutherans, Pentecostals, and many others may begin to rely on their good behavior to get them into God's good graces. That just puts everything backward. We need to rely solely on God's grace for entry into a relationship with Him, and then rely on His power for the good works that He wants us to do.

Close the session in prayer, thanking God for His grace and asking Him for power to live rightly.

DIFFERENT STROKES

Orthodox and Catholic

The East-West split in 1054 was officially a leadership dispute, but it also arose from various differences that had been brewing for some time.

Differences
Leadership style—

Allowances for geographical differences—

Later adjustments in Catholic teaching—

Hallmarks of the Orthodox faith
Mysticism—

Elaborate worship—

Icons—

Catholic and Protestant

The Protestant Reformation was sparked in 1517 by Martin Luther's response to indulgence selling, but Europe was already a political, social, and religious powderkeg just waiting to explode.

Dividing issues
Salvation by faith, not works—

Priesthood of the believer—

Availability of Scripture—

Hallmarks of the Protestant faith
Emphasis on the individual's faith response to God—

Emphasis on spiritual continuity,
rather than on historical continuity—

Hallmarks of the Catholic faith
Living righteously with faith and good works is essential—

Unity/centralized leadership—

Continuity with the historical church—

MTV MEETS ML

ZAP: Hey, what's hoppin', dudes and dudettes? Welcome to the MTV History Hap. Hey, we got a special guest on the show today. Straight outta the history books and onto your screen. It's Doctor Martin Luther. *(To Luther)* 'Sup, G.

LUTHER: Uh, hello.

ZAP: Let me say first of all, my man, that I really dig that "I Have a Dream" speech. It is like *honkin'*. I mean, the man can communicate with a capital K, if you know what I'm sayin'.

LUTHER: I think you have me confused with someone else. I'm the one who said, "Here I stand. I can do no other."

ZAP: Run that by me again?

LUTHER: Here I stand. I can do no other. *(Gets no reaction from ZAP.)* I really liked it at the time.

ZAP: Here I stand?

LUTHER: They were trying to get me to recant, to give up my views about the changes that needed to be made in the church. I couldn't do it. That was where I stood, and there was nothing else I could do.

ZAP: Oh, I get it! Took a while, but I'm groovin' with ya now. You're the guy with the Protestant Restitution.

LUTHER: Reformation.

ZAP: So what exactly was the problem?

LUTHER: The problem was that the church was corrupt from top to bottom. The people had forgotten the simple message of God's grace, and they had substituted this whole system of doing religious works.

ZAP: Hey, I know people like that today!

LUTHER: Well, I guess there will always be people who try to work their way into God's favor. But that's not what the Bible says. It says that those who are righteous will live by *faith*.

ZAP: Hold on a second, Doctor M. Like this is blowin' my already fragile mind, OK? Are you tellin' me we don't have to be good?

LUTHER: Are you good?

ZAP: Good? I'm great! Just read a self-esteem book and I am floatin' away on myself.

LUTHER: But *morally*, are you good enough for God?

ZAP: Uh . . . well . . . if you put it that way . . . *morally* . . . uh . . . no.

LUTHER: Then join the club. None of us are good enough for God. But the good news is that God doesn't accept us on the basis of how good our behavior is. He accepts us on the basis of His grace and mercy in Jesus Christ. When we believe in Christ, then God can help us behave properly.

ZAP: Well, sorry to say it, big guy, but your fifteen seconds of fame are way gone. Back to our Smash-and-Grab Top Ten Countdown. See ya.

STEP 1

Have kids form two teams for some kind of a contest—perhaps a kickball or volleyball game. Rather than appointing a captain for each team, see how well team members do in organizing themselves. For instance, if you're playing kickball, how do teams determine their kicking order? How do they determine who plays what position? Pay particular attention to whether there's any disagreement or disgruntlement on the part of team members. Let kids play the game for a while. Afterward, use this activity to introduce the idea that leadership styles and methods of decision-making are two elements that distinguish certain denominations from each other.

STEP 2

Begin Step 2 with a game of Red Rover. Have kids form two teams. Instruct the teams to stand several feet apart, facing each other. Have the members of each team spread out in a horizontal line, holding hands. To begin the game, one team will call to the other, "Red rover, red rover, let [the name of someone on the other team] come over." The person whose name is called will then run at the challenging team, trying to "split the team" by breaking the connection between two players. If the player succeeds, he or she gets to take one player from the challenging team back to his or her team; if the player fails, he or she must join the challenging team. Play several rounds of the game. Afterward, use the activity to introduce the splits that occurred in early church history.

STEP 1

If you don't have enough people to form groups for ordering pizzas, keep everyone in one group. Say: **I'm willing to buy pizza for this group—that is, if you can agree on what you want. But don't say anything out loud. I want you to write down your orders. If all of the orders are the same, then I'll assume we're in agreement and I'll place the order. If you don't agree, however, I might cause more hard feelings than goodwill by ordering pizza.** Hand out paper and pencils; let group members write down what kind of pizza they would like. It is very unlikely that all will be in agreement. After a few minutes, collect the orders and read them aloud. Ask: **Do you think we could come to some agreement on what to order, or should we just forget about it?** See if kids compromise on their initial requests. While waiting for the pizza to arrive, discuss how churches have to make similar decisions—come to agreement or forget about trying to compromise and go their separate ways.

STEP 4

Again, you will probably want to work as a single group rather than smaller groups as you discuss the Ephesians passage. As you read the passage aloud, instruct half of your group members to listen for action verbs; instruct the other half to listen for passive ones. Try to do whatever it takes to keep everyone involved and to keep group members interacting with one another. When someone asks a question, see what others in the group think before you jump in with the answer. Try to help kids get excited about the opportunity to work together as a small group to better understand Scripture—and each other.

STEP 1

Pass out paper and pencils to your group members. Explain to them that you are going to call out various categories of consumer products. When group members hear the category, they are to write down the names of what they think are the top 3 selling brands (in that order—1st, 2nd, 3rd) of that type of product. Some examples of products you might ask are: soda pop, jeans, cars bought in the United States, cereals, athletic shoes, toothpaste, etc. (Note: This is information you will have to obtain.) Afterward, state the correct answers as group members "grade" each other's papers. Award some prize to the person who had the most correct. Then make the point that just like all the different brands of products on the market today had to come from a few original products, church denominations are the same way. There were a few big original denominations that all other denominations have evolved from. Then say that those three—Catholic, Orthodox, and Protestant—are what you are going to take a look at and study today.

STEP 3

Have kids form teams of three or four. Hand out paper and pencils. Announce that the teams will be competing to see which can be the first to write down 95 different complaints about school. Explain that the complaints may be as specific as "My desk in history class has 10 pieces of gum stuck to the bottom of it" or as general as "The teachers are mean." See how long it takes for kids to come up with 95 complaints. Award prizes to the winning team. Use this activity to introduce the topic of Martin Luther's 95 complaints concerning the Catholic Church.

STEP 1

At the end of Step 1, give your kids an opportunity to show what they know concerning the three major divisions of Christian groups. Ask: **How many of you have ever attended an Orthodox worship service? How many of you have ever attended a Catholic service? How many of you have ever attended a Protestant service? What are some of the differences between the three styles of worship?** Encourage several kids to offer their opinions as to the pros and cons of each style; then ask them to tell you which style they prefer and explain why.

STEP 2

Have kids form groups. Instruct each group to come up with a scenario that explains how and why the splits occurred that eventually resulted in the formation of the Orthodox, Catholic, and Protestant churches of today. Encourage the groups to be as outrageous and humorous (without being offensive) as possible in their scenarios—the crazier the explanations, the better. After a few minutes, have each group share its scenario. Afterward, vote as a group on the best one. Lead in to a discussion of the actual reasons for the divisions.

STEP 2

Kids with little Bible background may perceive "the church" as being something that some people go to and others don't. Depending on kids' previous experience, you will probably want to condense the information in this step. The differences between the Orthodox church and the Roman Catholic church may not be as pressing to your group members as the differences between church people who put fish insignia on their cars and those who don't. You want your group members to know church history, but at this point you need to keep it balanced with what's happening now. Until young people understand the current situation, church history isn't likely to matter a lot to them.

STEP 3

This step also contains a lot of material that you might want to condense. Perhaps the discussion about Martin Luther will raise questions about other "church people" your group members have heard of, but don't know much about. Be sure to look ahead to the next session to see who will be introduced later, but be ready to answer questions about other people who aren't included in this series. Ideally, the questions at this point will concern the differences between Catholicism and Protestantism, but your group members may not know enough to keep their questions to that narrow a focus. Also use this time to help your group members be completely clear on the salvation-by-faith concept. It's more important for them to understand this essential doctrine than to know about selling indulgences.

STEP 1

Have kids form teams. Instruct the members of each team to plan a trip for their spring break. Emphasize that they need to cover *all* of the details of the trip—from deciding on a destination to choosing where they'll stay to determining how they'll take care of meals. After a few minutes, have each group share its plans. Then ask members from each group to talk about their experiences in making decisions regarding the trip. Ask: **How easy or difficult was this process? What areas were the most difficult to work out? Did people have strong opinions or did they not really care?** At the end of the discussion, point out that planning even a one-week trip can cause disagreements between people. Imagine what can happen between people when the destination is heaven, and the "visit" is for eternity!

STEP 4

Write "Mercy is not getting what we deserve; grace is getting what we don't deserve" on the board. Briefly discuss the statement as a group to make sure that your kids understand it. Hand out paper and pencils. Instruct kids to make two columns on their sheet, labeling one column "Grace" and the other column "Mercy." Give group members a few minutes to fill in their columns with examples of grace and mercy that they've seen in their lives. After a few minutes, ask volunteers to share some of the things that they wrote. Close the session by having kids sing or listen to a recording of "Amazing Grace."

MOSTLY GIRLS

STEP 1

When you set up your "pizza parlor," rather than arranging tables, set up stations at which your group members can make real pizzas. Provide each group with all of the necessary ingredients for making a pizza—including an array of possible toppings. Give the groups the same instructions that are in the session plan. When the pizzas are finished, pop them in the oven so that they'll be ready to munch on at the end of the session.

STEP 3

As you prepare for the skit on Repro Resource 4, you may wish to invite a male from your church to portray Martin Luther. A rather fun option, however, would be to provide a monk costume for one of your girls and let her play the part. If you get any complaints about playing a guy's role, point out that in Shakespeare's day women weren't allowed to act; men played all of the roles—male and female—in a performance. Turnabout is fair play!

MOSTLY GUYS

STEP 3

Hand out paper and pencils. After you discuss the boldness of Martin Luther, ask your guys to write out a list of things that they would like to see changed about your church. When they finish, they should nail (or tack) their lists to a nearby bulletin board. Since the category is so general, you may get a wide variety of ideas in many areas—what to study, new facilities to build, things to eliminate, and so forth. Encourage your guys to be outspoken about what they believe. Even though they will need to learn to work with other people in order to accomplish their desires, explain that strong feelings are a good start for establishing and maintaining commitment in the church.

STEP 4

Begin this step by having guys describe something they have built that they are pretty proud of. This can be anything from a ship in a bottle to a solar system science project to a really delicious submarine sandwich. Try to get your guys to identify with the satisfaction of their *workmanship*. Then, when they get to the discussion of Ephesians 2:10 and discover that they are God's workmanship, perhaps they will relate more strongly to His pride in having created them. Consequently, they should be more willing to place their confidence in Him rather than trying to work out their own salvation, which is sometimes a "guy" attitude toward Christianity.

EXTRA FUN

STEP 1

A variation of the opening activity is to let group members create their own pizzas. You should provide the individual crusts and a variety of ingredients, but then let each person assemble his or her own. Don't bring up the theme of the session until everyone is finished. As the pizzas are cooking, have kids describe what they put on their pizzas. See if any two are alike. Then use your kids' natural propensity for variety to explain why there is such a variety of different churches today. Point out that while some things remain the same in essentially all pizzas (crust, cheese, etc.) and churches, the choice of "toppings" can create a vast number of combinations.

STEP 4

If you open with the variety-of-pizzas approach to church, conclude with a unity-of-dessert example. Have a dessert item prepared that you know all of your group members enjoy. Challenge kids to remember that in spite of the fact that churches come in all varieties, the members of each church need to strive for unity. Sometimes we must sacrifice personal preference for the good of the group as a whole. So while some of the people may have preferred banana splits, they might have to "settle" in this case for chocolate chip cookies. Thank them for their sacrificial attitudes in this case (and, it is hoped, in more serious instances in the future).

STEP 1

Begin the session by playing several brief snippets of songs by Christian artists. Try to include as many different styles of music (rap, pop, country, easy listening, heavy metal, soul, blues, etc.) as possible. After you've played several song clips, have kids vote on which song (or music style) they'd like to hear more of. Ideally, you should get a variety of responses. Then ask: **If we divided up our group according to the music styles that we prefer, how many different groups would we have?** Use the idea of dividing the group according to differing personal tastes and styles to introduce the divisions that occurred in the early church.

STEP 3

Expand the "trinket" idea at the beginning of Step 3. Have kids form groups. Give each group one of the trinkets suggested in the text. Instruct the group to create a sales presentation for its item to present on the "Church Shopping Network." The presentation should be as exaggerated and humorous (without being offensive) as possible. After a few minutes, set up your "Church Shopping Network" camera and record each group's presentation. Afterward, play back the tape for your kids to enjoy. Use this activity to introduce the "trinket selling" and other practices of the Roman Catholic Church that Martin Luther objected to.

STEP 1

For a shorter opener, try a game of "What's the Difference?" Explain that you'll call out two items; after you do, the first person to stand and name three differences between the two items gets a point. The person with the most points at the end of the game is the winner. Among the pairs of items you might use are crocodile/alligator, Mississippi/Alabama, and dictionary/thesaurus. Use this activity to lead in to a discussion of the differences between Orthodox, Catholic, and Protestant beliefs.

STEP 4

Writing questions on the board and having kids form groups to answer them may take longer than you have time for at the end of your session. Instead, simply read aloud Ephesians 2:1-10. Then ask: **What does this passage tell us about good works?** (We are saved by the grace of God, and not by the works that we do. However, we are God's "good work." God has created us to be good. Having received His grace, we can begin to live as He intended all along.) Close the session in prayer, thanking God for His grace and asking Him for the power to live rightly.

STEP 1

Have kids form groups. Give each group $1,000 in play money. Explain that the money has been earmarked to help inner-city youth. Each group's assignment is to determine exactly how the money should be put to use. For instance, should it be used to help renovate an abandoned building to use as a youth center? Should it be used for drug-awareness education? Should it be used to fund an after-school program? Do *not* appoint a leader for each group. See what happens as the members of each group try to reach a consensus on how to spend the money. After a few minutes, have each group share its plan. Then ask members from each group to talk about their decision-making process. Use this activity to introduce the idea that methods of decision making (or leadership styles) distinguish certain denominations from each other.

STEP 3

To begin this step, ask: **Do you think church services in the suburbs or in rural areas are different from church services in the city? If so, how are they different?** Encourage several group members to offer their opinions. Then ask: **Why do you think these differences exist?** Lead in to a discussion of the history of Christianity, focusing specifically on the differences that led to various splits in the church.

STEP 2

To help kids see that people are different even when they live in the same general area, divide the group into smaller groups according to the schools they attend. If this will not give you a good balance (or if all of your kids go to one school), divide the group evenly; then assign the members of each small group a school in their area with which they would be familiar. However you divide the group, make sure that junior highers and high schoolers are on separate teams. Hand out paper and pencil. Instruct the members of each group to list as many distinctives as they can think of about their school in the following areas: clothing, slang, sports, clubs, and academics. After groups have assembled their lists, discuss differences and similarities. Then talk about some of the reasons for these differences (age of students, economics of the surrounding neighborhoods, fads that catch on because of unique circumstances, and so on) Point out that there are many factors that influence people's behavior, whether you're talking about school or church.

STEP 3

When group members hear about the Reformation, they may be thinking, *So what? We all have complaints about the church.* Bring up this possibility. Then have kids form small groups, making sure that you have an even mix of junior and senior highers in each group. Hand out paper and pencils. Instruct the members of each group to come up with their own list of grievances about the church. However, each grievance must have some kind of biblical support. After a few minutes, have each group share and explain its list. Discuss as a group the grievances on each list. [NOTE: This activity is not designed to give kids a forum for ragging about their church. Instead, it's designed to help them see that often what people complain about are things that are not at all essential to our faith and salvation.]

STEP 2

Bring in several books on church history and several books that address the beliefs of Orthodox, Catholic, and Protestant churches. Have kids form three groups. Give each group a stack of books and assign it one of the three major church categories. Instruct the group to find out all it can in 15-20 minutes about the history of its assigned church and the key beliefs that separate its church from the other two. When time is up, have each group present its findings. Discuss any findings that seem to contradict the findings of another group. Use the material in Steps 2 and 3 to supplement and clarify the information provided by the groups.

STEP 3

After discussing the practices of the Catholic Church that caused Martin Luther to protest, ask your group members to consider whether there are any practices in Christianity today—perhaps in an area like Christian broadcasting—that might cause someone to protest. Spend a few minutes discussing why such practices might cause a protest; then move on to Step 4.

DATE USED:

Approx. Time

STEP 1: *Pizza! Pizza!* _____
- ❏ Extra Action
- ❏ Small Group
- ❏ Large Group
- ❏ Heard It All Before
- ❏ Fellowship & Worship
- ❏ Mostly Girls
- ❏ Extra Fun
- ❏ Media
- ❏ Short Meeting Time
- ❏ Urban
- Things needed:

STEP 2: *As Far As the East Is from the West* _____
- ❏ Extra Action
- ❏ Heard It All Before
- ❏ Little Bible Background
- ❏ Combined Junior High/High School
- ❏ Extra Challenge
- Things needed:

STEP 3: *Nailed to the Door* _____
- ❏ Large Group
- ❏ Little Bible Background
- ❏ Mostly Girls
- ❏ Mostly Guys
- ❏ Media
- ❏ Urban
- ❏ Combined Junior High/High School
- ❏ Extra Challenge
- Things needed:

STEP 4: *Saved by Grace* _____
- ❏ Small Group
- ❏ Fellowship & Worship
- ❏ Mostly Guys
- ❏ Extra Fun
- ❏ Short Meeting Time
- Things needed:

SESSION 3

Who's Protesting What?

(An Overview of Major Protestant Denominations)

YOUR GOALS FOR THIS SESSION:

Choose one or more

☐ To help kids learn the basics of the history and distinctives of major Protestant denominations.

☐ To help kids understand some of the issues of theology and church life that brought these denominations into being.

☐ To help kids determine to live in the love and power of God's Spirit.

☐ Other:_____
_____

Your Bible Base:

Ephesians 6:10-13
1 Timothy 1:3-7
Revelation 2:1-6

Going Overboard

(Needed: Materials to make signs)

After welcoming group members, say: **Today we'll be focusing on Protestant denominations. How many Protestant denominations can you think of?** Get a list of several denominations.

Can you think of any denominations that believe pretty much the same thing that we in our church or denomination believe? Be prepared to mention some.

So why do we have different denominations if they believe pretty much the same thing? Let kids take a few stabs at the question. If no one mentions it, point out that it comes down to history. Different groups came into being for different reasons at different times.

Ask: **What does the word *Protestant* mean?** (Protesters. Protestants came into being because they protested certain practices of the Catholic Church. Protestant groups have continued protesting, forming new groups along the way. Some of the protests have been rather petty, but others have helped to bring new life to dead churches.)

Invite all of your group members to join in a roleplay. Explain that they will act out a parable concerning lifeboats that may help them understand denominations.

Say: **We're all in a big ship, crossing the ocean. What's the name of the ship?** Select a name for the ship. Have someone write it on poster board and hold it aloft. **Suddenly a storm comes up and we start to take on water. Who's the captain?** Select a captain. **The captain must get everyone bailing water so that the ship can stay afloat.**

But there are some people on board who feel that the ship is doomed. These people feel it's best to abandon ship, that no amount of bailing will help. Who's the leader of this rebel group? Select a leader. **This leader must convince people to abandon ship and climb into a lifeboat.**

Let the rebel leader lobby for the lifeboat while the captain urges people to stay and bail water. Then divide the lifeboat people (make sure there's at least one other besides the rebel leader) from the ship people. Ask the lifeboat people to choose a name for their vessel and write it on poster board.

Then say: **So now there are two vessels on the ocean—the ship and the lifeboat. The ship gets through the storm, but** pretty soon some questions arise. The captain seems to be a bit wacky now. Some of you think he's going in the wrong direction. Who's the leader of this new rebel group? Select a leader. You feel that it's best to take another lifeboat out and set off in the right direction. So you, rebel leader, try to drum up support as you, Captain, try to keep people on board, in your wacky way.

Once again, divide this new group of protesters from the main ship. Have members of the new group choose a name for their lifeboat and write it on poster board.

Then say: Meanwhile, back on the first lifeboat, the passengers are having problems. It seems that the people on one side of the boat can't stand people on the other side. Why? Have the lifeboat passengers choose a reason for the rift—bad breath, loud snoring coming from one side of the ship, or whatever. So the people on one side of the boat decide to inflate the raft on this lifeboat and set out on their own.

Divide the people on one side of the boat from the people on the other side. Have the "rafters" choose a new name for their raft and write it on poster board.

Then say: Now we have four vessels on the high seas. There might be five more lifeboats on the ship, each one with a raft inside, so we could keep splitting up if need be. But what are the differences among these four groups?

Interview someone from each of the groups. Ask about that person's attitude toward those in the other groups (within the roleplay, of course). How do the two lifeboat groups differ from each other? Actually, they don't differ very much at all. It's simply a matter of when and why they left the boat. Maybe even some of the raft people, after a few days, realize that their disagreement with the lifeboat people was pretty silly. These groups have a lot of similarity, just like many denominations, but the history of their voyage has put them in different boats.

Explain: Once you set out in a different boat, it's hard to get back together with your old boat. That's true of denominations too. Each denomination develops its own leadership, its own way of doing business, and its own way of worship. Even if the differences are small, it's hard to merge those things with another denomination. There have been a few mergers in recent years. Several Lutheran groups decided to come together. And Northern Presbyterians and Southern Presbyterians, divided by the Civil War, decided to get back together after 120 years of separation. But these have been exceptions to the rule. Once divided, it's hard to reunite. And, as long as you're not fighting with those in the other lifeboats, that may be just fine.

Four-Lane Highway

(Needed: Copies of Repro Resource 5, pencils)

Ask: **Who was Martin Luther? What did he do? Why?** (Luther sparked the Protestant Reformation with his opposition to corruption in the Roman Catholic Church.)

Explain: **Martin Luther was not the only one who was unhappy with what was going on in the Catholic Church. There were many others who were thinking about reform. In fact, we can identify four main streams of the Reformation. Once we understand these, we can better understand the different denominations in our world today.**

Hand out copies of "Streams of the Reformation" (Repro Resource 5) and pencils. Have kids form four groups. Assign each group one of the "streams" on the sheet. Instruct each group to read its assigned section and come up with five key words to describe that "stream." Give the groups a few minutes to work. When everyone is finished, ask each group to share and explain its five key words.

Afterward, point out that Repro Resource 5 deals only with the four historical streams that emerged in the 1500s. These are four "lifeboats," if you will. There have been many "rafts" that have set off from these movements since then.

In God We Crust

(Needed: Copies of Repro Resource 6, copies of Repro Resource 7, pencils)

Ask: **Have you ever done something that was really fun at first, but then got old and boring? If so, what was it?** Be prepared to share an example from your own life. **Why did the activity get old and boring?** (We humans tend to like new things. In this generation especially, things get boring fast.)

Explain: **There's something that happens with church movements that's very similar. You might call it the "crusting" of the church. I could take a luscious piece of bread and put it right here, but what would it look like a week from now? A month from now?** (It would get stale, crusty, moldy, and disgusting.) **It might start off as a great nutritious treat, but after a while, it gets all crusted over and worthless. A similar thing can happen with churches and denominations.**

Hand out copies of "Two Later Streams" (Repro Resource 6). Give group members a few minutes to read through the sheet.

Then say: **The Anglican Church had begun partly because the English didn't want the Roman Catholics telling them what to do. But then the Anglicans began ruling England with a heavier fist, and people who dissented with the official church were arrested. That's how the Baptists came into being, in the early 1600s. It was a dissenting group that actually had to flee from England and go to Holland for a while. There they met some Mennonites and were influenced by Anabaptist teachings. To this day, Baptists believe in believer's baptism and the separation of church and state—two hallmarks of Anabaptist theology.**

The Methodist Church came into being late in the 1700s as a renewal movement within the Anglican Church. Though the Anglicans had started with a wave of spiritual energy, by this time, some felt that they were crusting over, getting a bit moldy. Christianity was a matter of regular churchgoing and good theology, but it didn't seem to be changing people's lives very much. In addition, many poor people didn't feel welcome in the church. John Wesley began to teach people a "method" of Christian growth. Wesley emphasized spiritual exercises, particularly meeting with small groups. But a new spiritual fervency swept through England, and the Methodist Church was born.

Interestingly, within the next century, there were times when the Methodist Church seemed to lose its spark, and other movements broke off in attempts to recapture the original spirit. Among these were the Salvation Army, the Wesleyans, the Nazarenes, the Free Methodists, the Church of God in Christ—and, in a way, the Pentecostal movement.

The following skit may illustrate this pattern of encrusting and renewal. Ask for four volunteers to perform a brief skit. Hand out copies of "Crust and Decay" (Repro Resource 7) to the volunteers. Give them a few minutes to read through the script; then have them perform. [NOTE: We are not saying that any of the churches in the skit—Anglican, Catholic, or Methodist—are now "dead" or "crusty." As with the lifeboats, some people stay in the ship and keep bailing.]

O P T I O N S

EXTRA **ACTION**

MOSTLY **GIRLS**

MOSTLY **GUYS**

EXTRA **FUN**

EXTRA **CHALLENGE**

All of these groups have had significant renewal movements that have stayed within the denomination.]

Afterward, ask: **What was the pattern here? How do you think you'd feel if you were in a church that was getting "crusty"? Why?** Get several responses.

Then say: **There's a new issue that has arisen in the twentieth century. Churches have divided along liberal-conservative lines. Thinkers in some of the major Protestant denominations adopted controversial policies regarding the authority of the Bible; the factuality of Jesus' virgin birth, miracles, and resurrection; women's role in church leadership; the power of the church hierarchy; and other social issues. Some conservatives have felt compelled to spin off new denominations that upheld traditional views of these issues.**

Now, many Christians care more about your conservative or liberal stance on the issues than on your denomination. For example, a conservative Presbyterian has more in common with a conservative Methodist than with a liberal Presbyterian.

First Love

(Needed: Bibles)

Ask kids to turn to Revelation 2:1-6. Read the first verse. Then ask: **Who is speaking? To whom is He speaking?** (Jesus is giving His critique of seven different churches. At this point, He's speaking to the church at Ephesus, the same church that Paul wrote Ephesians to, and where Timothy served as pastor for a while.)

What's this business about the stars and lampstands? (The lampstands represent the churches [see Revelation 1:20]. The point is that Jesus is in control.)

Read Revelation 2:2-3. Ask: **What good things does Jesus say about the church at Ephesus?** (The people have worked hard and persevered, presumably under difficult circumstances. They have rejected "wicked men" and tested those who claimed to be apostles. They seem to be strong defenders of the true faith.)

Ask volunteers to read Ephesians 6:10-13 and I Timothy 1:3-7. Explain that both of these passages were written to this same church in Ephesus about 30 years earlier.

Afterward, ask: **What feeling do you get from these verses? What were the people supposed to do? From what we just read in Revelation, do you think they were doing this?** (The earlier texts give us a feeling of battle. There would be false teachers who would have to be stopped. It would be hard work defending the true faith. From the Revelation passage, it would seem that the people did good work.)

Read Revelation 2:4. Ask: **What criticism does Jesus have for this church? What does this mean? How important do you think this is?** (The people had "forsaken [their] first love." This could mean [a] the things they loved to do at first they weren't doing anymore; [b] they had a love for Christ at the beginning that they weren't showing anymore; or [c] they weren't loving *each other* the way they had earlier.)

Do you think this could be an "occupational hazard" for people who are fighting to defend the faith? (It's a leading question, but yes. In the I Timothy passage read earlier, it was stated that the goal of opposing false teachers is love. But that's easy to forget.)

Does this help us understand the history of denominations that we've been learning about? If so, how? (It's not an exact correlation, but it's interesting to see how even the members of a biblical congregation start to "lose it." They're doing everything right, but they forget how to love. That initial spark gets lost in the day-to-day grind. We need to keep reminding ourselves of where we started.)

Read Revelation 2:5-6. Ask: **What does Jesus want this church to do?** (Repent; change its ways; go back to genuine love.)

Do you think it can be done? If so, how? If not, why not? Get several responses.

Explain: **The Nicolaitans were probably a group that compromised with the surrounding culture. They probably engaged in idol worship and various immorality while still considering themselves good Christians. It's interesting that even after calling the church back to love, Christ affirms the need for righteousness. He's not saying, "Just love everybody and everything will be all right." Our love for God results in righteous behavior. But righteousness without love has no point to it** (see I Cor. 13:1-3).

Ask: **Is there a point in your Christian life that you need to go back to? Have you dropped something important along the way? It can happen to denominations. It can also happen to individuals—like you and me.**

Close the session with a time of silent prayer, giving kids an opportunity to rediscover their "first love."

OPTIONS

HEARD IT ALL BEFORE

LITTLE BIBLE BACKGROUND

FELLOWSHIP & WORSHIP

MOSTLY GIRLS

URBAN

JR. HIGH / HIGH SCHOOL COMBINED

EXTRA CHALLENGE

STREAMS OF THE REFORMATION

1. LUTHERAN

At first, Martin Luther didn't intend to start a new church; he was merely trying to open a theological discussion within the Catholic Church. But he was thrown out of the Catholic Church, and he got backing from a number of German leaders to start a new group.

Luther was most concerned about good theology. He didn't have a problem with all of the liturgical practices of the Catholic Church, so the Lutherans kept a number of these. Even today, some elements of Lutheran worship look a lot like Catholic worship. But Lutherans emphasize the basics of Protestant theology—salvation by grace, the authority of the Bible, and the priesthood of the believer.

Fact File

Spark: Luther's nailing his 95 complaints on the door of the church in Wittenburg, Germany, in 1517; Luther's being thrown out of the Catholic Church in 1521

Location: Lutheranism was originally strong in northern Europe, especially Germany and Scandinavia.

Pioneers: Martin Luther and Philip Melanchthon

Church leadership: Elected bishops

Emphases: Theology; justification by faith

Modern movements: Lutheran churches

2. CALVINIST (REFORMED)

What became known as the "Calvinist" movement actually began before Calvin's conversion, with a priest named Ulrich Zwingli. Serving in Zurich, Switzerland, Zwingli simply began to preach the Bible. This "back to the Bible" movement gained many followers, as people began to question Catholic teachings they believed were not based on Scripture. In 1523, the city-state of Zurich broke from Roman Catholic control and officially sided with Zwingli. Later, the French scholar John Calvin got involved with the Reform movement and wrote its most important books.

While Luther was satisfied to keep some Catholic practices that were based on good theology, the Reform movement wanted to strip away everything that was not found in Scripture. Thus, it rejected much of the ornate ceremony and even the great tradition of religious art. Church buildings were simple, and worship was centered on the reading and preaching of God's Word.

Even today, churches in the Presbyterian and Reformed tradition favor simplicity over ceremony.

Fact File

Spark: Zurich's decision to follow Zwingli in 1523; the publication of Calvin's master work The Institutes in 1536

Location: Calvinism was originally strong in south central Europe, especially Switzerland and France, and in Scotland and Holland.

Pioneers: Ulrich Zwingli, John Calvin, and John Knox

Church leadership: Presbyterian, which means "by elders." Calvinists could not find bishops over lesser officials in the Bible, but they found many teachings about elders. Thus, pastors are viewed as "teaching elders" in the church and serve, along with the "ruling elders" in the region, on the council that runs the churches.

Emphases: The sovereignty of God; God's control of everything

Modern movements: Presbyterian churches (in several different denominations); Reformed churches

STREAMS OF THE REFORMATION

3. ANGLICAN

An independence movement was brewing in England long before the Reformation broke out on the continent of Europe. On its own island, the English church was always rather insular, even when officially connected to Rome. Bible translators John Wycliffe (about 1380) and William Tyndale (1525) had attempted to put the Bible in the language of the people. They were met with official opposition, but gained popular support. Increasingly, Christians in England were concerned about Rome's excesses. But the official break with the Roman Church occurred under embarrassing circumstances.

King Henry VIII wanted a divorce, and the Pope would not grant it. So Henry appointed a new archbishop of the English church and ordered him to grant the divorce. In 1534, the English Parliament declared that the King of England was head of the English church and was no longer under the Pope's authority.

So was this just an independent Catholic church or did it open the door to a full-fledged Reformation in England? No one was sure. Lutherans and Calvinists tried to gain power in this theological vacuum, and there was still a large group of Catholic loyalists. Power went back and forth for more than a century. Ultimately, the Anglican Church forged a middle option that was sort of Catholic and sort of Reformed.

To this day, Anglican and (in America) Episcopal churches promote the unity of the church. Their ways of worship run the gamut from simple Protestant to ornate Catholic.

Fact File

Spark: England's Act of Supremacy, in which King Henry VIII became leader of the church in 1534 (although substantial reform didn't start until Edward VI came to the throne in 1547)
Location: England and, later, the United States, Canada, and Australia
Pioneers: Thomas Cranmer and Thomas Cromwell
Church leadership: Episcopal, which means "by bishops." The structure seems similar to the Catholic Church, but the power comes more from below—bishops are elected from among the priests. The head bishop, the Archbishop of Canterbury, is not seen as infallible.
Emphases: Church unity and worship
Modern movements: Anglican and Episcopal churches and major "spinoffs," including the Methodists, Congregationalists, and Baptists

4. ANABAPTIST

Anabaptists were the radical alternative of the Reformation. According to them, no one was reforming the church *enough*. Anabaptist means "those who are baptized again," and it comes from its adherents' insistence on believers' baptism as adults. It's not enough to be sprinkled as a baby, they say; you also have to make a conscious decision to follow Christ and seal that with baptism by a person of sufficient age.

Anabaptists also rejected the church-state connection that other Reformers took for granted. The church, they felt, had a spiritual power independent of any political structure. Anabaptists sought to obey Scripture radically—pushing pacifism, voluntary poverty, personal discipleship, and Christian community.

Of course, they were way too radical for most people in those days. They were persecuted by Catholics, Lutherans, and Calvinists alike. As those three groups carved up the political spoils of Europe in the 1600s, the Anabaptists were virtually ignored.

Some found a home in Holland, which tended to accept everyone. There the Mennonites were founded, and they had a major influence on a group of English rebels who later became known as Baptists.

Fact File

Spark: The rejection of the Anabaptist leaders by the Zurich Council in 1525, which brought new coherence to the group of rebels
Location: Scattered throughout central Europe and, later, Holland
Pioneers: Michael Sattler and Menno Simons
Church leadership: Congregational. Each believer has authority and is accountable to God. Christians may elect leaders, but official hierarchies are avoided.
Emphases: Individual commitment of faith; separation of church and state; authority from Scripture alone
Modern movements: Mennonites (who strongly influenced the early Baptists), Brethren, and Moravians

TWO LATER STREAMS

*There are many denominations
that flowed out of the original "streams of the Reformation." Here are two
of the most notable.*

1. BAPTIST

John Smyth was a courageous young preacher who started an illegal Separatist (non-Anglican) church in England. The congregation was forced to flee to Amsterdam. There, they met with some Mennonites, who shared their Anabaptist theology. Some of the English group decided to join the Mennonites, while others returned to England as the first Baptist church.

Fact File

Spark: Smyth's "re-baptizing" of his congregation in 1608

Location: England and America

Pioneers: John Smyth, Thomas Helwys, and Roger Williams (in America)

Church leadership: Pastors chosen by congregation

Emphases: The Bible; individual response of faith; believer's baptism; separation of church and state

Modern movements: Baptist churches

2. METHODIST

John and Charles Wesley were brothers who were serious about their faith. They were Anglican scholars, preachers, and even missionaries, trying hard to earn favor with God. But then each of these brothers had an eye-opening experience of God's grace. They accepted God's forgiveness and assurance in Jesus Christ and began preaching that Good News wherever they could.

Fact File

Spark: The Wesleys' conversion, three days apart, in 1738

Location: England and America

Pioneers: John and Charles Wesley; Francis Asbury (in America)

Church leadership: Elected bishops

Emphases: Personal response of faith; holy living as an outworking of the Spirit's transformation

Modern movements: Methodists and later "spinoffs," including Nazarenes, Wesleyans, the Salvation Army, the Church of God in Christ, and to some extent, the Assemblies of God

The prim and proper Anglicans weren't sure what to make of the spiritual energy of the Wesleys. When the churches closed their doors to them, the Wesleys and George Whitefield would preach in the streets and fields of England. The common people responded in droves.

The Wesleys really weren't trying to start a new denomination, but the Anglican Church was not welcoming this renewal movement. So eventually the Methodists organized as a distinct church.

CRUST AND DECAY

(A, B, C, and D stand together.)
ALL: We are the church of Jesus Christ.
A: This is exciting!
B: We are preaching the Good News that anyone can know God through Jesus.
C: He forgives our sins!
D: We are showing His love.
(ALL stop and suddenly look very tired.)
A: But now it's the 1500s. We are the Catholic Church.
B: There's a lot of stuff you have to do in order to really know God.
C: He'll still forgive your sins—for a fee!
D: After all, we have this building program.
A: Wait! Something's wrong here!
B: Yeah! Let's get back to the true Gospel!
C: Let's preach the love and forgiveness of Christ!
(A, B, and C separate from D.)
D: Hey, where are you going?
C: We are the Anglican Church now.
B: We're going to do things right!
A: This is exciting!
(A, B, and C stop and suddenly look very tired again.)
A: But now it's the 1700s. We're the Anglican Church—very proper.
B: Knowing God is good, I guess, as long as you're polite about it.
C: Surely God forgives *our* sins, but we don't commit very many. We're good people, unlike those commoners.
A: Wait! Something's wrong here!
B: Yeah! The true Gospel has to be for everyone, rich and poor alike!
(A and B separate from C.)
C: Hey, where are you going?
B: We are the Methodist Church now. We're going to welcome the common people!
A: This is exciting!
(A and B stop and suddenly look very tired again.)
A: But now it's the late 1800s. We're the Methodist Church *(yawn)* and we're kind of bored.
B: Do you remember where we put the Gospel? It was here a second ago.
A: What does it look like?
B: I forget.
A: Wait! Something's wrong here! Christianity can't be just going through the motions. We have to get busy helping people, to trust Christ to change our lives and theirs. It should be exciting!
(A separates from B.)
B: Hey, where are you going?
A: Now I'm the Salvation Army, or the Wesleyans, or the Assemblies of God. This is exciting! But maybe someday I'll forget why I started too.

STEP 1

Begin the session with a game of dodge ball, using three or four playground balls. Start out playing in the traditional way, with two teams throwing balls at each other from behind a line in the middle of the room. When a person is hit by a ball, he or she is out. The first team to eliminate all opposing players is the winner. After the first game, divide each team in half and play a second game using four teams (with the room divided into four sections). Continue dividing the teams until, for the last game, it's every person for himself or herself. Use this activity to introduce your discussion of the splits that have occurred among Protestant denominations.

STEP 3

Have kids take turns creating structures out of dominoes or building blocks and then knocking the structures over. Continue the exercise long enough for every person to have several turns. See how long it takes for the "newness" of the activity to wear off and for kids to get bored and start looking for alternatives to the activity. Use this exercise to lead in to the skit on Repro Resource 7.

STEP 1

The thought of churches breaking apart and people going separate ways can be a bit scary for a group that is already small. After the lifeboat exercise, ask: **How would you determine whether to compromise what you believe and try to stay "with the boat" or stick by what you believe—even if that means "sailing on your own" for a while?** Have kids consider whether or not the following issues would be important enough to cause them to leave the church and go elsewhere.

• **The board decrees that girls must wear dresses and guys must wear coats and ties to all church meetings.**

• **You can no longer meet in your usual area. You must meet in homes instead.**

• **The church stops believing that Jesus was born of a virgin and rose from the dead.**

• **You wanted the new carpet to be red, but the majority voted for blue.**

• **The pastor leaves and is replaced with a much older man.**

STEP 2

The Repro Resource 5 assignment will need to be assigned to individuals or pairs rather than to groups. This might be a bit awkward for some kids because the material tends to be a bit weighty, with unfamiliar names and words and new information. Before you hand out the sheets, give kids a few words of encouragement and challenge them to do the best they can at picking out five key words. Explain that you'll answer everyone's questions as you go along. Then provide plenty of time for your slower readers to soak in all they can and assimilate the information to the best of their ability.

STEP 1

With a large group, you might want to use a real-life example instead of the lifeboat exercise. Instruct your group members to begin planning some kind of event. As kids begin to discuss the details of the event, it's likely that there will be some disagreements. If so, have kids divide into groups based on the sides they take during the disagreements. For example, you might ask: **Should we plan a retreat, a fund-raiser, or an outreach event?** Kids will then form three groups based on which format they choose. After kids have formed their new groups, you might ask: **Should we be responsible for the food that's served at the event or should the event be catered?** Instruct kids to divide into even smaller groups based on their responses. Continue asking questions to divide the groups until only two or three people remain in each one. Then introduce the topic of denominations, adapting the last paragraph in Step 1.

STEP 2

Rather than simply having groups look for five key words in their assigned material, instruct them to come up with a creative way to present the information in their section to the rest of the groups. For example, one group might use a skit to present its information. Another group might create a song. Encourage the groups to be creative in their presentations. After a few minutes, let each group make its presentation.

HEARD IT ALL BEFORE

LITTLE BIBLE BACKGROUND

FELLOWSHIP & WORSHIP

STEP 2

If your kids are familiar with the details of the Protestant Reformation, try to put a modern spin on the material. Ask: **Are there any issues in the church today that could cause a major split like the one that Martin Luther instigated? If so, what are those issues? If not, why do you suppose that is?** Encourage several group members to offer their opinions.

STEP 4

Kids who've been taught about the differences between certain Protestant denominations may never have had a chance to interact with people of different denominations. If this is the case with your group members, plan some kind of activity that can include youth groups from several other churches (of different denominations) in your area. As you plan the activity, encourage your kids to get to know the members of other groups, to discuss not only the differences between their denominations, but the similarities as well.

STEP 1

To begin the session, ask: **Do you trust what I teach you at these sessions? If so, why? If you doubted some of the things I say, what would you do about it?** Give kids some time to consider this. Some might not yet think to question anything a church teacher would tell them. Some might have had questions, but were not comfortable enough to bring them up. Others might even be uncomfortable at the suggestion that someone might mislead them in their spiritual blindness. If your kids are new to the Bible and want to learn more, they essentially need to trust someone to help them learn and grow spiritually. But they should begin to see eventually that the Bible itself should be their authority more than any human teacher. Explain that many of the groups you will be discussing today were in a similar situation—looking for spiritual truth and trusting their religious leaders. Some of them were eventually misled and had to seek truth and freedom of religion in new settings.

STEP 4

When you get to the Bible study, begin with Ephesians 6:10-13 and I Timothy 1:3-7. Explain that these passages were written in regard to the church at Ephesus. Have kids suppose that they were in a church that received these letters from a pastor who had been away for a while. How would they feel? How would they respond to the challenges laid out for them? After discussing this, introduce the passage from Revelation. If kids new to Scripture become sidetracked by the prophetic tone and supernatural message from Jesus to John, they will already have discussed the other passages. Kids will also be better able to see that the church in Ephesus started out strong, but gradually lost sight of its "first love."

STEP 1

When kids arrive, have some lively music playing, some food spread out, and some balloons and streamers (or other decorations) adorning the room. In short, get ready for a party! After kids have mingled for a while, stop the music and instruct them to split into groups according to the school they attend, the color of their hair, or some another arbitrary factor that won't cause too many groups to form. Ask the members of each group to talk about the fact that their differences didn't prevent them at all from enjoying the party. In fact, when they weren't focused on their differences, they probably didn't even notice them. Explain: **When we all get to heaven, that's just how it will be. The differences that we see between our denomination and other denominations will disappear. It's good to understand others and their beliefs while we're here on earth, but when we get to heaven, those differences will all be gone.**

STEP 4

Challenge your kids to think back over the past few years of their lives to identify what point they need to return to. Hand out paper and writing utensils (colored markers would probably work best). Instruct group members to make a map of their faith, identifying the point they've left, the obstacles along the way that led them astray, and the road they need to take to return. (For example, let's say a person who never had a problem previously with gossip started hanging out with a crowd that gossiped a lot, causing the person to begin to gossip. That person might need to either change friends or learn to tame his or her tongue to not gossip any longer.) After kids have completed their maps, spend some time thanking God for His spiritual guidance—for being our compass—and praising Him for His love for us.

STEP 3

Say: **We've been looking at many different churches, started by many different men. Have you ever wondered what a movement founded by women might be like?** Refer group members back to Repro Resources 5 and 6, instructing them to focus on the distinctives of each group. Then, in groups of three or four, have them put together their "own" movement, based on Scripture and what *they* feel is important. After a few minutes, ask each group to share what it came up with.

STEP 4

Say: **We've talked a lot about some strong men of faith; now let's look at some women.** Bring in resource materials on women such as Catherine Booth, Joan of Arc, Catherine Marshall, Saint Margaret of Scotland, Saint Bridget of Sweden, Saint Clare of Assisi, or any other women that you may admire. Allow your girls time to peruse the material and discuss things about these women that they admire. There are many examples of strong women of faith throughout history. Your girls deserve to know them!

STEP 2

Since the church has had such a male-dominated history, let your guys present the material from Repro Resource 5 in the roles of the men who were responsible. Some guys may portray the church founders (Luther, Zwingli, Calvin, Wycliffe and Tyndale, the two Wesleys, and so forth). Others may portray historical figures who were partially responsible (popes, King Henry VIII, or whomever). As much as possible, have guys make their reports in first person, with comments as appropriate from "supporting characters."

STEP 3

Explain during this step that you've been looking exclusively at churches, but that's only part of the potential problem. Yes, if a church isn't careful, it can get "crusty" and lose its "fresh" influence for God on a community. That's the part of the problem this series has dealt with so far. But another problem to be considered is whether the church members truly give the church an opportunity to be influential. Sometimes it's the people who get crusty and leave the church without ever giving it a fair chance. Ask: **If your current spiritual life were represented by a piece of bread, would it be (a) a fresh, hot homemade roll right out of the oven; (b) a piece of bread from the center of a loaf, an entire week prior to its expiration date; (c) the end piece of a loaf from the day-old shelf; or (d) a crouton?** After your guys answer, ask: **What other foods would you compare yourself to, in a spiritual sense? Why?**

STEP 2

If you think your kids can handle it, try to have them write funny skits that symbolize the conflicts of the people described on Repro Resource 5 rather than approaching them purely from a historical context. For example, Martin Luther's opposition to the existing leaders of the Catholic church could be presented as a well-thought-out verbal presentation. Or it could be acted out as a World Federation Wrestling Match, an encounter on "American Gladiators," a confrontation with pirates in which Luther is forced to "walk the plank," an arm-wrestling challenge, or any number of things. After kids have fun with their presentations, you can quickly summarize the historical truth of the skits that have been acted out.

STEP 3

Have several volunteers agree to set up churches of their own and try to sway the rest of the group members to leave your church to join theirs. One person might have a refreshment-oriented church where every service includes doughnuts. Another person might have a "singles" church where guys and girls go to church together—and frequently out to lunch together afterward. Another person might have a church of leisure—with no services longer than fifteen minutes and little, if any, commitment required. Give your volunteers some ideas or see what they can come up with on their own. Then see if they can persuade the other group members to "come on over" to their church. Afterward, make it clear that the Reformation wasn't the result of such petty and cosmetic changes in church function, but was due to significant theological differences.

STEP I

To begin the session, play some scenes (which you've prescreened) from recent video releases that feature characters attending and worshiping in a Protestant church. If you can't find any recent releases that fit the bill, try using an older movie like *Footloose*. Compare the portrayals of Protestant worship services in the movies to the worship service of your own church. How are they similar? How are they different?

STEP 2

Before the session, you'll need to record some clips (perhaps from TV newscasts) of various types of protests. If possible, try to show some peaceful protests as well as some protests that turned violent. Show the clips to your group members. Then ask your group members what they think the various protests against the Roman Catholic church (by Martin Luther, Ulrich Zwingli, and others) were like. Lead in to a discussion of the various Protestant denominations that were formed as a result of those protests.

STEP I

Rather than going through the time-consuming lifeboat exercise, try a shorter, simpler method for splitting up your group members. For example, you might have kids form four groups based on the following criteria: kids who have no siblings, kids with one sibling, kids with two siblings, and kids with two or more siblings. After kids have formed groups accordingly, you might divide them further by using categories such as kids who are satisfied with the size of their family and kids who wish their family was a different size. At that point, each group would then split into subgroups. Continue dividing the groups until only one or two people remain in each one. Then introduce the topic of denominations, adapting the last paragraph in Step 1.

STEP 2

Combine Steps 2 and 3 by presenting Repro Resources 5 and 6 at the same time. Summarize the information in each section in one or two sentences. (For example, to summarize the "Lutheran" section, you might say: **After splitting from the Catholic church, Luther kept a number of the church's liturgical practices. And while some elements of Lutheran worship today look a lot like Catholic worship, Lutherans emphasize the basics of Protestant theology.**) Skip the "Fact File" sections, except perhaps to mention the "modern movements" of each group. Briefly go through the information in the session regarding the Anglican church and the Methodist church. Skip Repro Resource 7 and move directly to Step 4.

STEP 2

To begin this step, ask group members to name as many things as they can think of that people protest. Kids may name things like abortion, job conditions, court rulings, government actions, and so forth. Briefly discuss as a group some of the different forms that protest takes (boycotts, letter-writing campaigns, picket lines, and so on). Then ask: **Have you ever felt so strongly about something that you protested? If so, what was it? Why did you feel so strongly about it?** Lead in to a discussion of the protests against the Roman Catholic church that led to the Protestant Reformation.

STEP 4

Invite representatives from one or more Protestant denominations to your meeting. Ask each representative to talk about some of things his or her denomination is doing in the inner city. Perhaps each representative might discuss some of the programs his or her denomination runs for the homeless and needy, some of the organizations the denomination sponsors, and so on. Also encourage each representative to share some information on what your group members can do if they're interested in getting involved in one or more of the denomination's programs.

STEP 2

Repro Resource 5 may be a bit difficult for your junior highers. You may wish to pair them with high schoolers as you're dividing into groups to work on the sheet. Or you may want to make a chart of the information on Repro Resource 5 and place it where all can see it easily. Then you could work through Repro Resource 5 together, discussing the information as a group.

STEP 4

Many adults have difficulty understanding the Book of Revelation, so this step may be a real challenge for your junior highers. Prior to your meeting, create a poster that displays each of the symbols mentioned and explains what each represents. As you read the verses together, refer to the poster to help your kids discern the message included in the passage.

STEP 3

Bring in some kind of chart or diagram that shows the various divisions and formations of Protestant denominations throughout history. Let your group members spend some time discovering which groups split from which organizations and when. If your church belongs to a Protestant denomination, let your kids trace the "family tree" of your denomination. Your group members may be surprised to discover how many different denominations and groups there are within the realm of Protestantism.

STEP 4

Bring in several reference books that explain the beliefs of various Protestant denominations—preferably books that contrast and compare the different beliefs. Instruct your group members to create a pamphlet that explains how the beliefs and practices of various denominations differ from the beliefs and practices of your church. If done well, the pamphlet could be used as a resource in your church's library.

DATE USED:

Approx. Time

STEP 1: *Going Overboard* _____
- ❑ Extra Action
- ❑ Small Group
- ❑ Large Group
- ❑ Little Bible Background
- ❑ Fellowship & Worship
- ❑ Media
- ❑ Short Meeting Time

Things needed:

STEP 2: *Four-Lane Highway* _____
- ❑ Small Group
- ❑ Large Group
- ❑ Heard It All Before
- ❑ Mostly Guys
- ❑ Extra Fun
- ❑ Media
- ❑ Short Meeting Time
- ❑ Urban
- ❑ Combined Junior High/High School

Things needed:

STEP 3: *In God We Crust* _____
- ❑ Extra Action
- ❑ Mostly Girls
- ❑ Mostly Guys
- ❑ Extra Fun
- ❑ Extra Challenge

Things needed:

STEP 4: *First Love* _____
- ❑ Heard It All Before
- ❑ Little Bible Background
- ❑ Fellowship & Worship
- ❑ Mostly Girls
- ❑ Urban
- ❑ Combined Junior High/High School
- ❑ Extra Challenge

Things needed:

When the Spirit Moves
(What Pentecostals and Charismatics Believe)

YOUR GOALS FOR THIS SESSION:
Choose one or more

☐ To help kids learn the basics of the history and distinctives of Pentecostals and Charismatics.

☐ To help kids understand what the Bible teaches about the Holy Spirit.

☐ To help kids tap into God's power for their own lives.

☐ Other:_____

Your Bible Base:

Acts 2:1-4
I Corinthians 12:4-11;
13:8-13; 14:1-20, 22-33
Galatians 5:22-26

Plan Scan

Have kids form small groups. Ask each group to make plans for a social activity for your youth group or Sunday school class. Give the groups freedom to plan any kind of activity they want. (Of course, that doesn't mean the activity is going to happen.) Emphasize that you're looking for a *plan*, not just an idea. The groups must consider as many details as possible—specifically the arrangements that will need to be made—as they come up with their plans. Give the groups about five minutes to make their plans. When everyone is finished, have each group share its plan.

Afterward, ask: **As you made these plans in your groups, did you find that some people were very detail-oriented, while others wanted to play it by ear?** Ask who was which kind of person. **How did that affect the way you worked together?** Get a couple of responses.

Say: **There are various personality tests that are used to figure out the different ways people think. One of the frequently mentioned differences is that some people seem to play everything by ear, while others need everything decided specifically. One group says things like, "We'll cross that bridge when we get to it." The other group says things like, "If you fail to plan, you plan to fail."**

Ask: **If you had to characterize God and the way He deals with us as one of these two types, which would it be?** Of course, there's no right or wrong answer here. Scripture presents God as decisive and constant, but at the same time flexible and surprising.

Explain: **Today we'll be talking about Pentecostals and Charismatics. We will deal with a number of questions about the Bible and how to interpret it. But there are also personality questions involved. Charismatic worship tends to be more free-flowing—in the Spirit's control.** [NOTE: We're not suggesting that all Pentecostals are one way and all non-Pentecostals are another. But the personality questions add to the mix of theological and biblical issues.]

Say: **As we investigate these issues today, let's get past personality biases. Don't just say "That's weird" or "That's cool." Let's look at what the Bible says about how God works.**

How It Started

(Needed: Copies of Repro Resource 8)

Hand out copies of "The Pentecostal and Charismatic Movements" (Repro Resource 8). Give kids a few minutes to read through the sheet.

Have someone read Acts 2:1-4. Then ask: **When the church started on the day of Pentecost, how did the Holy Spirit let people know He was there?** (He gave the apostles the power to speak in tongues.)

To supplement your discussion of Repro Resource 8, use as much or as little of the following information as you desire:

Bible students debate whether Bible texts refer to mysterious empowerment to speak other languages or whether this was some heavenly language that the Spirit allowed the hearers to understand. The result at Pentecost was that people from many nations understood what was said—three thousand of whom became Christians that day.

Throughout the Book of Acts, there are several more occasions when newly converted people were filled with God's Spirit and spoke in tongues.

At various times throughout church history, there were reports of isolated groups or individuals expressing their worship in "pentecostal" ways—with tongues and sort of a spiritual "moshing."

But the modern Pentecostal movement erupted in Los Angeles in 1906. Revival meetings were held at a beat-up old church building on Azusa Street. People were not only getting saved and sanctified, they were speaking in tongues. Soon similar meetings were being held around the country and around the world. Within the next decade or two, several institutions and denominations were formed to promote this "Pentecostal" faith. Among these were the Assemblies of God, which is now the largest Pentecostal denomination.

Pentecostals believe the full Christian experience can only come through the baptism of the Spirit. This, they teach, is a second experience, after salvation. According to most Pentecostal groups, the baptism of the Spirit is almost always accompanied by tongues-speaking.

Pentecostals are also noted for their belief in other gifts of the Spirit such as prophecy and healing. Their worship services are filled not only with tongues-speaking, but also with other phenomena such as "singing in the Spirit" and being "slain in the Spirit."

OPTIONS

EXTRA ACTION

HEARD IT ALL BEFORE

MOSTLY GIRLS

MOSTLY GUYS

EXTRA FUN

MEDIA

URBAN

148

In many other respects, Pentecostals tend to be like other fundamentalist Protestants. They believe the Bible and tend to take it quite literally. And they emphasize the importance of personal holiness, sometimes observing strict codes of conduct.

A second wave occurred in the 1960s. This became known as the Charismatic Movement, and it grew out of non-Pentecostal churches. Suddenly there were pockets of people in Episcopal, Lutheran, and even Catholic churches who were being "baptized in the Spirit" and speaking in tongues. In some cases, entire churches "went Charismatic." Some churches split over the issue. And in many non-Charismatic churches, there are small Charismatic groups that meet regularly for worship and sharing. There are also some new Charismatic churches that have been started in the last thirty years or so.

For the most part, these Charismatic groups are not tied in with the traditional Pentecostal churches, even though their theology is similar. The Charismatic Movement has been known for its new style of worship—guitars, choruses, informal sharing, hand-raising—which is probably a throwback to the decade when it started, the 1960s. But many non-Charismatic churches have also adopted this style of worship, without accepting the teaching about modern tongues-speaking or other spectacular spiritual gifts.

STEP 3

Back to the Bible

(Needed: Bibles, copies of Repro Resource 9, pencils)

Say: **Let's look at some of the key Bible texts about spiritual gifts and speaking in tongues.**

Have kids form four groups. Hand out copies of "Spirit Search" (Repro Resource 9) and pencils. Assign the following passages:

Group 1—I Corinthians 12:4-11; Group 2—I Corinthians 13:8-13; Group 3—I Corinthians 14:1-20; Group 4—I Corinthians 14:22-33

Give the groups a few minutes to read their assigned passages and answer the questions on the sheet. When everyone is finished, have each group share its responses. Use the following information to supplement the groups' responses, as needed.

Group 1—I Corinthians 12:4-11

What would you say is the main point of this passage? (The unity of the church amid the diversity of spiritual gifts.)

OPTIONS

SMALL GROUP

LARGE GROUP

LITTLE BIBLE BACKGROUND

MEDIA

JR. HIGH HIGH SCHOOL COMBINED

EXTRA CHALLENGE

Why are spiritual gifts—the "manifestation of the Spirit" (12:7)—given?
("For the common good"—not for anyone's individual privilege.)

Have you seen a Christian use any of the gifts mentioned here? If so, how were the gifts used? Be prepared to share examples you've seen.

How would you define "the message of wisdom" (12:8)? "The message of knowledge" (12:8)? "Distinguishing between spirits" (12:10)? (Non-Pentecostals are likely to define "the message of wisdom" as good leadership, "the message of knowledge" as good teaching, and "distinguishing between spirits" as keen perception about people's motives. The Pentecostal interpretations of those gifts are more spectacular, involving God's giving specific messages to the church through gifted individuals.)

Group 2—I Corinthians 13:8-13
What would you say is the main point of this passage? (Love is the most important thing for a Christian.)

What things will "cease," "be stilled," or "pass away" (13:8)? What do you think this means? (Prophecies, tongues, and knowledge. Compared to love, these are all temporary. Our experience of knowing and expressing God is partial now, but love draws us into the eternal heart of God.)

What do you think "childish ways" (13:11) might include? (In context, all three gifts—prophecy, tongues, and knowledge—would have to be included. It could be that the Corinthians were childishly fighting over the gifts, and that Paul was chastising them by reminding them that all gifts are childish compared to love.)

Some non-Pentecostals say that this passage refers to the stopping of the "supernatural" gifts, such as speaking in tongues. These gifts, they say, were intended as signs for the early church that God was at work, but that the church would eventually outgrow its need for these gifts. Do you agree or disagree with this theory? Why? Be prepared to share your church's beliefs on this matter here.

Group 3—I Corinthians 14:1-20
What would you say is the main point of this passage? (Prophecy is a more helpful gift than speaking in tongues. It is preferable to be understood.)

What gift does the author, Paul, seem to prefer over speaking in tongues? Why? (Prophecy, because all can understand it.)

What does Paul say about his own personal devotions (14:18)? (He spoke in tongues frequently in private, but not in the church.)

In what way do you think the Corinthians were "thinking like children" (14:20)? (Perhaps in their bickering over their spiritual gifts. Perhaps in desiring the more spectacular gifts.)

Group 4—I Corinthians 14:22-33
What would you say is the main point of this passage? (Worship should be both orderly and intelligible to the outsider.)

What does the author, Paul, say about the purpose of speaking in tongues? (It's a sign for unbelievers—possibly to say, "Hey! Something really cool is going on here! Pay attention!")

What instructions does Paul give for speaking in tongues in church? (Only two or three should speak in a meeting—one at a time. There must be an interpreter. It should be orderly.)

What does Paul mean by "the spirits of prophets are subject to the control of prophets" (14:32)? (Those who proclaim God's truth are not out of control. They should not enter into some ecstatic frenzy as some pagan prophets did.)

STEP 4

Voices

(Needed: Copies of Repro Resource 10)

Hand out copies of "Voices in the Wind" (Repro Resource 10). Explain that these statements reflect the way some young people might feel about Pentecostal or Charismatic groups. Go through the statements one at a time. After you read each one, ask: **What would you say to this person? Do you think this person is reacting well? What cautions or corrections would you suggest to the person regarding her reaction?**

Use the following information to supplement your discussion of Repro Resource 10. (Your responses will, of course, depend on your church's attitude toward the charismatic gifts, the baptism of the Holy Spirit, and speaking in tongues.)

Marty seems to be reacting to the external appearance of charismatic worship. She needs to get past the "weirdness" and really deal with the underlying beliefs.

Michelle obviously had some stagnation in her Christian life. For Charismatics, this is a classic case of someone in need of Spirit baptism. Non-Charismatics might see this as a spiritual reawakening, an energizing—even a "filling" with the Spirit—but not the first-time entry of the Spirit. Can we affirm Michelle's new commitment, even if we don't agree with the Charismatic interpretation of what happened to her?

Tara is having the problem that many non-Charismatics have with Charismatics. It's the promise of a higher level. This is the central theological difference between the two camps. Is there a second blessing required? Does the Spirit enter the believer at a point beyond salvation, or is it all a "package deal"?

As you close the session, read Galatians 5:22-26. Encourage your group members to "keep in step with the Spirit" in their daily lives.

OPTIONS

HEARD IT ALL BEFORE

LITTLE BIBLE BACKGROUND

FELLOWSHIP & WORSHIP

MOSTLY GIRLS

MOSTLY GUYS

SHORT MEETING TIME

URBAN

JR.HIGH HIGH SCHOOL COMBINED

EXTRA CHALLENGE

The PENTECOSTAL and CHARISMATIC MOVEMENTS

ORIGINS
Pentecostal: There were some stirrings in late 1800s, but the movement erupted in 1906 in Los Angeles. Revival meetings spread and new denominations were formed.
Charismatic: The movement began in 1960, in an Episcopal Church in Van Nuys, California, and spread through small groups in mainline Protestant and Catholic churches.

KEY BELIEFS
• *Baptism by the Holy Spirit as a second blessing.* Salvation is step one. For the full experience of Christ, one must be filled with the Spirit.
• *Speaking in tongues.* This always accompanies Spirit baptism. It is the evidence that one has received the baptism. (Some Charismatics are less dogmatic than others about the necessity of speaking in tongues.)
• *All spiritual gifts are active today.* While many other Christians believe that "supernatural" gifts such as healing were intended only for the early church, Pentecostals and Charismatics see no reason why these gifts should not be used today.

CHARACTERISTICS
• *Lively worship.* If the Spirit is running the show, who knows what will happen? The Charismatic movement in particular has developed an accessible, energetic worship style.
• *Personal holiness.* If one is filled by the Spirit, his or her life should please the Spirit. The traditional Pentecostal churches especially emphasize the "sanctified" lifestyle and sometimes place strict requirements on behavior.
• *Emotional devotion.* While other Christians may emphasize a mental understanding of God's Word, Pentecostals and Charismatics tend to emphasize the emotional side. Worship services are often highly emotional, as are the individuals' personal worship times.

PRACTICES THAT MAY NEED EXPLANATION
• *Speaking in tongues.* This is considered a heavenly praise language. Sometimes God gives a message to the church through someone speaking in tongues, in which case an interpreter must translate for the congregation.

• *Healing.* Pentecostals and Charismatics still uphold this biblical gift, although they maintain that only certain people possess the gift. "Laying on of hands" is often the way this power is transmitted.
• *Prophecy.* Pentecostals and Charismatics still uphold this biblical gift, which involves relating a message from God concerning future events. Most non-Charismatics who are uneasy about getting new messages from God interpret this gift as preaching, the proclamation of God's Word.
• *The word of knowledge.* A person with this gift can tell another person exactly what's wrong with him or her and exactly what to do, even if the two have never met before. This is another biblical gift that non-Charismatics interpret in a less supernatural way.
• *Singing in the Spirit.* This is a worship activity in which a song starts in the congregation and just flows along, led by the Spirit. People may be singing different tunes and different words, or no words at all, but the intention is Spirit-led praise.
• *Being "slain in the Spirit."* This is a popular practice among traveling preachers and faith healers. A person is "touched" with the power of God and falls back, as if dead. It is seen as a testimony to God's power and perhaps as a kind of baptism—death and new life.

Spirit Search

Group 1—I Corinthians 12:4-11
What would you say is the main point of this passage?

Why are spiritual gifts—the "manifestation of the Spirit" (12:7)—given?

Have you ever seen a Christian use any of the gifts mentioned here? If so, how were the gifts used?

How would you define "the message of wisdom" (12:8)? "The message of knowledge" (12:8)? "Distinguishing between spirits" (12:10)?

Group 2—I Corinthians 13:8-13
What would you say is the main point of this passage?

What things will "cease," "be stilled," or "pass away" (13:8)? What do you think this means?

What do you think "childish ways" (13:11) might include?

Some non-Pentecostals say that this passage refers to the stopping of the "supernatural" gifts, such as speaking in tongues. These gifts, they say, were intended as signs for the early church that God was at work, but that the church would eventually outgrow its need for these gifts. Do you agree or disagree with this theory? Why?

Group 3—I Corinthians 14:1-20
What would you say is the main point of this passage?

What gift does the author, Paul, seem to prefer over speaking in tongues? Why?

What does Paul say about his own personal devotions (14:18)?

In what way do you think the Corinthians were "thinking like children" (14:20)?

Group 4—I Corinthians 14:22-33
What would you say is the main point of this passage?

What does the author, Paul, say about the purpose of speaking in tongues?

What instructions does Paul give for speaking in tongues in church?

What does Paul mean by "the spirits of prophets are subject to the control of prophets" (14:32)?

Voices in the Wind

Marty

A friend of mine invited me to her church service, but I didn't know what I was getting into. She told me the church was "charismatic," but I honestly thought that just meant the people were really friendly. Everything seemed normal, at first. We sang these choruses for a while, but then it got really weird. This strange kind of song started. Everyone was singing something different. It got louder, and then softer, and then louder again. It was like we were on Mars or something. Then people started standing up and talking gibberish, and everyone was raising his or her hands in the air. Somebody cried out that he'd been healed. Somebody else said that he knew there was someone in the room who had doubts and he looked right at me. I just wanted to get out of there. They say they're Christians, and maybe they are, but I don't see why they can't just worship like normal people.

Michelle

I've been a Christian all of my life—well, since I was six. I tried to live right and all, but it was always kind of dull. You know? Like I was missing something. So then I went on this retreat with some friends. They were Christians, too, but they weren't from my church. They started talking about the Holy Spirit, and it was, like, really obvious that they were talking about something I didn't have. I mean joy and excitement. I always believed in the Holy Spirit, but I didn't know much about Him. So they were all praying for me that I would get baptized in the Spirit, and they told me how I'd just start speaking in tongues and all. And then it happened. It was such an incredible thing. I was blanking out with joy and saying things I didn't understand. But it was really cool. Anyway, now I'm back home and going to my old church. The people here don't believe in speaking in tongues. I'm afraid to tell anyone, because he or she might think I was really wrong. But I just know it's right. You know?

Tara

My cousin goes to a Pentecostal church and she's been spending the summer with my family. She's pretty cool, but all summer she's been ragging me about my faith. I'm a Christian. I was saved three years ago. But she says I need something more. She says I need the Holy Spirit to come upon me or else I'm not a "full" Christian. I really hate it when she says that because it makes me feel like she's holy and I'm not. But do I really need that? I thought the Holy Spirit was inside me *now*. That's what I was always taught. Is there really something else I need? My cousin points out every bad thing I do now and tells me that I need the Spirit. If I was baptized in the Spirit, she says, I wouldn't do those bad things. I don't know what to do.

STEP 1

Try a more active opener. Ask a series of personal-preference questions. For each question, kids will indicate their responses by moving to one side of the room or the other. For example, you might ask: **Would you rather play a sport yourself or watch someone else play it on TV?** Designate one side of the room as "Play it yourself" and the other side as "Watch it on TV." Kids should not only choose which side of the room to move to, but should also indicate the strength of their feelings by standing as close to or as far away from the wall on that side of the room as is appropriate. The closer someone stands to a wall, the more strongly he or she feels about the issue. You might ask questions concerning kids' preference between junk food and gourmet meals, between living in a warm climate and a living in cold climate, and so on. For the final question, ask: **Do you prefer an orderly, restrained worship service or a free-flowing, active service?** After kids respond, move to Step 2.

STEP 2

Play a variation of the old TV game show "To Tell the Truth," using Repro Resource 8. Before you distribute copies of the sheet, hand out index cards to six volunteers. Each card should have one of the "Practices That May Need Explanation" written on it, along with the accompanying explanation. Instruct each of your volunteers to come up with two other plausible-sounding explanations for his or her assigned practice. Explain that the volunteers' goal is to trick other group members into believing one of the made-up explanations. After a few minutes, have each volunteer identify his or her practice and then read the three explanations. See how many of your group members can identify the correct explanation. Afterward, hand out copies of Repro Resource 8 and go through the sheet as a group.

STEP 1

A small group might not have as many different types of people as the average large group, so you may need to adapt the opening activity. Designate one wall of the room as "Totally True" and the opposite wall as "Completely False." Then read a number of statements and have kids stand (literally) where they stand (philosophically) in response to each statement. Here are some statements you might use:

• **I am a spontaneous person. I like things to happen that I don't expect.**

• **If I were told I could go to Florida for a week—all expenses paid— if I could get ready in 15 minutes, you could count on me to be there in 10.**

• **I know where I want to go to college.**

• **I know what I want to be when I get out of college.**

Use statements that will help your kids show whether they're "play it by ear" people or "I need to have a plan" people.

STEP 3

You have a lot of biblical material to cover, so you'll probably need to divide into groups—even though you may have groups of only one or two people. Be careful not to make your small groups responsible for knowing all of the answers to your questions. Many kids feel awkward enough in a group of five or six, much less when they're expected to deal with a difficult passage on their own or in pairs. When you're asking questions, help your kids with their answers. You'll probably be in a hurry to cover so much material, but don't forget to affirm your kids as you go along. Some of what you're assigning is from passages of Scripture that your church may not cover on a regular basis. It might be completely new to your kids, so help them through it as much as you can.

STEP 1

Begin the session by letting group members sing one of their favorite up-tempo songs or choruses. Sing it through the first time as you normally would. For the second time, incorporate hand clapping and foot stomping. For the third time, let group members create some hand motions or dance steps to accompany the song. Each time group members sing the song, encourage them to be a little more active and raucous. See what happens on about the fifth or sixth time through the song. Afterward, ask your group members whether they prefer a more orderly, restrained style of worship or a more free-flowing, active form of worship. Use the discussion to introduce the material on Repro Resource 8.

STEP 3

Rather than simply having groups answer their assigned questions, instruct each group to come up with a creative way to present the information in its passage to the rest of the groups. For example, Group 1 might use a skit to present the information in I Corinthians 12:4-11. Group 2 might create a song or a rap to communicate the information in I Corinthians 13:8-13. Encourage the groups to be imaginative in their presentations. However, emphasize that all of the group's assigned questions must be answered in the course of the presentation. After a few minutes, let each group make its presentation.

STEP 2

If your kids are convinced that they know everything there is to know about Pentecostal and Charismatic beliefs, give them a chance to prove it. Test them on the material on Repro Resource 8. For example, you might ask: **According to Pentecostal belief, what does it mean to be "filled with the Spirit"? What does it mean to be "slain in the Spirit"?** To make things more interesting, you might set up an agreement with your group members before they take the test. You might decide that if they get a certain number of answers right on the test, they will get to choose the closing activity for the session. If, however, they don't get a certain number of answers right, they must spend the last 10 minutes of the session cleaning up your meeting area (or doing some other unpleasant task).

STEP 4

If your church is non-Pentecostal and non-Charismatic, you may find that some of your kids have preconceived notions about what Pentecostals and Charismatics are like. If so, give your group members an opportunity to rub elbows with kids from a Pentecostal or Charismatic church in your area. Invite your visitors over for an afternoon or evening of fellowship, competition, and discussion. Give your group members (as well as the kids from the visiting church) a chance to discover not only the differences between the two groups, but the similarities as well.

STEP 3

If your kids don't know much about Scripture, this would be a very difficult place for them to begin to explore on their own. Consequently, it would probably be better for you to study each passage as a single group—even if you need to reduce the amount of Scripture covered. It will probably be best if *you* read each passage as group members follow along. Then, as you ask the questions, kids can look together for the answers. That way, they can also work together when any of them have questions of their own. Also be sure to tailor the questions to apply more to "first-timers" than to people already comfortable with Scripture and the workings of a church.

STEP 4

Of all of the Scripture covered in this session, the closing passage from Galatians 5:22-26 is probably the most important for kids who haven't accumulated a lot of Bible knowledge. Don't skip it or rush through it. After dealing with the working of the Holy Spirit in ways that may seem strange to your kids (especially if your church is not Pentecostal or Charismatic), be sure to let them see the very practical ways that the Holy Spirit equips *all* Christians. Let each person rate the presence of each of the nine spiritual qualities (vss. 22, 23) in his or her life on a scale of one (least) to 10 (most). The easiest way to do this is to read one quality at a time and let each person hold up a number of fingers to indicate how well-equipped the person feels in that area. Explain that only by becoming more sensitive to the presence of the Holy Spirit in our lives and keeping in step with Him will we be able to improve the scores we have given ourselves.

STEP 1

When the group arrives, have several different flavors of popcorn available throughout the room. As kids mingle, encourage them to choose their favorite flavor. When you're ready to start the session, take a survey of who preferred which flavor. Then ask: **Does the fact that some of you prefer caramel corn while others prefer cheese popcorn change the fact that both groups like popcorn?** (No. They're just variations on the same theme.) **In a similar vein, do you think differences in worship styles really matter as long as the worship goes to God?** You may need to be careful here. Point out that not just any worship is OK; it must be biblically based. There are many ways to interpret Scripture, however; as long as the worship foundation is on target, differences in style probably don't matter much.

STEP 4

After reading Galatians 5:22-26, ask: **What does this passage say to you today? What areas of your life does it address?** Hand out paper and pencils. Challenge group members to write a prayer to God, asking His for help in areas of their life that need work and offering praise for areas in their life that are "in step with the Spirit."

STEP 2

Before you begin Step 2, hand out paper and pencils. Ask your girls to write down what they think of when they hear the words *Pentecostal* and *Charismatic*. Explain: **Many of us who are not familiar with these worship styles have our own ideas—and sometimes our own misconceptions—of what they are.** Work through Repro Resource 8; then come back to your group members' lists to discuss how accurate their ideas were.

STEP 4

Have your group members form pairs. Encourage the members of each pair to share with each other something that they know they need to do this week in order to "keep in step with the Spirit." Allow time for your girls to pray with their partners; then challenge them to pray for each other throughout the rest of the week.

STEP 2

Begin this step by letting guys imitate their favorite TV preachers. Many guys, when they see a preacher on TV once or twice, tend to form immediate opinions. They particularly tend to criticize and make fun of things they don't understand. Consequently, guys from non-Charismatic churches may tend to make fun when they see people being "slain in the Spirit" or healed, or when they see other things that aren't done in their own churches. After you witness the performances of your guys, you'll probably be able to tell which preachers (and denominations) kids have been watching. It should also clue you in to any advance prejudices you should deal with during the session.

STEP 4

Many times guys are overly critical of church things—especially things that are new to them. But it's surprising to see how accepting they can become as soon as they begin to date girls who attend churches where all of those "strange" things are going on. Adapt the three readings on Repro Resource 10 to represent guys talking about girls they really like and are dating. In the context of trying to maintain a strong relationship with a member of the opposite sex, your guys are likely to become immediately more sensitive and helpful. Their advice will probably be more from the heart in such cases rather than merely from the head.

STEP 1

Hand out paper and pencils. Have kids write down a number of questions that begin with the phrase "Would you rather . . . ?" For each question, they should try to think of some very hard decisions for someone to make. For example, they might ask, "Would you rather eat a big piece of liver or get kissed by your great-aunt who always slobbers all over your face?" or "Would you rather go on a date with someone who annoys you half to death or stay home with your parents who annoy you half to death?" After a few minutes, collect the sheets. Then, one at a time, have kids draw a slip and answer the question. If kids come up with some good questions, it will be interesting to watch the reactions of the people who answer. Some are likely to be decisive and sure of themselves in almost every case. Others are likely to waffle back and forth for a while before answering. This activity can replace the planning exercise that opens the session and can lead in to the discussion of the different forms of worship.

STEP 2

Let group members write out (or simply tell about) their most unusual or embarrassing church experience. In many cases, stories are likely to originate from visits to churches where kids were unfamiliar with the procedure. If you have kids write out their stories, you have the option of collecting the sheets, reading one story at a time, and letting others guess which story is whose. But there's a lot of material to be covered in this session, so you might want to simply let a few kids relate some anecdotes to help keep the tone of the meeting light and a little more personal.

STEP 2

Before the session, record a Christian television broadcast that features a Pentecostal or Charismatic worship service or evangelistic meeting. If possible, try to include segments that feature people speaking in tongues and being "slain in the Spirit." While your group members are watching the tape, ask: **What things do you like about this service? Why? What things make you uncomfortable? Why?** After you get a few responses, move on to Repro Resource 8.

STEP 3

To begin this step, play several clips of songs that are sung in different languages. If possible, try to find songs that are sung in Spanish, Italian, German, French, Norwegian, Irish, Japanese, and so forth. See if your group members can identify each foreign language. You might want to make a game out of it by awarding points for each correct answer. Afterward, discuss as a group which of the languages were easiest to identify and which were hardest. Use this activity to introduce the discussion of speaking in tongues.

STEP 1

If you're short on time, skip Step 1. To introduce Repro Resource 8 (and the session topic), ask your group members to name the first things that come to mind when you mention the words "Pentecostal" and "Charismatic." Write kids' responses on the board. Then, as you go through Repro Resource 8, compare the information on the sheet with your kids' responses on the board to see how accurate your group members' first impressions were.

STEP 4

Rather than going through the statements on Repro Resource 10, ask one of your group members to share an experience he or she had in a Pentecostal/Charismatic church or an encounter he or she had with a Pentecostal/Charismatic acquaintance. Then, as a group, discuss ways that the person might have responded differently (or ways that the person might respond differently in the future). As necessary, incorporate the comments in the session plan concerning the examples on Repro Resource 10.

STEP 2

Ask group members to think of the different nationalities that are represented in their neighborhood. Ask: **How many different languages are spoken by the people who live in your area?** See which group member identifies the most languages in his or her neighborhood. Then ask: **How many of these people of other nationalities could you communicate with if you had to?** Get a few responses. Then point out that Peter and the rest of the apostles faced a similar situation at Passover. Lead in to a discussion of Acts 2:1-12. Then hand out copies of Repro Resource 8 and continue the session as written.

STEP 4

Invite representatives from one or more Pentecostal or Charismatic churches in your area to your meeting. Ask each representative to talk about some of the things his or her church is doing in the inner city. Perhaps each representative might discuss some of the programs his or her church runs for the homeless and needy, some of the organizations the church sponsors, and so on. After the representatives have shared, spend some time discussing ways that your group could work together with one or more of the churches to further urban ministry in your area.

STEP 3

If your junior highers (or even your high schoolers) aren't familiar with spiritual gifts—what they are or how they are used—take a few minutes to talk about your church's position on spiritual gifts. Read I Corinthians 12:14-31 and Romans 12:3-8. Talk about the different gifts mentioned and how they are visible in your congregation.

STEP 4

After reading Galatians 5:22-26, close the session with a fruit party. Bring in nine kinds of fruit, each labeled with a fruit of the spirit. Let the kids put together a fruit salad of their choice. As they're eating, talk about which fruits they see most often and which ones they see least often in people around them. (However, emphasize that no one should mention any names.)

STEP 3

One of the best ways to make sure that your group members have a handle on Pentecostal/Charismatic beliefs is to stage a debate. Have kids form two teams. Assign one team to argue from the perspective of Pentecostals and Charismatics. Assign the other team to argue from the perspective of non-Pentecostals and non-Charismatics. Among the topics teams might debate are speaking in tongues, being filled with the Spirit, healing, and being "slain in the Spirit." Give the teams a few minutes to prepare by reviewing Repro Resources, notes from the session, and relevant Scripture passages. In the debate, you will introduce a topic; each team will then have two minutes to present its argument, followed by one minute apiece for each team's rebuttal. Afterward, discuss as a group some of the points that were made during the debate.

STEP 4

Bring in several books that explain (in language even a non-seminarian can understand) the beliefs and practices of Pentecostal and Charismatic churches. Give your kids a few minutes to look through the books, marking important sections. Then instruct group members to work together to create a pamphlet that explains how the beliefs and practices of Pentecostals and Charismatics differ from the beliefs and practices of your church. If done well, the pamphlet could be used as a resource in your church's library.

DATE USED:

Approx. Time

STEP 1: *Plan Scan* _____
- ❏ Extra Action
- ❏ Small Group
- ❏ Large Group
- ❏ Fellowship & Worship
- ❏ Extra Fun
- ❏ Short Meeting Time

Things needed:

STEP 2: *How It Started* _____
- ❏ Extra Action
- ❏ Heard It All Before
- ❏ Mostly Girls
- ❏ Mostly Guys
- ❏ Extra Fun
- ❏ Media
- ❏ Urban

Things needed:

STEP 3: *Back t❏ the Bible* _____
- ❏ Small Group
- ❏ Large Group
- ❏ Little Bible Background
- ❏ Media
- ❏ Combined Junior High/High School
- ❏ Extra Challenge

Things needed:

STEP 4: *Voices* _____
- ❏ Heard It All Before
- ❏ Little Bible Background
- ❏ Fellowship & Worship
- ❏ Mostly Girls
- ❏ Mostly Guys
- ❏ Short Meeting Time
- ❏ Urban
- ❏ Combined Junior High/High School
- ❏ Extra Challenge

Things needed:

SESSION 5

Common Ground and Negotiables

(Affirming the Common Heritage of the Church Universal)

YOUR GOALS FOR THIS SESSION:
Choose one or more

☐ To help kids learn what the Bible teaches about the unity of the church.

☐ To help kids understand which differences between religious groups are important and which are not.

☐ To help kids connect with believers of other denominations.

☐ Other:_____

_____

Your Bible Base:

I Corinthians 1:10-13;
2:1-5; 3:3-9
Ephesians 4:1-6

I've Got Your Number

(Needed: Prepared index cards)

Before the session, you'll need to prepare index cards with the following numbers or number categories on them:
- 28
- Even numbers
- 8
- Any number between 1 and 13
- The last digit of your phone number
- Any number with a 5 or a 3 in it
- Odd numbers
- Your age
- The age of any member of your family
- Numbers that can be divided by 7 with no remainder
- Any number greater than 23

Make sure you have enough cards so that each group member gets one. If you need more cards, come up with numbers or number categories similar to the ones listed above.

To begin the session, hand one card to each group member. Explain: **Each person needs to connect with two other people. You connect by finding a number or number category that you have in common with another person. For example, if your card has "8" on it, you might connect with someone whose card has "Even numbers" on it. When you connect with someone, keep that person by your side. Our goal is to make a circle of connections that includes everyone in the room.**

Give group members a few minutes to search for connections. After a while, you may need to undo some connections in order to regroup in a way that includes everyone. You may also need to "cheat" by claiming a number for yourself that completes the circle.

After you've completed the circle, ask: **How is this circle like the denominations we've been studying?**

If group members can't figure out the connection, say: **Denominations are very different. What can an Anglican possibly share with a Baptist? But what does an even number have in common with an odd number? They're both numbers! And with the help of a few others, we can make a connection.**

If we focus only on our differences, we will always be apart. But can we find some common ground? Sure we can—in our common worship of Jesus Christ. This is not to say that our differences don't matter. Naturally, we think we have some things right that others have wrong. But we can still talk together, fellowship together, possibly even worship together with those who honor Christ too.

STEP
2

All for One

(Needed: Bibles, copies of Repro Resource 11, pencils)

OPTIONS

SMALL GROUP

LITTLE BIBLE BACKGROUND

SHORT MEETING TIME

JR. HIGH HIGH SCHOOL COMBINED

Have kids form small groups. Hand out copies of "Long Division" (Repro Resource 11) and pencils. Instruct each group to complete all three sections on the sheet. Explain that (a) the author, Paul, had started the church in Corinth a few years earlier; (b) another Christian preacher, Apollos, who was apparently a very skilled preacher, had gained a following in the area; and (c) Cephas was another name for the apostle Peter. (You may want to read Acts 18 yourself as background.)

Give the groups a few minutes to work. When everyone is finished, go through the sheet one section at a time. After each group has shared its title for the first passage, vote as a group on which title is best. Ideally, this voting process will cause some debate among your kids. This activity is designed to stir up division—exactly what the text warns against.

After some debate, ask: **Why does there have to be one supreme title? Can't we learn from the way others have looked at the text?** Get a few responses.

Then say: **In the same way, we can view our faith a certain way, but still learn from people of other denominations.**

Use the following information as needed to supplement your discussion of the Scripture passages on Repro Resource 11.

I Corinthians 1:10-13

What title would you give these verses? (Perhaps "Unity" or "Breaking Up Is Easy to Do.")

What was the problem in Corinth? (Factions. People were arguing over which preacher's teaching to follow.)

Do you think there was anything wrong with the "I follow Christ" group? Explain. (Maybe, maybe not. It's possible that these people were purists who claimed to follow Christ *instead* of other teachers. Or perhaps they thought that they were the only ones who had the truth.)

I Corinthians 2:1-5

How did Paul come to the Corinthians? (He came in weakness and fear, with much trembling. He was not eloquent. In contrast, Apollos was quite eloquent. We know that other preachers of the time prided themselves on their smooth delivery.)

Why was it important for him to come to the Corinthians in this way? Why was it important for him to remind the Corinthians of this? (It was obvious that Paul was not promoting himself when he came to the Corinthians; rather, he was simply preaching God's message.)

What attitude does Paul seem to be recommending for the church? How might that attitude change things? (Perhaps Paul is recommending an attitude of humility and vulnerability. Such an attitude would severely limit the number of arguments and fights in the church.)

I Corinthians 3:3-9

Why does Paul call the Corinthians worldly? (In the world system that doesn't follow Christ, people are always fighting to get their way.)

How does Paul describe Apollos and himself and their work? (Paul described Apollos and himself as "fellow workers," each with a job to do. Their work complemented each other's.)

What do you think is the main point of these verses? (All Christians are teammates in ministry. It's not about us, but about God's work.)

The $64,000,000,000 Question

How do you think Paul's teachings in I Corinthians should affect the way we think about Christian denominations? (Baptists, Presbyterians, Methodists, and the rest may disagree on theological points, but if we are serving Christ, we can work together. We should act with love and humility—and keep the focus on Christ.)

Agreeing to Disagree

(Needed: Copies of Repro Resource 12)

Ask for three volunteers to perform a skit. Hand a copy of "Spies Like Us" (Repro Resource 12) to each volunteer. Give your actors a minute or two to read through the script; then have them perform.

Afterward, ask: **What was the Professor's conclusion?** (The strange beast was an elephant. Each investigator touched only part of it. Since it wasn't a dangerous beast, they could leave it alone.)

Explain: **So it is with denominations sometimes. Each one focuses on a certain aspect of God, which may be different from the focus of a different denomination.**

Is God sovereign, in control of the events of our lives and our world? Absolutely! The Presbyterians have that idea down pat.

Do we also have a responsibility to respond to God's invitations? You bet. That's something the Methodists and Baptists are especially good at.

Can the Holy Spirit be a powerful, transforming force in our lives? Yes! Even if you're not a Pentecostal or Charismatic, you can appreciate their emphasis on the Spirit's power.

The most important thing is Jesus Christ. If we agree that He is our Savior, we can agree to disagree on other issues.

I may like tuna fish and you may hate it. I may think the Dallas Cowboys are the best football team on the planet, and you may violently disagree. I may like classical music and you may despise it. In each case, we can still be friends. We agree to disagree.

In the same way, I may think that the Methodist [or Baptist or Mennonite] church across the street is dead wrong on certain issues. But if we can agree that Jesus Christ died for our sins, we can have fellowship in Christ.

School Days

(Needed: Copies of Repro Resource 13)

Hand out copies of "Alone Together: A Personal Memoir" (Repro Resource 13). Have a volunteer read aloud the "personal memoir."

Afterward, ask: **How does your experience compare with this? How do you normally feel about people of other denominations? How could you establish Christian friendships with people of other denominations?** Get several responses to each of these questions from your group members.

As you wrap up the session, focus on the bottom section of Repro Resource 13, asking group members to consider their response to the series. Give them a minute or two of silence to think and pray about this. Then, to close the session, read aloud Ephesians 4:1-6.

LONG DIVISION

Read each of the passages silently and then discuss the questions that follow.

I Corinthians 1:10-13
What title would you give these verses?

What was the problem in Corinth?

Do you think there was anything wrong with the "I follow Christ" group? Explain.

I Corinthians 2:1-5
How did Paul come to the Corinthians?

Why was it important for him to come to the Corinthians in this way? Why was it important for him to remind the Corinthians of this?

What attitude does Paul seem to be recommending for the church? How might that attitude change things?

I Corinthians 3:3-9
Why does Paul call the Corinthians worldly?

How does Paul describe Apollos and himself and their work?

What do you think is the main point of these verses?

The $64,000,000,000 Question
How do you think Paul's teachings in I Corinthians should affect the way we think about Christian denominations?

SPIES LIKE US

ALPHONSE: I have called this meeting of our village elders to discuss a serious threat. As you may have heard, there is an invader that comes at night to the lagoon outside the village. Three nights ago, I heard its eerie whining sounds. So, with great courage, I crept out in the darkness to investigate what sort of creature this was.

BERNIE: And what did you find, O Great One?

ALPHONSE: It was dark, you understand, but I managed to touch the beast. It is a thick, tall creature—like a giant tree—with leathery skin.

So I propose that we get the town chainsaw and make this beast into firewood.

BERNIE: I beg to differ, O Great One. Two nights ago, I too crept out to the lagoon under the moonless sky. What I felt with my bare hands was this: a giant worm with two hollow eyes and leathery skin. I propose that we go to the village salt supply and sprinkle salt on this disgusting creature, because we know that salt makes worms shrivel up and die.

CECILIA: I say this with all due respect, but you are both crazy. I went out there last night to check out this thing for myself. It's a bird, I'm telling you. In the darkness, I felt its leathery wing, large and flexible, like the flap of a tent. I fear that this vulture could fly over our town in an instant and devour anyone it set its keen eyes upon. I propose that we take our hairpins and pin its wings down so that it will not be able to fly.

BERNIE: Your idea is really stupid.

CECILIA: *My* idea is stupid? You're going to sprinkle *salt* on the creature! How about a little oregano to go with it?

ALPHONSE: Clearly, you both are missing the point.

CECILIA: I wouldn't talk, Mr. Magoo. Where do you get this "big tree" nonsense anyway?

BERNIE: He probably made a wrong turn and went into the woods. It really *was* a tree!

ALPHONSE: I thought we might have some disagreement, so I invited the Professor and his able assistant, Mary Ann, to hear our testimony and recommend the proper course of action. Professor, you have studied the creatures of many lands. What do you have to say about this strange beast? What is it?

WHAT DID THE PROFESSOR SAY?

Alone Together:
A Personal Memoir

There was a time when the prophet Elijah thought he was the only true believer in Israel. He thought everyone else had started worshiping idols. "I am the only one left," he cried (I Kings 19:10).

I felt like that as a high school student. But I didn't need to.

I attended an exciting Conservative Baptist church, but most of the kids in my youth group lived in other towns. Only one went to my high school, and she was rather shy. When I looked for Christian fellowship in the halls and classrooms of Gateway High, I couldn't find it.

My classmates were nice, and I got along with them well. Most were Catholic, but some were Methodist and Presbyterian—one even went to a "liberal" Baptist church. But somewhere I got the notion that none of those churches could be trusted. Those kids probably weren't "true" Christians, I thought. They might say they believed in Jesus, but did they really trust Him as their personal Savior? Probably not. I was too bashful to ask them point-blank.

In my senior year, I managed to start a Bible study in a school classroom at the end of the day. (Today I'd get sued for that, but then I wasn't thinking about legal issues.) The Bible study wasn't huge, but maybe a dozen would show up from time to time. And these were Methodists and Presbyterians—people I had written off before. As we talked, I realized these were "true" believers, just as I was, starving for some Christian friendships.

I was sorry it took me that long to reach across those denominational lines. When Elijah was depressed, God reminded him that there were still 7,000 faithful people in Israel. Elijah was not alone. And neither was I.

Based on what we've learned in this series, I think God would like me to . . .
(Check all that apply.)

___ Get to know the beliefs and history of my own denomination.

___ Connect with another Christian in my school or community who may be of another denomination.

___ Explore the beliefs of other denominations.

___ Focus more on the one essential thing: trusting Jesus.

Here's what I can do in the next month to start making that happen:

NOTES

STEP 1

Begin the session with a game of "Tribond." This board game challenges players to figure out the common bond between three seemingly unrelated items. (For example, if the words *cat*, *dog*, and *angel* were given, players would have to figure out that they are all types of fish.) Have kids form teams. Rather than having each team move its playing pieces around the game board according to the game's instructions, simply read one set of clues to each team and give the team 15 seconds to figure out the common bond. Award one point for each correct guess. The team with the most points at the end of the game is the winner. Use this activity to introduce the idea of common bonds between different denominations.

STEP 3

Before the session, put together a jigsaw puzzle that has about 100 pieces in it. After putting the puzzle together, divide it into four sections. Put the pieces from each section (after taking them apart) in a separate envelope. At this point in the session, have kids form four teams. Give each team one of the envelopes. Instruct each team to put together its section of the puzzle as quickly as possible. When the teams are finished, put the four sections together to complete the entire puzzle. Use this activity to introduce the idea that different denominations focus on different aspects of God. Suggest that when we look at the emphases of different denominations, we get a better view of the "complete picture" of God.

STEP 1

If you don't think you have enough group members to make the number game challenging, try a different activity. Announce that you will do something special for group members (perhaps take them out to eat), if they can list 25 different things that they all have in common. This may sound like an unrealistic challenge at first; but after a while, some of your sharper kids will likely begin to expand the perimeters of their thinking. After all, your group members are all people; they're all under 10 feet tall; they're all from Earth; and so forth. Keep urging kids on until they find 25 reasonably valid things they have in common. Afterward, point out that we tend to treat each other as many church denominations do—we tend to focus much more on our differences than we do on our similarities.

STEP 2

Conduct the Bible study as a single group, letting different people read the Scripture passages and respond to the questions (though after the first person answers, try to encourage additional comments or differences of opinion from others). It shouldn't take long for a small group to get through these questions and have a reasonably in-depth discussion. At the end of the study, add a few questions: **What do you think our church needs to learn from Paul's writings? What is the most important thing you think you should remember from these passages? Have you ever been involved in "competition" of a spiritual nature? If so, what was the situation? How was it resolved?**

STEP 1

The numbers activity may be difficult for a large group, so you may want to replace it with a different opener. Divide your kids into groups of six, trying as much as possible to separate kids who usually hang around together. Hand out paper and pencils to each group. Explain that the groups will be competing to see which one can form the strongest bond among its members. The members of each group will form their bonds by finding things that all of them have in common. The team that comes up with the longest list of common bonds in five minutes is the winner. Encourage kids to be as imaginative as possible in their lists. Emphasize that almost nothing is too obscure to be considered a common bond. (For example, if all six group members were born in an even-numbered month, that would be considered an acceptable common bond.) After five minutes, collect the lists and read each one aloud. Award prizes to the group with the longest list. Use this activity to introduce the topic of common bonds between different denominations.

STEP 3

After volunteers go through the skit on Repro Resource 12, have group members form teams. Instruct each team to create a riddle scenario similar to the one on Repro Resource 12, in which three different characters have three different (limited) views as to what something is. After a few minutes, have each team share its riddle scenario. See if any of your other group members can solve the riddle. Afterward, draw comparisons to the way different denominations focus on different aspects of God.

HEARD IT ALL BEFORE

LITTLE BIBLE BACKGROUND

FELLOWSHIP & WORSHIP

STEP 3

Kids who have spent most of their lives in the same church may assume that all church worship services are fairly standard. If such is the case with your group members, try an activity that will help your kids recognize the differences (as well as some of the similarities) between the worship services of various denominations. During the week before the session, collect several bulletins (or sheets that list the order of service) from several different churches (of different denominations) in your area. Let your group members look through the bulletins, noting similarities and differences of worship procedures in the various churches. Is the order of service relatively consistent from church to church? Do any of the churches include worship elements that your church doesn't? Are any of the same hymns sung in different churches? Do the sermon topics have anything in common? After a few minutes, discuss your group members' findings.

STEP 4

As you wrap up the session (and this series), throw a curveball at your heard-it-all-before kids. After discussing the common ground of different denominations, ask: **If Christians have these things in common, then why do we need denominations?** Group members' answers to this question should give you a clue as to how well they've been listening during the past few weeks. As needed, review material from the first four sessions of the book.

STEP 2

The Bible passages covered are good ones for a group without much Bible background. But you might want to take an approach other than simply asking the questions presented in the session. Instead, ask your group members to suppose that they are writing a book entitled *Everything You Need to Know about Starting a Church and Keeping It Going Strong*. Explain that these passages have been recommended as excellent sources for research. After you read each passage, ask: **What can we learn about starting and maintaining a church from this source? What would be a good chapter title to describe this information? Can you think of personal stories from our church or youth group that might be included in this chapter?**

STEP 4

This series covers a lot of material that your group members are likely to forget before long. So try to give kids something to remember. As time permits at the end of the session, see how much of the closing passage (Ephesians 4:1-6) kids can memorize before they leave. Start by having kids first memorize verses 4-6. Then, if there is still time, go back to verse 3; then to verse 2; and, last but not least, to verse 1. Some of your better memorizers may be able to quote the entire passage by the time they leave. If so, challenge them to keep saying it every day for a while until they are sure they won't forget it.

STEP 1

To begin the session, say: **So far in this series, we've learned a lot about different denominations. Let's list some of the things that we've learned.** Encourage group members to name some similarities and differences between your church's denomination and other denominations. Also encourage kids to share things they've learned about other denominations that they didn't know before. Afterward, read Ephesians 4:1-6. Talk about the fact that ultimately, we all focus on God. Spend a few minutes in prayer, thanking God for creating both unity and diversity.

STEP 4

The best way for your kids to understand another denomination is to visit a worship service. Line up some visits for your youth group to various area churches. You may even wish to talk to other youth leaders to set up a time of sharing between the two groups. Continually remind your group members that regardless of our differences, all denominations have the same goal—to worship and honor God.

MOSTLY GIRLS

STEP 1

Have your girls form groups of three or four. Ask the members of each group to describe what they think the church universal might be like if we humans didn't get so caught up in focusing on everyone's differences. Let group members use paper, pencils, crayons, markers, magazines, or anything else they need to create a representation of their "united" church. They may use words, pictures, colors, or anything they want. After a few minutes, ask each group to share and explain its creation.

STEP 4

After your girls have completed Repro Resource 13, encourage them to share with the group some of their thoughts on this series—what they've learned and what they need to work on. Then have group members form pairs. Instruct the members of each pair to pray for each other, mentioning specifically the goals for the next month as listed on Repro Resource 13. Close the session by reading Ephesians 4:1-6 and offering prayer for the group as whole.

MOSTLY GUYS

STEP 1

Tailor the categories of the number game specifically to guys and then let them play it as written. Here are some categories to get you started:

• Number of times you've worn your gym shorts since you washed them

• Number of times you've eaten today

• Number of girls you've had a crush on this year

• The last two numbers of anyone's phone number you know from memory

• Number of CDs you've bought during the past month

• Number on any uniform you've ever worn

STEP 3

Try to convey the information in this step in the form of a couple of skits. Have two volunteers play the roles of guys who are meeting for the first time. The first guy should try to start a conversation to get to know the other guy better. But the second guy should strongly disagree with every opinion the first guy expresses. Group members should see clearly how difficult it is to make new friends while maintaining a negative attitude. Then do a second skit in which the first guy does exactly the same thing—tries to get to know the other guy. But this time, the second guy—while he may disagree with the first guy's opinions—should try to do so in a gentle way that would not offend him. In many cases, he might agree up to a point, but then express a slight difference of opinion. Your guys should see that the attitudes they have toward other people may be much more important than they realize. Ask: **What can we learn from these two skits about getting along with people who belong to other denominations?**

EXTRA FUN

STEP 1

Have kids form two teams to play "tug-of-war." Start by using a cheap piece of thin string or ribbon that is sure to break. Try again by doubling the string, then tripling it, and so forth, until it eventually becomes unbreakable. Afterward, point out that our "ties" to other people may be broken if we have only one thing in common with them. But the better we become at finding additional ties and common bonds, the stronger the connection becomes. Soon the relationship becomes so strong that, no matter how hard we pull (or how much we disagree), the bond will not break. We need to develop as many common bonds as we can with people of other denominations before we start focusing on differences of opinions.

STEP 4

Conclude the session by having your kids play a few rounds of the game Taboo. The object of the game is to communicate a word or phrase to someone else without using five "taboo" words. After playing a while, point out that with practice, we can learn to communicate with people of other denominations without keying on the things that cause disagreement. Emphasize that we need to practice focusing on the things that are OK to discuss before we move on to more "taboo" areas of conversation.

STEP 1

Play portions of three seemingly unrelated songs and see if your kids can guess what the common bond is that links the three songs. For example, you might play "Hey Jude" by the Beatles, "The End of the Road" by Boyz II Men, and "She Talks to Angels" by the Black Crowes. The common bond is that the songs are all performed by groups whose names start with the letter *B*. Play three or four rounds, using a different set of songs for each round. Depending on how well-versed your group members are in pop music, you may make the common bonds as obvious or as obscure as you like. Use this activity to introduce the idea of common bonds between different denominations.

STEP 4

Bring in a couple of videos that contain scenes of people coming together for a common purpose. For example, you might show the scene at the end of *It's a Wonderful Life* in which all of George Bailey's friends gather to help him out. Or you might show the scene at the end of *How the Grinch Stole Christmas* in which the residents of Whoville join together to celebrate Christmas. After showing the scenes, ask: **Is this how you picture people of different denominations coming together? If not, how do you picture it?** Use the ensuing discussion to get ideas from your group members on how they might go about establishing contact with kids from other denominations.

STEP 1

Rather than using the numbers activity, try a shorter opener. Have kids form groups of three or four. Give each group a piece of paper and a pencil. See which group can be the first to discover 10 things that all of its members have in common. The first team to list 10 common bonds and then hand its list to you is the winner. Use this activity to introduce the topic of common bonds between different denominations.

STEP 2

If you're short on time, use only the I Corinthians 1:10-13 and I Corinthians 3:3-9 passages on Repro Resource 11. Rather than having kids form small groups to assign titles to the passages, simply read each passage and then discuss as a group the questions on the sheet. In Step 3, skip Repro Resource 12. Briefly point out the emphases of different denominations and affirm that the important thing is that we agree that Jesus is our Savior. Then move on to Step 4 to wrap up the session (and the series).

STEP 3

Before you begin Step 4, ask your group members to list some of the obstacles that prevent or hinder them from getting to know people of other denominations. Encourage kids to call out as many obstacles as they can think of, no matter how minor the obstacles may seem. Compile a list on the board of the obstacles your group members name. After you've got a fairly sizable list, brainstorm as a group some ways to overcome the obstacles listed on the board. Your group members may surprise you (and themselves) with the helpful suggestions they come up with. Encourage each person to choose one of the suggestions to put to use this week to establish contact with someone from another denomination. Allow some time at the beginning of your next meeting for group members to share the results of their efforts.

STEP 4

As you wrap up this session (and this series), have your kids plan a community project that will include youth groups from several different churches (of different denominations) in your area. Perhaps you might plan a cleanup day at a local park or playground in which young people can work side by side with members of other churches to beautify the community. Or perhaps you might contact a local mission or homeless shelter to see what your group of interdenominational kids can do there. Your goal is to help kids see what they can accomplish when they work in cooperation with fellow believers.

STEP 1

Ask your junior highers to move to one side of the room and your high schoolers to move to the other side. Explain that you will be calling out "dividers," things that will cause your kids to choose one side of an issue or another. To indicate their responses, kids will move to one side of the room or the other. For instance, you might say: **I believe that capital punishment is OK.** If kids agree with the statement, they should move to one side of the room; if they disagree, they should move to the other side. Spend a few minutes calling out a variety of dividers—some significant, some not. At various points throughout the game, point out that each side of the room contains both junior highers and high schoolers. At the end of the game, when kids are thoroughly combined, say: **Though we all didn't agree on all of the same things, it's clear that some of us have things in common that we didn't realize before.** Point out that the same is true with the church. Some denominations have more in common with certain denominations than with others, but we all have a common ground—Jesus Christ.

STEP 2

If you know that your junior highers will have trouble with Repro Resource 11, you may wish to try another option. Before the session, prepare a poster that summarizes the main points of each passage on Repro Resource 11. At this point in the session, read each portion of Scripture, talk about the main points you've summarized, and then ask volunteers to act out how they think the Corinthians might have reacted to Paul's message or how Paul might have delivered it. Encourage group members to look at each passage from various angles to see what they come up with.

STEP 3

At the end of Step 3, before you wrap up the session (and the series), give your kids a chance to test each other on what they've learned during the past few weeks. Have kids form two teams. Instruct each team to come up with seven questions that deal with denominations. The questions may address historical information about denominations (who started which denomination and why), scriptural principles, specific beliefs of various denominations, or any other denomination-related topic. However, the teams must know the correct answer for each question they come up with. After a few minutes, let the teams take turns firing questions at one another. Award one point for each time a team correctly answers one of its opponent's questions and one point for each time a team stumps its opponent with a question. If you wish, give prizes to the team with the most points at the end of the game.

STEP 4

Instruct your group members to do some research to find out what constitutes the "common ground" that most denominations and Christian groups agree on. If your kids are really ambitious, you might have them schedule times to talk with the pastors or board members of other churches (of different denominations) in your area to find out specific information regarding each church's beliefs and practices. Your kids can use the information they compile to plan an interdenominational worship service with several of the churches in your area.

DATE USED:

Approx. Time

STEP 1: *I've Got Your Number* _____
- ❑ Extra Action
- ❑ Small Group
- ❑ Large Group
- ❑ Fellowship & Worship
- ❑ Mostly Girls
- ❑ Mostly Guys
- ❑ Extra Fun
- ❑ Media
- ❑ Short Meeting Time
- ❑ Combined Junior High/High School

Things needed:

STEP 2: *All for One* _____
- ❑ Small Group
- ❑ Little Bible Background
- ❑ Short Meeting Time
- ❑ Combined Junior High/High School

Things needed:

STEP 3: *Agreeing to Disagree* _____
- ❑ Extra Action
- ❑ Large Group
- ❑ Heard It All Before
- ❑ Mostly Guys
- ❑ Urban
- ❑ Extra Challenge

Things needed:

STEP 4: *School Days* _____
- ❑ Heard It All Before
- ❑ Little Bible Background
- ❑ Fellowship & Worship
- ❑ Mostly Girls
- ❑ Extra Fun
- ❑ Media
- ❑ Urban
- ❑ Extra Challenge

Things needed:

Unit Three: Your Bible's Alive!

How to Handle a Double-Edged Sword

by Fran and Jill Sciacca

As you introduce *Your Bible's Alive!* keep in mind that your group probably consists of a mixed bag of Bible students. At one extreme, you may have kids who don't know Chronicles from Corinthians. At the other extreme, you may have some whose eyes have glazed over from too much Bible input and too little output. As a high school Bible teacher, I'm faced with both types each day. You may safely assume one thing about almost *all* of your kids: They probably have an incomplete understanding of what the Bible is.

Someone wisely said, "The Bible is a window into the very heart and mind of God Himself. Don't spend your life merely polishing the glass!" I like this statement because it is consistent with the Bible's description of itself. In speaking of Jesus, the Living Word, John wrote, "No one has ever seen God, but God the One and Only, who is at the Father's side, has made him known" (John 1:18). God became a human in order to save humans beings. But there remains the staggering reality that deep within the purposes of God, the intention was also present that we could know the Lord more fully. The Incarnation was intended to reveal the very nature and character of God to us. Therefore, the Bible *really* is a "window" into the heart and mind of God. With it, we can explore His thoughts and purpose for our life. Help students see the incredible truth that what they hold in their hands is not merely a book; it is a window through which we can see and know God.

There Are People on These Pages, Not Just Print!

The Bible is a real book about real people. God has painstakingly filled the pages of His Word with accounts of men, women, children, kings, queens, heroes, and failures. In glowing technicolor we see the results of good choices, and the consequences of bad choices. Paul's statement in Romans 15:4 ("For everything that was written in the past was written to teach us, so that through endurance and the encouragement of the Scriptures we might have hope") highlights one of God's intentions for spending so much time on *people* in the Bible. He wants us to *learn* from them!

High school students relate best to real-life people. In this unit you have avenues of opportunity to let biblical principles take on human form as you help group members see that the Bible is a book about people *like them.* Doors will open for discussions about deep (possibly painful) truths, and *you* will not be doing the "talking." Your Bible character can do most of the teaching for you!

Don't be afraid to discuss the failures in the Bible. Many of today's teens have a resumé filled with incidents they would like to forget. Likewise, the Bible reveals people who failed. But some repented, and found forgiveness and hope. They learned from their mistakes and moved on. Other's didn't. Too often, we parade a string of successes before our teens, assuming that they will be challenged to higher living. What kids really need is to recognize that the Bible addresses ordinary struggling people.

Looking through the Writer's Eyes

I'll never forget one class period when I was teaching the importance of properly interpreting Scripture. I slowly read a note to the class that a student had written. After each paragraph, I would make an interpretation of what the letter meant to me. I deliberately distorted the obvious meaning. When I finished, my students were frustrated. It was unfair, they said, for me to put my own interpretation into the note. They all insisted that the student who wrote it meant specific things by the chosen words. My obligation was to understand what the writer meant, not what I perceived he or she meant.

The same principle holds true regarding God's Word. Help your group members see that we need to place ourselves in the role of the first readers of any Bible book. Teach your kids to ask questions like "What was going on when this letter was written?" and "Why was this letter written?" Just as I had no right to reinterpret my student's note, we cannot preface a statement from God's Word with "Well, to *me* this passage means …" or "What *I* think this means is …" The author used the words he did for a reason.

You may also want to bring in a Bible encyclopedia, dictionary, and/or commentary. Introduce your group members to enlightening and helpful works that have been written to help us better understand God's Word. Often, what seems confusing or even contradictory when we read or study God's Word is simply a matter of understanding the culture or context of the passage.

Balancing Relevance and Reverence

Because of the variety and creativity in humanity, the Bible is full of unusual, sometimes even comical stories. You can have some good-natured fun with these stories, but be careful in the process. Some youth workers assume that the Bible is not relevant for today's teen; so they seek to *make it relevant*. In the process, the Bible is sometimes cheapened. Remember, God's truth is *always* relevant because its message is eternal. The problem is not relevancy, it is comprehension. When young people understand a passage of Scripture, it becomes personal and applicable to their lives. Do not sacrifice a sense of reverence for the Bible in an attempt to prove "relevance."

Prophecy's Primary Purpose

Teens turn to prophecy full of curiosity and intrigue. Every year, my students groan in disbelief when they discover that we're only going to spend one day on the Book of Revelation. (I teach a year-long Bible survey class.) Young people are attracted to topics that tend to generate a lot of heat, but very little light!

God has given us a clear statement on the purpose of predictive prophecy in 2 Peter 3:11, 12, 14: "Since everything will be destroyed in this way, what kind of people ought you to be? You ought to live holy and godly lives as you look forward to the day of God and speed its coming. … So then, dear friends, since you are looking forward to this, make every effort to be found spotless, blameless and at peace with him."

We have a sneak preview (but not the whole picture) of the last page of history. We know this life is a gateway into eternity, that God will be glorified and Satan will be crushed. But we are not to focus on finding out *when* this will happen. Help your group understand that our knowledge of the Lord's return should cause us to live our daily lives in such a way that we are found "blameless" when He appears.

Your Bible's Alive! is designed to help your group members discover and embrace the truth of Hebrews 4:12: "For the word of God is living and active. Sharper than any double-edged sword, it penetrates even to dividing soul and spirit, joints and marrow; it judges the thoughts and attitudes of the heart."

In the process of preparing for this unit, I trust that you will be stimulated to become a more faithful student of Scripture. Our most important message is to communicate a love for God's Word rather than just a knowledge of what He has said. The best teaching tool to use with this curriculum is your own life. If your students see the Word of God leading you to a more intimate walk with God, they will be challenged to see Scripture come alive for themselves. What a *privilege*!

Fran and Jill Sciacca have been involved in youth ministry for two decades. Fran is a graduate of Denver Seminary. He has been teaching high school Bible since 1980. Jill has a degree in journalism and sociology and is a full-time homemaker and free-lance writer/editor.

The images on these two pages are designed to help you promote this course within your church and community. Feel free to photocopy anything here and adapt it to fit your publicity needs. The stuff on this page could be used as a flier that you send or hand out to kids— or as a bulletin insert. The stuff on the next page could be used to add visual interest to newsletters, calendars, bulletin boards, or other promotions. Be creative and have fun!

Watch Bible Characters Come to Life Before Your Very Eyes!

If you think Jonah was just a guy who took a weird fishing trip and David was just a guy who had good aim with a slingshot, you're in for a big surprise. Join us as we begin a new course called *Your Bible's Alive!* You'll discover some incredible facts about these and other Bible characters. Facts that you may never have heard before. Facts that may leave you eager to learn more.

Who:

When:

Where:

Questions? Call:

WISEGUY

Find out
what the
Bible has to say.

SESSION 1

By the Book

BIBLE = X+2YZ

YOUR GOALS FOR THIS SESSION:

Choose one or more

☐ To help kids see that the Bible, as the written Word of God, is much more than just another self-help/advice book, and contains the answers and wisdom they need to make the best possible decisions.

☐ To help kids differentiate truth from misperception in regard to what the Bible is, and to help kids understand that the Bible is for them.

☐ To help kids put together a plan to get more out of the Bible.

☐ Other:_____
_____

Your Bible Base:

Psalm 119
John 5:39-40

Getting Some Answers

(Needed: Fortune cookies)

Have each group member think of a decision he or she needs to make soon. Some decisions may be serious concerns (what college to attend, what to major in, whether or not to join the military, etc.). Others may be quite frivolous (who to ask out this weekend, what color of jacket to buy, whether or not to go swimming this evening, etc.). Have everyone write down his or her dilemma. Then hand out fortune cookies. Say (tongue in cheek): **We're going to try to get some answers for your questions today. These fortune cookies contain excellent advice, and your job will be to apply the wisdom of your fortune cookie to your specific question.**

Let everyone open the cookies and struggle to make sense of what is written there. Have some volunteers share their decisions and fortunes, and then explain how the advice of the cookie applies to their concern. In many cases there is not likely to be any kind of direct application, which is OK. In such cases, have kids force some kind of connection. If the person can't come up with anything on his or her own, let other group members help stretch the meaning of the fortune to answer the question—in bizarre ways if necessary. (Creative people will make some kind of connection.)

Afterward, ask: **Are you ready to make your decision now? Why or why not?** Perhaps some of your group members selected situations they had already made up their minds about, and will be willing to make a decision. Most kids, however, will probably express how ludicrous it would be to act based on the musings of a fortune cookie.

Ask: **If you're not yet ready, what will need to happen before you *will be* ready to make a decision?** Let group members respond. Their answers should provide a number of sources they go to for advice—asking friends or parents, doing research in books or other media, consulting advice columns, and so forth. Considering the setting, some are likely to include "pray about it" or "see what the Bible has to say" as options. If so, press to see how they think the Bible might apply to each of the decisions they are struggling with. But don't take too long at this point. Group members will have an opportunity later in the session to put together a more complete plan to apply the Bible to their daily decisions.

Supply and (Too Little) Demand

(Needed: Copies of Repro Resource 1)

Hand out copies of "The Parable of the Benevolent Scientist" (Repro Resource 1). Give group members a few minutes to read the parable.

Then ask: **What do you think of the man who had a valuable and needed resource at his disposal, yet didn't use it? Why?**

How do you think the scientist must have felt to have his great invention ignored?

Since this is a parable, it must be symbolic of something else. What do you think this story might be trying to tell us? (We have God's Word at our disposal, yet we frequently choose to ignore it while we try to solve problems and find answers by our own efforts.)

How do you think God feels when He sees us stumbling around in the "garbage" of sin and confusion, rejecting all of the resources He has given us?

Why do you think so many people—especially young people—aren't more committed to searching the Bible for answers to their questions? (The language is too difficult to understand [this issue is dealt with in Session 3 of this book]; they don't know how to use the Bible to find specific help; they already suspect the Bible will conflict with what they *want* to do, and they don't want to confirm their suspicions; they don't actually believe [or care] that the Bible is God's Word; etc.)

Try to deal with each of the issues named by group members. But quickly bring the focus back to *your* group rather than young people as a whole. If other people don't want to use or believe the Bible, we can't be responsible. Yet we *are* accountable for our own knowledge and use (or lack of use) of God's written Word.

Ask: **What are your personal complaints about using the Bible? What questions do you have about how to use the Bible, or about its reliability?** Encourage group members to be completely honest about their feelings toward Bible study and their current levels of involvement. If they don't express themselves honestly, there is little hope for their getting past the problem to try some solutions that might help.

OPTIONS

HEARD IT ALL BEFORE

MOSTLY GIRLS

EXTRA FUN

URBAN

JR. HIGH / HIGH SCHOOL COMBINED

A Long-Playing Psalm

(Needed: Bibles, chalkboard and chalk or newsprint and marker)

Explain: **We may not get much out of Bible study until we begin to understand exactly how important the Bible is. It's not like Aesop's Fables, even though it contains many stories with moral points. It's not merely like Shakespeare, even though it contains much "classic" literature. It's not simply like *Bartlett's Quotations,* even though it is quoted perhaps more than any other book. The most important thing about the Bible is that it's God's Word that has been recorded for us. When we read the Bible, it's as if God is speaking to us. So using the Bible shouldn't be a boring or dreaded task. Rather than seeing it as a reference book with little practical application, we should see it as a love letter from Someone who cares about us more than anyone else ever will. It's something we need to cherish and read for the sheer thrill rather than from a mere sense of obligation.**

To help group members see how high a regard we should have for God's Word, have everyone turn to Psalm 119. (If some group members are in the habit of sharing Bibles or letting other people look up the passages, be sure each individual has a Bible and the opportunity to interact with Scripture during this exercise.) Explain that when God's Word begins to mean something to us personally, we are more likely to devote more time to reading it.

Give a little background to explain the uniqueness of this particular psalm. It's not identified as one of David's psalms, but the author has a tremendous respect for the Word of God. It is certainly the longest psalm, partially because it is written in an acrostic form. More specifically, each of the first eight verses begins with the first letter of the Hebrew alphabet. The next eight verses each begin with the second Hebrew letter. And each consecutive set of eight verses work their way in the same manner through the entire Hebrew alphabet of 22 letters (22 x 8 = 176 verses total). Throughout the entire psalm, the author continually turns his focus to the importance of God's Word.

Ask: **As you look through this psalm, what are some of the words used as synonyms for God's Word?** The following are several possible answers (interpreted from the original Hebrew, taken from *The Bible Knowledge Commentary* [Victor]):

- Law—Denotes direction or instruction
- Word—A general term for God's revelation
- Saying—A synonym for *word*
- Command(ment)—A definite, authoritative instruction
- Statutes (translated as *decrees*)—Literally, "things inscribed," referring to enacted laws
- Judgment—A judicial decision that sets a precedent; a binding law
- Precepts—A poetical word for injunctions
- Testimony (translated as *statutes*)—A solemn declaration of the will of God
- Way—A metaphor to describe a pattern of life marked out by God's Law
- Path—Similar to *way*

After group members have listed several words, ask: **Why do you think so many different words were used?** (The different words used reveal a variety of purposes of Scripture.)

Point out that God's Word contains laws and commandments that should be obeyed regardless of how we feel, but it also is a way and a path to help us feel safe, protected, and secure. We should *want* to do what God says rather than do so simply out of obligation. Another term not included on the previous list, yet that sharp-eyed group members might discover is *promise* (vs. 140, for example), or righteous promise (vs. 123). The Bible is more than a bunch of rules and regulations. It reveals the many things that God has in store for those who choose to follow Him.

Since Psalm 119 is too lengthy to study completely, assign groups (or individuals) random sets of eight verses each to examine. Ask each group to report on what can be gained from a better understanding of God's Word, the Bible. Psalm 119 contains several great themes: God's Word as a lamp and light (vs. 105); the "sweet" taste of God's words (vs. 103); the importance of young people living according to the Word of God (vs. 9); the strength we receive from Scripture during turbulent times (vss. 25-32); etc. As the groups report their findings, compile a master list on the board to show what an ongoing devotion through Bible study has to offer your group members.

Just Words on a Page

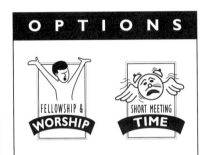

Now that you've covered some of the things that the Bible is, spend a bit of time considering what it *isn't.* Begin by reading a number of statements and letting group members respond to them. Kids should stand if they feel a statement is true and sit if they think it is false. Here are some statements you might use:

- **The Bible is the most important book in the world.**
- **Christianity and the church would quickly deteriorate without the Bible.**
- **The Bible is a holy book and should be treated with the utmost respect.**
- **A good knowledge of the Bible ensures a good relationship with God.**
- **It's impossible to succeed in life without knowing a lot about the Bible.**
- **The Bible contains a lot of good suggestions for how people should live.**
- **Somewhere in the Bible you can find an answer to every problem you have.**

These are all broad statements. Kids' responses will probably depend on how they interpret each statement. In several cases, both "true" and "false" answers can be supported. For example, the Bible certainly contains a lot of material about how people should live, but some kids could argue (justifiably) that such things are *commands* rather than *suggestions.* The Bible might be the most important book in the world, but it won't be the most important book in the world *to us* unless we know more about it than we do any of our textbooks or favorite novels. Try to show through this exercise that some of the things we assume about the Bible may not be as black and white as we may think.

After some discussion, present a final true-false statement: **Diligent study of the Bible leads to eternal life.** Let kids respond.

Then have someone read aloud John 5:39-40. Ask: **What do you think Jesus is trying to tell us in these verses?** It is important to see that *knowledge* of biblical truth is of little use unless it leads to *application* of that truth. God's Word should lead us to God Himself. Knowledge of Scripture is not the key to the kingdom. Jesus alone is the way, the truth, and the life (John 14:6).

Ask: **What if you really liked someone and wanted to establish a relationship, but you never actually made personal contact with the person? You write letters and talk on the phone every once in a while, yet you never make any effort to get together in person. How strong do you think that relationship would be? How long do you think it would last?** Point out that a relationship with a living God is not likely to grow or flourish if we try to relate to His Word without relating to Him personally. If we don't apply what we read in Scripture, it does us little more good than a fortune cookie. Even "diligent" study of the Bible is not enough. The Bible isn't a magical book that will take care of our problems simply because we read words on a page. But as we learn to identify principles from Bible passages and apply those principles to our own lives, our knowledge of Scripture will draw us closer to God.

STEP 5

Word Study

(Needed: Copies of Repro Resource 2)

Few topics are discussed as frequently in Christian youth groups as the importance of Bible study. Yet one reason for the recurring theme is that it's relatively easy to *discuss* the topic in a group without getting around to *doing* much about it as individuals. "What Does the Bible Say about the Bible?" (Repro Resource 2) is a "get started" resource for kids to take home. It contains a list of ten passages that deal with the importance of the Word of God and/or Bible study. Hand out a copy to each person. Ask kids to read and think about one (or more) of the passages each day during the next week. If many of your kids already have a daily devotional routine, don't have them interfere with it. But for those who don't have a regular time alone with God through His Word, have them agree to select one of the passages to do each day during the following week. Every day they will get a new insight into the value and significance of God's Word. Then at the next meeting, provide an opportunity for kids to ask questions they had during the week. You may also want to have ready another resource for daily Bible study by next week to encourage group members to continue what they start this week.

Close with a prayer of thanks to God for His written Word, as well as for Jesus, the Word who became flesh (a concept also included on the take-home Repro Resource). Ask for wisdom as group members prepare to look into the truths of Scripture during the next week.

OPTIONS

EXTRA ACTION

SMALL GROUP

LITTLE BIBLE BACKGROUND

MEDIA

URBAN

JR.HIGH HIGH SCHOOL COMBINED

EXTRA CHALLENGE

THE PARABLE OF THE
BENEVOLENT SCIENTIST

Once upon a time there was a scientist who was devoted to helping people. Each day as he went to work, he would see hungry and homeless people who begged for food. He wished that no one had to go to bed hungry, so he set about inventing something that would help. Eventually he discovered a way to rearrange certain kinds of molecules, so that he could actually manufacture food out of microscopic particles contained in the air. And rather than rush to write scientific papers about his miraculous invention or go on talk shows to get famous, he instead chose to give away his new device to someone who really needed it.

On his way to work the next day, he took his pocket-sized invention with him. A man stood on the corner with a "Will Work for Food" sign, so the scientist stopped and asked if he was hungry. "I'm starving," the man said. "I haven't had anything substantial in almost a week."

The scientist smiled, handed the man the device, and explained how it worked. "All you do," he said, "is press the button to get the food you want. Here's a list with a thousand different possibilities, including chicken soup, T-bone steaks, angel hair pasta with pesto sauce, double cheeseburgers, fries, hot fudge sundaes, and just about anything else you can think of. Just key in the number of whatever you want, and the food appears."

The man on the street hit the numbers for ham, eggs over easy, hash browns, and coffee. Each item appeared in turn. The man devoured the food on the spot, and was shocked beyond words when the scientist insisted that he keep the device. The scientist then continued on to work, prepared to create another device and write out the instructions so the machines could be mass produced to feed the hungry people of the world. He was still working on his second model two weeks later when, on the way to work, he saw the guy he had given the first device to. The man was back on the streets, begging for food.

The scientist was dismayed. He stopped and asked the man, "What's wrong? Did the food device malfunction? Did you lose it? Was it stolen?"

"No," answered the man. "I still have it, and it works fine. It's back in the alley in a shopping cart with all of my other possessions."

"Then why are you out here begging for food?" asked the kind scientist.

"Well, I tried most of the things that the machine can manufacture, and it's some of the most delicious stuff I've ever eaten. But it just seems too easy to press a button and get whatever I want. Sometimes I'd just rather try to do things myself, you know? When I go through garbage cans or ask people for food, I never know what I'm going to get. Like last month I found the remains of a bucket of chicken. It must have been pretty old, because I was sick for about a week after eating it. But it was satisfying to take care of myself. Your machine makes it too easy."

The scientist walked away, disappointed. He never made another machine. Instead, he went into the field of behavioral psychology to try to understand what makes people act in such strange ways. The hungry man is still hungry. Meanwhile, the scientist's machine is still out there somewhere–lying unused in an alley or perhaps collecting dust on someone's coffee table.

WHAT DOES THE BIBLE SAY ABOUT THE BIBLE?

Most people could stand to know a little more than they do about the Bible. Sometimes it seems that the more we learn about God's Word, the less we actually know. Even though we may be aware of many of the stories and key verses, there's still a lot of material that escapes our notice.

Below is a list of passages that no one should miss. You've probably seen most of them before, but if so, take a closer look at them this time. Each one should tell you a little more about the Bible itself—and the importance of reading and studying it more often. There are ten passages. Don't do them all at once. In fact, don't read more than one a day. Then spend whatever time you have left *thinking* about what each one says.

After you read each passage, answer the following questions:
• Are any symbols used to describe God's Word? (Some passages may not have any.)
• What can you learn about the Bible (the Word of God) from this passage?
• How can you apply what this passage says to your own life? Be specific.
• What questions come to mind as you read and think about the passage? (Write them down for later discussion, even if you eventually figure out the answer on your own.)
Here are your assignments. Take your time each day and see what you can learn.

DAY 1: PROVERBS 30:5, 6

DAY 2: ISAIAH 55:8-11

DAY 3: JEREMIAH 23:25-29

DAY 4: MATTHEW 4:1-4

DAY 5: MARK 4:1-20

DAY 6: JOHN 1:1-14

DAY 7: EPHESIANS 6:10-17

DAY 8: II TIMOTHY 3:12-17

DAY 9: HEBREWS 4:12

DAY 10: JAMES 1:22-25

STEP 3

Bring several index cards. On each card, write one of the following objects that are used in the Bible as symbols for God's Word: *lamp* (Ps. 119:105), *mirror* (Jas. 1:23), *sword* (Heb. 4:12), *rain* (Isa. 55:10, 11), *snow* (Isa. 55:10-11), *fire* (Jer. 23:29), *hammer* (Jeremiah 23:29), *seed* (Mark 4:14), etc. Also throw in a few other words that sound like potential answers (*flowers, gavel, ocean, broom,* etc.) and some just for fun (*banana, Corvette, porcupine,* etc). Have kids form teams. You'll need one set of cards for each team. Have the teams line up on one side of the room. Place the cards on the other side. At your signal, the first person in each line will run to his or her team's pile of cards and separate them according to which ones are authentic symbols of God's Word and which aren't. After each person separates the cards, you will announce how many are incorrect. Then the next person on each team will run to the pile of cards and makes changes. Continue until one team correctly separates all of its cards.

STEP 5

Point out that the Bible contains plenty of action if we simply do what it says. To demonstrate, select a group member to lead a "Bible aerobics workout." Perhaps your kids can think of several "active" biblical instructions. If not, several are listed below. Spend a few minutes performing each action as if in an aerobics class. (But don't let anyone feel uncomfortable if he or she is out of shape. Keep the mood light.) Here are some activities to use:

- *"Keep in step* with the Spirit" (Gal. 5:25)—Walk briskly around the room.
- *"Run . . .* the race marked out for us" (Heb. 12:1)—Jog in place.
- *"Strengthen* your feeble arms and weak knees" (Heb. 12:12)—Do pushups or knee bends.
- *"Flee* the evil desires of youth" (2 Tim. 2:22)—Run around the room.
- *"Fight* the good fight of the faith" (1 Tim. 6:12)—Shadow box.

STEP 1

Rather than limiting your opening activity to fortune cookies, let each group member represent a different source of advice. One person might represent a gypsy fortune teller. Others might represent a palm reader, an advice columnist, a phrenologist (someone who interprets the shape of a person's skull and bumps on the head), a parent, and a youth leader. Have each person come up with an actual decision that needs to be made, as instructed in the session. But then everyone else should provide advice (in character) for that decision. Kids may also want to demonstrate the underlying motivations for certain advice givers (money for fortune tellers, popularity for advice columnists, etc.). Afterward, ask: **How good was the advice you received? What problems arise when you seek advice from people you don't know well? In light of these potential problems, why do you think so many people are drawn to fortune tellers, astrology, and so forth?**

STEP 5

Rather than hand out Repro Resource 2, which contains 10 days' worth of Bible studies, create a phone chain instead. Call one group member each day and give him or her the day's Bible study passage. He or she should then call one person and pass on the information. This chain should continue until all group members have received the information. [NOTE: This may take some advance planning—exchanging phone numbers, deciding on who calls whom, etc.] An advantage of this system is that no one can claim to forget about his or her devotional time or lose the sheet that contains the day's passage. In addition, a phone chain will get your young people talking to one another. Perhaps they might begin to discuss the passages and applications from earlier in the week. But if not, at least they will have the opportunity to build fellowship while discussing things other than church and youth group.

STEP 1

Rather than dealing with individual decisions, think of a decision that would affect the entire group. It should be phrased so that it can be answered either yes or no. ("Should we disband this group so that you have more time to do homework?" "Should we give up all the fun stuff in our meetings and just have Bible studies?" "Should we take over the church and make the older people do what we want?") Have kids form teams. Assign each team a method to determine a response (either yes or no) for the decision. For example, one team might toss a coin, with heads indicating yes and tails indicating no. Another team could spin a game spinner, with an even number indicating yes and an odd number indicating no. Another team might throw dice to reach a decision. Be creative in your methods. After you ask the question, let teams use their methods to determine the answer. Try to show how ludicrous it is to use such methods to make decisions. Also point out that such things are "detestable" to God if they are taken seriously (Deut. 18:10-12). When we have the Bible as a source of wisdom, it is more than foolish to use other methods of decision making—it is sinful as well.

STEP 3

With a large group, you can cover *all* of Psalm 119. Divide the 22 sections of the psalm among your kids. As they read their assigned verses, they should prepare to answer the following questions:
- **What words are used in this passage to describe God's Word?**
- **What instructions are we given?**
- **What promises are we given?**

Discuss each of the questions as a large group, letting individuals respond. Not all of the sections will contain answers to each question, but all kids will be able to contribute frequently. Afterward, point out how much the author of the psalm was influenced by God's Word. Challenge your kids to become involved with the Bible so it will become important to them as well.

STEP 2

If hearing has ceased to be effective with your group, try sight and smell to help get across a point. Prior to the meeting, set up a table of delicious-looking food in the room. As group members read the parable on Repro Resource 1, you might stroll over to the table and help yourself to what's there. You can also use the food on hand as examples of what the device in the parable could manufacture (eating as you describe). But don't allow group members to sample anything. Continue the session with the food in their presence. Only when the session draws to a conclusion and you begin to emphasize the importance of personal interaction with God's Word should you allow them to have some personal interaction with the food at hand.

STEP 3

Before beginning the Bible study, ask: **How would your life be affected if it could suddenly be proven that the laws of mathematics were not actually true? What if certain portions of history were shown to be different than how they have been described to you?** (While certain classes or homework assignments might need to be adapted, little if any personal regret is likely to take place.) Then ask: **How would your life be affected if the Bible were proven to be wrong? What changes would you expect to make?** Let several kids respond. Group members' responses are likely to reflect to what extent they depend on the Bible as a source of wisdom and a moral base. Continue: **How do you know the Bible isn't wrong?** Try to help kids see that the Bible shouldn't be just another book someone forces us to read and know. Help them understand that when we don't study the Scriptures on a regular basis, we are the ones who will ultimately suffer.

STEP 3

To introduce the importance of Bible study, play a recording of Amy Grant's "Thy Word" (from the album *Straight Ahead,* © 1983 Meadowgreen Music Co./Bug & Bear Music). The song is based on Psalm 119:105 and is a natural lead-in to the Bible study. After playing the song, ask: **Do you think the songwriter ever dreaded Bible study? Explain. According to the lyrics, what are some of the benefits of Bible study?** (Security of knowing God is near; courage; fellowship with God; remembrance of God's love; guidance.) **How is the writer's attitude toward Bible study similar to or different from yours?**

STEP 5

For a group with little Bible background, you should try to eliminate all possible reluctance group members might have to getting personally involved with the Bible. So after you hand out copies of Repro Resource 2, spend some time helping group members locate all of the references and write down the page numbers from their individual Bibles. This shouldn't take too long when done as a group, and it might remove a potential barrier for kids during the week. While it certainly would not be much trouble for someone to look up the books in a table of contents if necessary, the ease of having the page numbers available might make a difference for some kids.

STEP 3

After studying Psalm 119, let kids create their own acrostic thanksgiving/praise psalm. (You may want to have them work in small groups to accomplish this.) Their psalm can take any form they wish. It need not be 176 verses, nor consist of rhyming couplets. (Though if they want to challenge themselves in such ways, they should certainly give it a try.) Perhaps the easiest form would be to create a song/prayer in which each line begins with a different letter of the alphabet. For example:

All praise we give to God
Because of His wonderful love
Creator, shepherd, and loving Father
Defender of His people and giver of
Everything we need.

Some letters of the alphabet will probably be difficult for kids to use, but don't let them get discouraged. They should simply move on to the next letter and see how many they can use. Let them create their own rules as they go along, and they may surprise you with what they come up with.

STEP 4

Explain that the Bible is only effective to the extent that we do what it says. In most cases, kids will know quite a bit about what the Bible says, so try to move them to the next level—*application*. Don't force anyone to do this, but encourage volunteers to fill in this sentence: "Because God's Word says _____, I will try harder to _____." Specifically, it would be good for these statements to be directed to other group members or the group as a whole. If your goal is to build fellowship, a good starting point is the verbal affirmation to change for the better. Kids might express a need for improved levels of forgiveness, support, love, respect, or any number of other things. Then, as you continue to study the Bible in future meetings, keep coming back to this fill-in statement. Point out that any time we know something about the Bible, that knowledge should call for action on our part.

STEP 2

If none of your girls mentions that there are few women highlighted in the Bible, raise this issue yourself. Ask: **Why do you think women are focused on so little in the Bible?** (The events in the Bible occurred in a patriarchal, male-dominated society.) **Does this fact make it more difficult for you to relate to the Bible? Why or why not? If you could change one thing about the Bible, what would it be? Why?**

STEP 3

Many of your girls may never have thought of the Bible as something fun or interesting to read. Talk for a few minutes about the types of books your group members *do* like to read. Then make a list of what it is about those books they like. This list will likely include elements such as good stories, romance, interesting people and places, action, adventure, mystery, etc. After you've completed the list, go through the elements one at a time and try to think of parts of the Bible that contain the same elements. Your girls may be surprised to learn just how much "good stuff" the Bible contains.

STEP 1

One fortune cookie apiece may not do it for most guys. So get several dozen fortune cookies. Then, one at a time, let each guy describe what decision he needs to make, draw a cookie, and read the fortune. If possible, he should try to adapt the fortune to his problem. If he doesn't like the advice of the cookie, or if it makes no sense, he may draw another one (and keep going until he finds one he likes). Continue with various decisions until you run out of cookies. But to keep the cookies from running out too quickly, score the activity so that the person who uses the fewest cookies wins. Guys should make some attempt to apply the advice of the fortune to their problem. But if it makes no sense at all, allow them additional fortunes (and more cookies to eat).

STEP 3

As you study Psalm 119, dwell on the issue of *dependence* on God's Word. Ask: **Do most guys like to admit that they have to depend on anything or anyone? Why? Even if you agree that you need to depend on the Bible, are you ever embarrassed to admit it? If so, in what situations? Do you think biblical concepts such as purity and humility are important, or is being a pain and "sowing wild oats" part of growing up if you're a guy?** Let your group members express their opinions about these issues. Then point out the clear dependence expressed by the author of the psalm. Challenge your guys not to let preoccupation with image or attitude prevent them from depending on God. Encourage them to make every effort to let God's Word help them through life.

STEP 1

Have group members form teams. Instruct each team to brainstorm several trios of things that have a common bond. For example, the trio of "angel," "cat," and "sword" have the common bond of being kinds of fish. The trio of "Black," "Enchanted," and "Sherwood" have the common bond of being names of forests. Explain that each team should write down a number of trios. The goal is to make them difficult, but not too obscure. After a few minutes, have the teams play against each other. (You will act as judge if someone claims that a particular trio of words is not logical, or if a team comes up with a correct answer that isn't the intended answer.) If you have four teams, one team will read a trio of words. The other three teams will then huddle and see if they can think of the common bond. Have the teams write down their answers. Then at your signal, have them tell you what they wrote. Keep score to see which team does best. To wrap up the activity and move to the next part of the session, give a trio of your own: **Lamp, Sword, and Mirror.** (All are words used to describe God's Word.)

STEP 2

Create a play from the parable on Repro Resource 1. Write dialogue from the narrative portions wherever possible, and use a narrator for the rest. Add new characters if you wish (fellow scientists, other street people, etc.). As you put together the play, adapt it for a particular audience. It might be for your church congregation, another youth group, or a class of younger kids. Whatever the intended audience, try to make the characters and dialogue appropriate for them. As time permits, give thought to simple backgrounds you could create or props and costumes to use. If possible, group members should perform the play for another group (and be ready to explain what they've learned in this session).

STEP 1

Instead of using the fortune-cookie opening, tape record a number of kids asking questions about the decisions they need to make. Don't explain why you're doing it. Simply get them to share some of the decisions that loom in their future, as well as any difficulties they face in trying to make the decisions. Then as you begin the session, set up the room as a radio studio in which a call-in talk-show host has a panel of "experts" discussing decision making. One at a time, announce that you have a "caller" and play a section of the tape you made. Let your student panel try to offer the best advice possible about making the decision that is described. Afterward, have group members express whether or not the advice was helpful. Then ask: **When you need to make a major decision, what media do you use? Besides media, where do you go for help with your big choices? Which of these sources is consistently most beneficial?**

STEP 5

Bring in some children's ABC books. Give kids a few minutes to look them over. Then explain that group members will be using the letters in the book to describe the Bible. Write each letter of the alphabet on a separate slip of paper. Put the slips into a container. Have each group member draw one or more slips (depending on the size of your group). Instruct each person to use the letter(s) that he or she drew to complete this sentence: "The Bible is _____" (accurate, believable, comforting, etc.). [NOTE: For information's sake, "xciting" does not qualify as a word.] After everyone has shared his or her idea(s), compile this "ABCs of the Bible" list. You may even want to photocopy it, add some artwork, and sell it to parents as a fundraiser for your group.

STEP 3

With the length of Psalm 119, one option for conducting a short session is to spend the entire time studying the passage. Divide the psalm into sections. Assign each group member (or small group) a different section of the psalm to read and be prepared to talk about. Then lead the session by asking questions and letting group members respond. Start with simple questions like these: **From what you read, do you think the writer thought Bible study was valuable? How can you tell?** Then move on to specifics: **What can Bible study do for you? How can it help you during a time of stress? How can it help you when things are going really well?** Finally, spend time on personal application: **What would it take for you to get as enthused about Scripture as the writer of this psalm was? Of everything he says, what is most likely to convince you to "dig a little deeper" into the Bible? How can you prevent Bible reading from becoming monotonous and dull?**

STEP 4

Begin the session with Step 4. Allow group members to express their opinions about the Bible. Then move from their opinions to the importance of Scripture—not as a magic cure-all for our woes, but as a signpost that points us to a personal relationship with God Himself. Try to generate a number of questions. Then move back to Step 3 and discuss Psalm 119 as you search for answers to the questions that have been raised. Finally, hand out Repro Resource 2 as a take-home sheet.

STEP 2

Ask: **How many of you know people who try to use the latest slang or who think they know all about what's "in" as far as clothing, music, and movies are concerned—when they really haven't got a clue?** Most of your kids probably have opinions about such faux hipsters. Then ask if your kids ever think of the Bible in the same way— as something that pretends to be relevant today, but that is actually outdated. If your kids have such feelings about the Bible, it's likely that part of the reason has to do with the language of the Bible. So give your kids an opportunity to translate some of the "hard to understand" verses in the Bible into the *New Hype Version* (NHV). This NHV Bible should feature the language of the urban youth culture. Have kids form teams. Assign each team a passage of Scripture to translate. Explain that the NHV Bible will be available on videotape as well as in print, so teams should feel free to translate passages using writing, drama, music, dance, etc. After a few minutes, have each team share its translated passage.

STEP 5

Before you hand out Repro Resource 2, have a few people armed with rolls of toilet paper burst into the room. They should begin wrapping anyone in their path with the toilet paper. Some of your kids may prevent the invaders from wrapping them; others may allow themselves to be wrapped. After a few minutes, the volunteers should leave. Afterward, draw a parallel between this bizarre occurrence and the Bible. Point out that once God's Word is loosed, nothing can stop it—even though some people may reject being "wrapped up" in its security. Then hand out Repro Resource 2. As your kids work on the assignment during the week, they should consider how Scripture can be "let loose" in their life to "wrap" others with God's Word.

STEP 2

Separate your junior highers from your high schoolers to read and discuss the parable on Repro Resource 1. Ask the questions from Step 2 while the kids are in separate groups. Then have the two groups come back together and review their answers. Compare their answers. Are they similar? Or do the members of the two age groups have different observations and perspectives? Sometimes when you have a wide diversity of age groups, the two extremes can teach each other. The younger ones can learn from the maturity of some of the older ones. And the older group members, who may be becoming jaded by some of the harsh realities of adult life, can see the simplicity of younger kids and recall the joys of childlikeness. More often, the two extremes may tend to see the worst about each other. But with a little help, they may occasionally be able to learn something from each other.

STEP 5

After you hand out copies of Repro Resource 2, say: **In addition to the verses listed on the sheet, I think it would be good for us to add the verses we think are important.** Then ask each person to tell what his or her favorite verse is while everyone else writes down the references in a corner of the sheet. (Or, as an option, you can collect the list of verses, type them up, make copies, and provide new sheets next week.) If older group members have been devoted to Bible study and are becoming spiritually mature, they should have a variety of verses they've come across that left an impression on them. When the younger ones see this, they may be more inspired to give serious Bible study a try. But if few people can cite a verse other than John 3:16, you will have the opportunity to close with a challenge to explore other parts of the Bible individually, when God can "speak" through His Word and direct us to portions of Scripture that will give us help and hope.

STEP 3

After reading and discussing a 176-verse acrostic song, challenge group members to adapt other literary forms that will honor God. Whatever kids are studying in English class can probably be adapted: haiku (a non-rhyming poem with three lines of five, seven, and five syllables), limericks, parodies ("How do I love thee? Let me count the ways"), Dr. Seuss rhyme patterns, iambic pentameter, etc. Group members' efforts need not be long or complex—simply original and sincere. Have volunteers read what they create.

STEP 5

Frequently when young people discuss the importance of Scripture, questions arise about how we got the Bible and why we should trust it more than any other book. It is difficult to answer all such questions quickly, so it may be wise to schedule a follow-up session to deal exclusively with matters of canonicity and authenticity. One of the best ways to deal with the questions is to provide young people with good (understandable) resources and let *them* do a bit of research. As you wrap up this session, you might want to have group members brainstorm some initial questions they have. Then find some volunteers willing to look for specific answers to these questions. While new questions are likely to arise when you get into a full-scale discussion, at least you'll provide a starting point and get your young people involved.

DATE USED:

Approx. Time

STEP 1: *Getting Some Answers* _____
- ❏ Small Group
- ❏ Large Group
- ❏ Mostly Guys
- ❏ Extra Fun
- ❏ Media

STEP 2: *Supply and (Too Little) Demand* _____
- ❏ Heard It All Before
- ❏ Mostly Girls
- ❏ Extra Fun
- ❏ Urban
- ❏ Combined Jr. High/High School

STEP 3: *A Long-Playing Psalm* _____
- ❏ Extra Action
- ❏ Large Group
- ❏ Heard It All Before
- ❏ Little Bible Background
- ❏ Fellowship & Worship
- ❏ Mostly Girls
- ❏ Mostly Guys
- ❏ Short Meeting Time
- ❏ Extra Challenge

STEP 4: *Just Words on a Page* _____
- ❏ Fellowship & Worship
- ❏ Short Meeting Time

STEP 5: *Word Study* _____
- ❏ Extra Action
- ❏ Small Group
- ❏ Little Bible Background
- ❏ Media
- ❏ Urban
- ❏ Combined Jr. High/High School
- ❏ Extra Challenge

What a Bunch of Characters!

YOUR GOALS FOR THIS SESSION:

Choose one or more

☐ To help kids see that the Bible is essentially one long story—not just a random collection of short stories about a variety of interesting characters.

☐ To help kids begin to piece together some of the stories they know to see how the stories interrelate.

☐ To have kids interview Christians they know to see how those people—as well as the kids themselves—are part of the ongoing story of God's redemption of the world.

☐ Other:_____
_____

Your Bible Base:

Hebrews 11:32—12:3

STEP 1

The Piece That Passes Understanding

(Needed: Jigsaw puzzle [completed and broken into sections], envelopes, team prize [optional])

OPTIONS

EXTRA **ACTION**

LARGE GROUP

EXTRA **FUN**

MEDIA

SHORT MEETING **TIME**

Prior to the meeting, find a jigsaw puzzle that won't take too long to assemble, yet will present a bit of a challenge for your group members. First assemble the puzzle and then break it into sections that are approximately the same size. (Choose a number of sections that will correspond to the number of groups you wish to form during the meeting. So if your group usually breaks into four smaller groups for discussion, Bible study, and so forth, break the puzzle into fourths.) Keep the sections of the puzzle separated. Then mix the pieces within each section, placing the sections in individual envelopes. But before you do, take one key piece from the center of each section and put it in a *different* envelope. So each group will be missing one crucial piece of its section of puzzle and will have one piece that just doesn't fit at all.

At the beginning of the session, have kids form groups. Explain that you're going to have a contest to see which group can assemble its puzzle first. You might want to announce that the winning group will receive a prize (perhaps a bag of candy) if you think it will bring out the competitive nature of your group members. At your signal, groups should open their envelopes and begin to assemble their puzzle pieces.

It shouldn't take groups long to discover they have a "wrong" piece. Astute groups should also see that they have only a portion of the whole puzzle. They might want to "make a trade" with another group to complete the individual sections. Groups who figure this out should share the prize. Finally, have all of the groups combine their portions of the puzzle to see the complete picture.

Afterward, ask: **Did you ever work really hard to put a jigsaw puzzle together, only to discover at the end that a piece or two was missing? If so, how did you feel?**

When you put together jigsaw puzzles, is it more enjoyable when you're first starting or when you have only a small portion to go? Why? (It's usually easy to put together the "frame" or border of outside pieces. Then it becomes difficult to assemble the interior until there are only a few pieces left.)

Does the Bible ever seem like a "puzzle" to you? If so, in what ways? Many groups frequently deal with "puzzling" teachings of the Bible. This time, however, stress the importance of putting together individual pieces of Bible knowledge. Most young people know selected stories and assorted key passages, but we need to keep "working at the puzzle" until we can see how it *all* fits together. Missing pieces should frustrate us just the same as with a jigsaw puzzle.

STEP 2

Good Connections

(Needed: Copies of Repro Resource 3, pencils)

Hand out copies of "What's the Connection?" (Repro Resource 3) and pencils. Let group members see how many "connections" they can make between some of the primary characters in the Bible. If your group members have a good understanding of the Bible (or if you want to review something you've recently studied), have them add some lesser-known characters to their sheets. When they finish, have them add up the lines they drew and see who came up with the most connections.

Afterward, single out a few of the characters on the sheet and ask:
Who did you connect this person to?
Some of the basic connections are as follows:
   1. Adam—Eve—Cain—Abel
   2. Abraham—Sarah—Isaac—Jacob—Esau—Judah
   3. Moses—Aaron—Miriam—Pharaoh—Joshua—Caleb
   4. Deborah—Gideon—Samson
   5. Ruth—Naomi—Boaz
   6. Elijah—Ahab—Jezebel—Elisha
   7. David—Bathsheba—Solomon—Absalom
   8. Isaiah—Daniel—Micah—Jonah—Hosea
   9. Jesus—Peter—Andrew—Pilate—Barabbas—Nicodemus—
      Woman at the Well
   10. Paul—Silas—Timothy—Titus—Philemon
Most of these connections refer to family members or associates of the key person listed first. Consequently, many of the names that follow are related to each other as well. In a couple of instances, the connections involve job responsibility. (For example, all of the people for #4 are judges; all of the people for #8 are prophets.) Many connections can be made between numbers as well. For example, Boaz, David, and Jesus

O P T I O N S

SMALL GROUP

HEARD IT ALL BEFORE

LITTLE BIBLE BACKGROUND

MOSTLY GIRLS

MOSTLY GUYS

EXTRA FUN

EXTRA CHALLENGE

could all be connected to Judah since they were from his tribe. Paul encountered a post-resurrection Jesus on the road to Damascus and made references to Abraham, Moses, and others. And in a sense, all of the characters could be connected to Adam and Eve. Any connections your group members can make (and substantiate) should be accepted.

After group members total and discuss the connections they made between characters, use the groupings to review some of the basic periods of biblical history: Creation, the Patriarchs, Bondage and Deliverance, Judges, Kings, Captivity and the Prophets, the Life of Jesus, and the Formation and Continuation of the Church. Point out that as complex as it may seem from the number of stories and characters involved, the Bible is actually an ongoing account of God's relationship with humankind. That relationship began in perfection; then we sinned and distanced ourselves from God. But God forgave us and provided a way back to Him. And the Bible has a happy ending with God's people restored to full and perfect fellowship with Him.

Ask: **Why do you think the Bible contains so many stories about people? Wouldn't it be a lot shorter if God simply gave us a list of dos and don'ts and skipped all of the personal anecdotes?** Spend some time letting group members think about this. Among other things, they should discover that

- characters give the Bible a sense of history (the Persian kings, Augustus Caesar, etc.)
- through character studies we see consequences of obedience and rebellion
- we tend to relate better to people than to rules and regulations
- God is more concerned in the *application* of the "do's and don'ts" than in our simply knowing them.

We're Being Watched

(Needed: Bibles)

Ask: **Other than Jesus, who is your favorite Bible character? Why?** Let several group members respond.

Then ask: **Where in the Bible do you turn to read about your favorite character?** See if most of your group members can provide a quick reference. If not, perhaps some of them are drawing on stories they've *heard*, but haven't actually *read* in quite a while. Then explain that there is one place in the Bible where many of their chosen characters—Old Testament ones, anyway—are mentioned in the same place. Have group members turn to Hebrews 11 and skim the chapter to see if they find the characters they chose. Some may be named specifically. Others may be alluded to in the latter verses of the chapter.

Have someone read aloud Hebrews 11:32-38. Then ask: **Who do you think some of these unnamed people might be?** Any number of answers may be correct. For example, Solomon administered justice; Daniel withstood the lions' den; Deborah was a powerful judge; etc. Also note that there have been *many* people who were faithful to God in all of these ways, yet whose stories were never recorded.

Of all the sufferings mentioned here, which do you think would be most difficult to endure? Why?

What does it mean that "the world was not worthy of" the people who endured these sufferings? (They were living for God in a sinful world. In many cases, it seemed that they were the "losers"; but ultimately, it's only God's opinion that matters. In reality, these were exceptional people who would eventually receive great honor and rewards from God.)

Have someone read aloud Hebrews 11:39-40. Then ask: **What had been promised to these people that they hadn't yet received?** (A Messiah who, among other things, would restore the relationship between God and His people.)

What did God plan that would be "better for us"? (He provided a Savior. Today we can examine the person and work of Jesus to see what God has done for us and how we should act. We also have the Holy Spirit actively at work in our lives.)

How many of the characters named in Hebrews lived perfect lives? (Obviously none.)

OPTIONS

HEARD IT ALL BEFORE

LITTLE BIBLE BACKGROUND

FELLOWSHIP & WORSHIP

MOSTLY GIRLS

MOSTLY GUYS

SHORT MEETING TIME

URBAN

Then what was the big deal about *their* faith as opposed to ours? (They endured numerous obstacles and persevered as people of God based only on a *promise* of better things to come. They had few if any of the assurances we have today.)

Have someone read Hebrews 12:1-3. Then ask: **What should be our relationship with such faithful Old Testament characters?** (They played their roles early in God's story and "paved the way" for us. We need to acknowledge their contributions by learning all we can from them and making any needed changes in the way we live. As we heed their examples, we join them in what God desires for us [Hebrews 11:40].)

When you think of having these great people of the faith as "witnesses" of how you are currently living your life, how does it make you feel? Why?

What are some of the sins and hindrances that "entangle" many people your age? How, specifically, might they "throw off" each one?

If you sought really hard to lead a life that would please God, and if you suffered a lot along the way, how do you think you would feel if everyone just seemed to ignore you? (While we shouldn't live our lives to impress others, we might naturally hope to be good examples and influences on others. If they didn't seem to care about our dedication or the difficulties we faced, we might be somewhat disappointed or forlorn.) Point out that by learning from the examples of biblical characters, we give significance to their lives and help demonstrate that their sacrifices were not in vain.

To help show the importance of learning lessons from the lives of people recorded in the Bible, have volunteers look up and be ready to read the following pairs of passages:

- Jonah 1:17 and Matthew 12:38-41
- Genesis 19:24-28 and Luke 10:8-12
- Genesis 7:17-23 and Matthew 24:36-41

In each of these pairs, a well-known Bible story is alluded to by Jesus as He makes a point. Have group members first read both sets of verses and then explain what point Jesus was trying to make. Also explain that Jesus used both positive and negative examples from Scripture to help people understand what He was trying to say. The biblical accounts of the past were recorded to affect *our* present and future. They should be more than mere stories to us. We need to pay careful attention to the lives of those people and the lessons they can teach us.

STEP
4

Contemporary Characters

(Needed: Bibles, paper, pencils, panel of adults [optional])

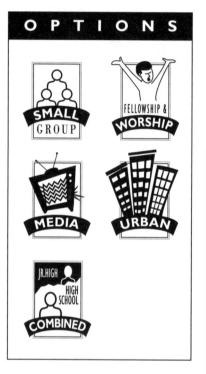

Some people may work very hard to examine the lives of Bible characters and draw out practical applications they can make based on those characters' lives. Yet those same people may tend to overlook God's people *today*—alive and active in their churches. If we were to become just a bit more observant and inquisitive, we might be likely to find all kinds of stories *from people we already know* that would help us lead better Christian lives and avoid a lot of potential mistakes.

If possible, arrange to have a panel of adults from your church available to be interviewed during this part of the session. Try to select people who can give concise but striking testimonies of how God has worked in their lives. Explain that as we look back on our lives, we often get a completely different perspective than we have while we're going through the various phases. We can sometimes see reasons for the things we could never understand before. We might see a time when God said no to something we desperately wanted—only to see Him provide something better. We might see amazing ways He directs us to spouses or close friends. And we might see, in retrospect, how important our faith was during those times (and how little good our whining and complaining did).

As you introduce each member of your panel, explain one of the things you think your group members might be able to learn from the person. (One panel member might have a high-school anecdote, another might have a choosing-a-college story, another might have a romantic remembrance, etc.) Then open the floor to questions from group members. You might want to have some queries ready in case kids are slow getting started. It shouldn't take long for group members to see that God still works just as frequently and powerfully (if not *quite* as miraculously) as He did for the characters in the Bible.

Even if you don't have the opportunity to set up a panel, don't pass up the opportunity to learn from some of your fellow Christians. Instead of the panel, have individuals or small groups plan to interview some people in your church. Perhaps your kids have witnessed traits of certain members (through testimonies, prayers, ability to handle crises, etc.) that would create a desire to know those members better. If so, have them try to set up some appointments with those church members. If your kids don't know other church members well, *you* might want to suggest some potential matches (putting student athletes with former ballplayers, putting student and adult musicians together, and so forth). Then spend some time letting kids write out several questions that they would want to ask the adults. They should also be thinking of things they could reveal about themselves that would allow the adults to know them better. Do what you can to facilitate the interviews, but leave the "work" to group members. At your next meeting, let group members report back on what they learned. They might be surprised to discover to what extent God is at work among your church and its members.

People of God: The Next Generation

(Needed: Copies of Repro Resource 4, pencils)

Summarize: **According to what we read in Hebrews, many people suffered in order for us to know more about God. We can also see God at work in the lives of people right here in our church. We have numerous books and films to show how the power of God has made profound changes in individuals and groups throughout history. But exactly what should all of this mean to us?** Let group members respond. Eventually, they should see that now it's *their* turn to set good examples for others. Explain that the story of God's love for humankind didn't end with the writing of the Bible. It still continues today. Your group members are "sequels" to the stories they read in the Bible. Your group members are accountable for learning from the characters of the past, and then applying that information to their lives so *they* will become better models for people in the present and future. They can have strong influences on friends, parents, brothers and sisters, teachers, neighbors, and even total strangers.

Hand out copies of "Take a Look at Yourself" (Repro Resource 4). Have group members recall their behavior during the last week, evaluate it, and record appropriate comments. When they finish, let volunteers share some of the observations they made about themselves.

Then ask: **What would you think about having your life recorded for posterity as a story in a holy book for people to study and learn from? Would those people be more likely**

OPTIONS

EXTRA ACTION

SMALL GROUP

JR. HIGH HIGH SCHOOL COMBINED

EXTRA CHALLENGE

to learn from the times when you performed bold acts of
faith, or the ones where you messed up? Let kids respond.

Then say: **When you look at the characters in the Bible,
you won't find much about their teenage years—in most
cases. Even as adults, it took most of them a while to discover that God had a special purpose for them. Moses,
Noah, Paul, Jesus' disciples, and Sarah are good examples
of this. Other times people found God's plan for their lives,
but then abandoned God's ways late in life—people such as
King Saul, Solomon, and Gideon. We need to study all of
these characters carefully so we can get an early start, but
avoid making the same mistakes. Thanks to these characters, we know the importance of starting *now* to be faithful
to God, and we can see what we have to lose if we don't
continue to grow in our relationship with Him.**

Close with a challenge for your group members to begin dealing
with any specific problem areas they've already noted on Repro
Resource 4. From there, they can move on to other problems they
discover in their lives. But the sooner they get started, the longer they
will be able to experience the wonderful things God can do for and
through them.

WHAT'S THE CONNECTION?

Sometimes the Bible may seem like just a bunch of stories about various characters. But many of those characters are connected to each other in one way or another. Look through the names below and draw a line to connect any that you know for sure have some kind of association. (No guessing! You must be able to explain the connection between the two people.)

CAIN

AARON

HOSEA   MIRIAM

SARAH

ABEL   CALEB

ISAAC   NAOMI

JOSHUA

DANIEL

ABRAHAM

ISAIAH   PAUL

DAVID

SILAS

ABSALOM

PETER

DEBORAH   JACOB

SOLOMON

ADAM

PHARAOH

ELIJAH

AHAB

JESUS   PHILEMON   TIMOTHY

ELISHA

ANDREW

JONAH   PILATE   TITUS

BARABBAS   ESAU

SAMSON   WOMAN AT THE WELL

MICAH

BATHSHEBA

RUTH

EVE

JUDAH

BOAZ   GIDEON   MOSES

JEZEBEL

NICODEMUS

TAKE A LOOK AT YOURSELF

Do you ever hear or read a Bible story and then become critical of the characters in the story? For example, do any of the following comments sound familiar?
- "Adam and Eve were in paradise, but they ate the forbidden fruit. How stupid!"
- "How dumb could Samson be to tell Delilah his secret and end up blind and imprisoned?"
- "That rich young guy could have followed Jesus, but he was just too selfish!"

Of course, it's easy to sit back and comment about the shortcomings of *other* people. But let's suppose people have been watching *your* every move for the past week. And suppose your words, thoughts, and actions were all recorded—just like those of Bible characters. After reading the story of your life during the previous week, what would someone be likely to say about the following things? (Be specific about the comments you would expect to receive.)

	Positive Comments	Negative Comments
Your language		
Your actions		
Your relationships (parents, friends, etc.)		
Your thoughts		
Your spiritual life		
Other miscellaneous observations		

"Don't let anyone look down on you because you are young, but set an example for the believers in speech, in life, in love, in faith and in purity" (I Timothy 4:12).

STEP 1

To begin the session, hand out several Tinker Toys or Legos to each group member. Instruct him or her to create something unique. Be sure to reserve a few pieces for yourself because you'll need them later. If possible, have group members work around a large table so that their creations can be moved without a lot of effort. After a few minutes, have each person display his or her work and describe what it is. Then after everyone has shared, try to connect all of the individual works (using the pieces you saved for yourself) to make one large creation. Use this activity to introduce the topic of Bible characters. Though each person has a special and unique story, in reality, each one merely contributes to the single story of God's love and redemption.

STEP 5

Wrap up the session with one of your group's favorite relay races—Lifesavers on toothpicks, eggs in spoons, or whatever. If your group doesn't have a favorite, try a traditional, pass-the-baton relay. The point you want to make is that just as an Olympic four-person relay depends heavily on individual contributions for the good of the team, so we all need to work hard as individuals for the good of the church. While some young people may be a little too hyperactive to absorb these truths at the end of a session, they may be more receptive after they've run the length of the room (or around the building) several times and are eager for a break.

STEP 2

Instead of using Repro Resource 2 as written, divide the characters on the sheet among your kids. Add others as needed so that each person has a list of at least five characters that no one else has. Announce a number of categories for which kids can get a certain number of points per character on their list. For instance, ask: **Can you name the parents of any of the people on your list?** If kids can name both parents, they get two points; if they can name one parent, they get one point. In some cases—such as Adam and Eve, or characters whose parents aren't mentioned—there will be no opportunity for points. But such instances should balance themselves out as you move on to other categories. Also, kids should be reasonably sure of their answers. You won't have time to look up wild guesses to see whether or not they are correct. Other categories might include the following:

- **Name a bad thing each person did.** (Maximum one point per character.)
- **Name the children of each person.** (One point per kid for each character.)
- **Quote something each person said.** (Maximum one point per character.)
- **Name the book(s) of the Bible in which you would find each character.** (One point per book for each character.)

STEP 4

Instruct each of your group members to think of a Bible character and a person he or she knows (personally) who share a common trait. For instance, someone might say, "Thomas—Jesus' disciple—and my grandfather both refuse to believe that something is true until they see it with their own eyes." Award prizes for the most creative comparisons.

STEP 1

Begin the session by forming a human machine. Have group members imagine they are cogs, levers, wheels, or any other machine part. Start with one or two people performing some mechanical function, and gradually add others until you have formed one enormous machine. Be sure to add a variety of sounds as well. The more group members respond to each other's movements, the better your "machine" will be. Use your human machine to demonstrate how many parts with various functions can have a single, unified goal. Similarly, the characters described in Scripture are unique and diverse, yet contribute to the unified story of God's salvation of the world.

STEP 5

Ask kids to name their favorite reading material—the types of books and magazines they most enjoy. You'll need to have available a large supply of various types of books and magazines. When a group member identifies what he or she most likes to read, hand him or her a sample of that reading material. It's likely that few, if any, of your kids will name the Bible as their favorite reading material. So after everyone has chosen a book, say: **Even though the Bible may not be our favorite thing to read, we need to make an effort to read it as regularly as possible. If we spend most of our time reading other things, the Bible can get lost in the shuffle.** To demonstrate this, place a Bible on the floor at the front of the room. Then have kids come forward one at a time to stack their book or magazine on top of the Bible. (For fun, you might see how high you can get the stack before it topples over.) Afterward, explain that it's OK to enjoy reading things other than the Bible—as long as the Bible doesn't get "lost" among them. Our first priority should be to spend time in God's Word.

HEARD IT ALL BEFORE

STEP 2

After kids complete Repro Resource 3, but before you discuss it, conduct a contest. Hand out paper and pens. Ask:

• **How many stories do you think are contained in the Bible?**

• **How many commandments are there for us to follow?**

After kids have written their answers for both questions, instruct them to add the two numbers together. Then announce that the sum they should have come up with is three. Explain: **The Bible is one ongoing story that begins with God's creation of a paradise and humankind's fall, moves forward to God's plan of salvation for His fallen people, and concludes with the restoration of the relationship—at which time God and His people are together again in His paradise. Everything else in the Bible is a subplot to that one main story. And as for the commandments, Jesus narrowed them down to two for us. He said, "'Love the Lord your God with all your heart and with all your soul and with all your mind.' This is the first and greatest commandment. And the second is like it: 'Love your neighbor as yourself.' All the Law and the Prophets hang on these two commandments"** (Matt. 22:37-40). Point out that sometimes we get too involved in the emphasis on "Bible trivia" and lose the perspective of the Bible as one cohesive story.

STEP 3

Emphasize how much Jesus knew about the Old Testament and how frequently He applied it to Himself and His teachings. Single out His comment about how His own experience would be like Jonah in the belly of a great fish (Matt. 12:40). Ask: **Who is your favorite Bible character? How does one of that person's experiences apply specifically to something you're currently facing?** Have volunteers share their responses.

LITTLE BIBLE BACKGROUND

STEP 2

Group members without much Bible background aren't likely to know the stories of all of the characters on Repro Resource 3 (or later in the session). If they don't seem to know many of the connections for some of the characters on the sheet, take some time to help them find the source of the stories in their Bibles. You need not have them read the story at this time, but encourage them to do so sometime during the following week. Explain that the best way to cover so much material is to do a little bit each day (or *almost* every day). Point out that if we try to understand the Bible only during church and/or youth group, we are almost certain to stay confused about much of it.

STEP 3

As you discuss the characters mentioned in Hebrews 11, try to determine their distinctive personalities rather than simply lumping them together as "the faithful people of the Bible." You may have to summarize some of the stories. After you do, explain: **If there had been "Faith Awards" during Bible times, these people would have been the winners. But since there weren't, which of today's awards do you think each of these people might have a chance to win?** Let group members try to think of appropriate matches between people and awards. For example, Samson might win a professional wrestler's championship belt. David, for all his psalms, might win a Grammy. Noah could win the America's Cup for sailing. Try to think of all kinds of awards, including the "Senior Superlatives" that many schools have (Most Likely to Succeed, Cutest Couple, Most Intelligent, etc.).

FELLOWSHIP & WORSHIP

STEP 3

During a study on the importance of knowing Scripture, the temptation may be to keep the discussion on an academic level. But since this session focuses on the vast assortment of human characters described in the Bible, you have a good opportunity to focus on fellowship. After going through the passage in Hebrews 11, have each group member focus on one Bible character that he or she finds particularly interesting, and complete this sentence: "I really appreciate _____ because he (or she) _____." Then have kids complete the same sentence using each other's names. Go from person to person as the rest of the group expresses reasons for appreciation. You should participate as well. Be prepared to express appreciation for kids who may be overlooked by others. Try to help everyone feel affirmed during this activity. As God's servants in the present and future, group members should feel just as important as His servants of the past.

STEP 4

If you can't assemble a panel of adults to interview, at least recognize the ones who have influenced your kids. Ask each group member to make a list of the adults who have been most influential in modeling faith. Each person's list should contain as many names as he or she can think of. After kids finish their lists, have them write a brief note to each person on the list, explaining why he or she has been influential in the young person's life. If you're short on time, come up with a single sentiment that can be copied and sent to everyone on your kids' lists. For instance, you might write "Your name was mentioned by our group members as someone whose outstanding faith and lifestyle is an inspiration to us." Then *everyone* can sign each card before you send them out. Your kids may be surprised at how much a small token of appreciation like this can mean to adults who are struggling to lead good Christian lives in today's world.

STEP 2

The end of this step offers a good opportunity to talk about the fact that though the Bible contains more stories of men than of women, it is—from cover to cover—a book about relationships, especially God's relationship with us. Point out that the keys and principles of relationships know no gender bounds. Ask: **What are some ingredients— good or bad—of a relationship that can be found in stories in the Bible?** List these ingredients on the board as your group members name them. After you've listed several ingredients, discuss which of your girls' relationships have similar qualities.

STEP 3

Have each of your girls choose a female character from the Bible whom she admires and would like to know more about. If your girls have trouble coming up with a character, offer some of the following ones to choose from: Sarah, Ruth, Esther, Mary, Elizabeth, Martha, etc. (Add some of your own favorite characters to the list.) After your girls have chosen their character, ask volunteers to share which character they chose and explain why they chose her. Challenge your group members to do a little digging in the Bible this week to see what else they can learn about the character they chose.

STEP 2

After completing Repro Resource 3, have group members list all of the female Bible characters they can think of who set a positive example. Then go through the list character by character. Ask: **What can we learn from the life of this woman?** If none of your guys mention them, point out the following facts:
• There are many positive female examples in the Bible—Sarah, Hannah, Deborah, Jael, the woman at the well, the woman who anointed Jesus' feet, Mary, Ruth, Esther, Lydia, and many others.

• Even so, the accounts of men greatly outnumber those of women.

• The faithful examples set by these women aren't just for other women; guys should learn from such examples as well.

After making these observations, discuss the importance of seeing similar examples in the lives of female *peers*. Challenge your guys to begin to deal with any gender bias they may be developing. If nowhere else, they should strive to set aside any potential for discrimination while at church and youth group.

STEP 3

Guys are sometimes reluctant to apply what they learn in Scripture to their own lives. Help them deal with this tendency by getting them to associate with the *feelings* of some of their Bible heroes. Ask: **Which Old Testament character are you most like? Why?** Or ask: **Which of Jesus' disciples are you most like? Why?** Then ask some follow-up questions to get your guys thinking about what the person actually experienced. So if someone replies, "Daniel," ask: **If it had been you standing in front of King Darius, knowing that to admit you were praying would lead to almost certain death, what would you have done?** Try to show your guys that faith is rarely as simple as we sometimes assume. It takes great courage and strength to stand firmly for God when to do so makes us unpopular

or otherwise at risk.

STEP 1

Rather than using the jigsaw-puzzle opening, try a storytelling activity. Designate someone to begin a story, making it up as he or she goes along. (Some of the best stories will include members of your group.) Before the storyteller gets too far into the plot, stop the person and designate someone else to take over. Keep letting various people take over the storytelling responsibilities until you finally ask someone to end the tale. While many such stories are not likely to make a lot of sense, use this fact to demonstrate that the Bible is really one long story—and it makes a lot more sense than the story your group came up with.

STEP 2

Assign each group member the identity of a Bible character. Then give kids five minutes to find as many other characters in the room as possible who have something in common with their character. Common characteristics might include things like being discussed in the same book of the Bible, being a witness to a miracle of God, etc. (Being male or female is *not* good enough to qualify as an acceptable common trait.) After five minutes, have group members share the common characteristics they found.

STEP 1

Before the session, collect a variety of images of cartoon characters—either in print or on video. (Some characters should be rather obscure, but not too unreasonable.) Also collect several pictures of Bible characters, using whatever preschool or primary art you can find—or perhaps an illustrated Bible story book. First, have a contest to see who can identify the most cartoon characters. After determining a winner, try it again—this time with the Bible characters. But when you show the characters, cover up any hints that would indicate who the person is. (Noah should be seen without an ark or animals; David should be seen without Goliath; etc.) Again determine a winner. Afterward, discuss how important a specific identity is to cartoon characters. Their creators don't want them to be confused with other characters. Yet sometimes when we think of Bible characters, we picture them as being rather generic (physically, at least). Therefore, we need to study their stories carefully so that we can easily differentiate Moses from Abraham and Noah, and Ruth from Esther and Mary. To lump them all together from childhood images makes us miss out on their most important individual contributions.

STEP 4

If you have a video camera available, consider shooting an "appreciation video" for the church as a whole. Put together a rough script of what various group members want to say. Some might express appreciation to specific people for specific reasons; others might thank the church as a whole. Explain that you will try to find an opportunity for the adults of the church to watch the video, so group members should make sure no one feels overlooked. Then find a way for the adults in your church to see what your group members put together—perhaps during the church service, at a congregational meeting, or (on a rotating basis) in various adult Sunday School classes and Bible studies.

STEP 1

Before the meeting, find a chart or time-line that summarizes Bible history. (The Good Things Company [Drawer N, Norman, Oklahoma 73070] offers a very detailed family tree of Jesus that would work well.) Place the chart in a central location and let it be the center of your meeting. First, have group members point out all of the names they recognize on the chart. (There will probably be many characters who are completely unfamiliar.) Then look for the main "action" of Bible history—the connection from Adam to Abraham to Judah to David to Jesus. Point out that history doesn't just "happen" as time goes on. In retrospect, group members should see that God has a specific plan, and each individual is part of that plan. As you examine the chart, let group members ask questions as you make relevant comments from the session.

STEP 3

Instead of a traditional sword drill, conduct a Bible *character* sword drill. Make a list of several Bible characters, specific stories that involve them, and the Scripture passages where the stories are found. Explain that when you call out the name of a character and a specific story (for example, **Elijah—being taken to heaven in a whirlwind**), kids may begin searching their Bible for the passage. The first person to find the passage (in this case, 2 Kings 2:11) must stand and call it out. You will then quickly summarize the story and move on to the next character. Award small prizes to each winner, if possible.

STEP 3

Many of your inner city kids are probably aware that they've lived *far* from perfect lives. In fact, this realization may be keeping some of them from receiving Christ as Savior. They may view God as a "big lightning bolt in the sky," waiting to "zap" them for their sins the minute they acknowledge Him. Read Romans 3:23 to your kids to assure them that "all have sinned and fall short of the glory of God"—even the faithful Old Testament characters mentioned in Hebrews 11. Follow up that verse by reading Philippians 3:13-14 ("Forgetting what is behind and straining toward what is ahead, I press on toward the goal to win the prize for which God has called me heavenward in Christ Jesus"). Point out that all we can do is keep our eyes on Christ, ask forgiveness for our past sins, and try to live for Him day by day.

STEP 4

If you can't find a panel of adults for your kids to interview, try using the testimonies of more famous Christians. You'll need to find several videotapes, books, and/or magazine articles in which Christian athletes like Mike Singletary (formerly of the Chicago Bears), Kevin Johnson, David Robinson, and A.C. Green share what God has done in their lives. Even though your kids won't be able to ask these people questions about their testimonies, it's likely that your group members will pay close attention to what they have to say.

STEP 4

As part of recognizing the *contemporary* faithful people of God, you might want to begin with a Parents Appreciation Night. Plan to set aside a future meeting time to give thanks for all that your kids' parents have done for them. (Daring groups might even want to try to cook a dinner for the parents.) Spend some time during this step clarifying what your group members would like to say and do to help parents feel more appreciated. Come up with a program (and perhaps a menu) to show parents how much they mean to your group members. Young people (especially junior highers) need to make strong efforts to stay close to their parents. This is a time of life when many parent-child relationships are tested. The more commitment the *kids* make to keeping the relationship strong, the more likely the parents will be to trust them and give them more freedom to grow. (And when you've planned your Parents Appreciation Night, a good sequel might be Pastor Appreciation Night.)

STEP 5

Instruct your high schoolers to write on the back of Repro Resource 4 the top three things they think junior highers notice about their (the high schoolers') lives. Some may list things like the way they talk and the way they treat others. Others may name things like the way they dress and the kind of car they drive. Then have your junior highers write down the top three things they *actually* notice about high schoolers. When everyone is finished, collect the lists (keeping the sheets of the two age groups separate). Then read the lists aloud. This activity should demonstrate to your high schoolers that they are role models for younger kids—whether they like it or not.

STEP 2

As you're discussing the various characters in the Bible, have group members form a "common bond chain" that connects as many characters as possible. Provide one name to get things started. Let's say you begin with Adam. The first person should then think of a character who has something in common with Adam. It might be Eve, his wife. It might be Noah, who also got in trouble while naked (Gen. 9:20-27). It might be Paul, who also had an encounter with a serpent (Acts 28:3-6). Once a character's name has been used, that character may not be used again—nor may the association. (Otherwise, group members might spend a half hour exhausting all of the *males* of the Bible.) This may be difficult at first, but challenge group members to make a game of this from time to time. It's a good exercise to make connections between stories that aren't usually associated. In addition to being a means of associating different stories, it also helps group members think in broad terms of the Bible as being a whole, rather than limiting their thinking to one independent story at a time.

STEP 5

Say: **Most of you probably think you know a lot about Bible characters. Here's your chance to prove it.** Write the names of several Bible characters on slips of paper and put them in a container. Have each group member draw a slip. Then instruct kids to write a half-page to one-page report on the character they picked. Encourage them to be creative in their reports, perhaps writing in first-person as the character. Throw a couple of not-so-well-known names into the mix to liven up the activity. Names like Achan and Hymenaeus may cause kids to do a double-take when they're expecting names like Adam and Moses. As you wrap up the session, remind group members to bring their reports to the next meeting so they can read them aloud to the group.

DATE USED:

Approx. Time

STEP 1: *The Piece That Passes Understanding* _____
❏ Extra Action
❏ Large Group
❏ Extra Fun
❏ Media
❏ Short Meeting Time

STEP 2: *Good Connections* _____
❏ Small Group
❏ Heard It All Before
❏ Little Bible Background
❏ Mostly Girls
❏ Mostly Guys
❏ Extra Fun
❏ Extra Challenge

STEP 3: *We're Being Watched* _____
❏ Heard It All Before
❏ Little Bible Background
❏ Fellowship & Worship
❏ Mostly Girls
❏ Mostly Guys
❏ Short Meeting Time
❏ Urban

STEP 4: *Contemporary Characters* _____
❏ Small Group
❏ Fellowship & Worship
❏ Media
❏ Urban
❏ Combined Jr. High/High School

STEP 5: *People of God: The Next Generation* _____
❏ Extra Action
❏ Large Group
❏ Combined Jr. High/High School
❏ Extra Challenge

Breaking the Code

Choose one or more

☐ To help kids see that the Bible isn't hard to comprehend if they seriously try to understand it.

☐ To help kids identify obstacles that prevent them from comprehending the Word of God, and to establish goals to get past such obstacles.

☐ To help kids learn to use available tools to figure out the parts of the Bible they just can't make any sense of.

☐ Other:_____

_____

Your Bible Base:

Matthew 13:1-23

Tales from the Cryptogram

(Needed: Copies of Repro Resource 5, pencils)

Hand out copies of "Code Dread" (Repro Resource 5) and pencils. Have group members work on the codes listed on the sheet. Some are fairly simple, but most are rather difficult. The goal is to have the kids struggle quite a bit and feel a certain sense of frustration, but not to make them feel stupid. Consequently, you might want to have them work in groups rather than individually. Also be ready to provide clues along the way (one word from the sentence, a couple of letters that have been substituted for other ones, etc.). One other clue you might want to give: The word *code* appears in every sentence.

After a while, see how many of the codes were broken by your group members. Also check to see how many of the codes were recognized by your young people. And while you will probably have no problem solving them yourself, here are the answers just in case:

1. "If you think this is Morse Code, you are absolutely right."
2. "If you read this sentence backward, you will break the code quickly."
3. "If these dots were raised, this would be a Braille code."
4. "In this code, each letter is shifted two letters down the alphabet." [A = C, B = D, etc.]
5. "These code numbers represent the positions of the letters in the alphabet." [1 = A, 2 = B, etc.]

Some of your group members might be able to figure out the Braille and Morse codes by working out the letter combinations. But explain that it certainly would have been much easier if they had the keys to each of the codes. It would then be no trouble to figure out the sentences, and frustration would have been greatly reduced. Point out that it's not that the sentences are unclear. It's simply that group members are missing something they need in order to "translate."

OPTIONS

EXTRA ACTION

LARGE GROUP

MOSTLY GUYS

URBAN

JR. HIGH / HIGH SCHOOL COMBINED

Wheel of Biblical Confusion

(Needed: Chalkboard and chalk or newsprint and marker, list of biblical words and phrases)

Ask: **Does it ever seem to you that the Bible is written in some kind of code? Explain.** Note group members' comments and try to deal with them as you go through the session. But first try to draw out some specific examples with a quick game of "Wheel of Fortune" (without the wheel). You may play with three volunteers at a time or you may divide into teams and let group members play as a team. Make a list of biblical names, places, phrases, etc. that might be obscure, difficult to understand, or otherwise challenging. Then write the category on the board and draw underlines to indicate the number of words and letters in the puzzle you have selected. Players may guess consonants until they miss. They may guess the solution at any time. But if they select a letter that isn't in the puzzle or guess the solution incorrectly, play resumes with the next person or team. Below are a few suggestions to get you started. (The terms may vary based on the Bible translation used. These are taken from the NIV translation.)

People
Melchizedek (Gen. 14)
King Nebuchadnezzar
   (Dan. 1–4)
King Xerxes and Queen Vashti
   (Es. 1)
Ananias and Sapphira (Acts 5)
Bildad the Shuhite (Job 2)

Places
Canaan (Num. 13)
Mount Nebo (Deut. 32)

Armageddon (Rev. 16)

The Negev (Gen. 12)
The third heaven (2 Cor. 12)

Things
Urim and Thummim (Ex. 28)
Asherah pole (Jud. 6)
Seraphs (Isa. 6)
Eunuch (Acts 8)
Leviathan (Isa. 27)

Words/Phrases
Day of Atonement (Lev. 16)
Feast of Ingathering (Ex. 23)
Son of Man (Matt. 8)
Sacrifice of praise (Heb. 13)
The abomination that causes
   desolation (Matt. 24)

Select words and phrases your group members have covered in the past and should know, yet may still be confused about. As each word or phrase is solved, quiz group members to see how much they know about it. Try to raise a number of questions concerning strange and unusual names and places, as well as the biblical style of writing itself. (Keep track of the questions at this point. In Step 5, you will have an opportunity to try to answer some of them.)

Explain that even when we figure out the spelling and pronunciation of such words, we still have to deal with some very unusual names, places, and objects.

Ask: **What do you do when you come across a portion of Scripture that you simply can't understand?** (Skip over the hard parts; give up trying to get *anything* out of the Bible; use reference materials to help understand; ask for help from someone who knows more; etc.)

STEP 3

Peter Pollin' Mary

Sometimes it's difficult for young people to clearly express what they think about certain topics, or to put their feelings into words. To facilitate your discussion of the difficulties of reading the Bible, read a number of statements and poll your group members to see whether they agree or disagree with each one. Group members should stand if they agree and remain seated if they disagree.

You may create your own list of agree/disagree statements, but here are a few to get you started:

- **I find many parts of the Bible too difficult to understand.**
- **More people would study the Bible if it wasn't so hard to comprehend.**
- **I have trouble finding what I'm looking for in the Bible.**
- **I think regular—almost daily—Bible reading is very important.**
- **I read and study the Bible almost every day.**
- **There's too much unnecessary stuff in the Bible.**
- **The Bible would be easier to understand if the names and places weren't so weird.**

Perhaps your group members' agree/disagree responses will generate some questions or discussion. If so, deal with any issues that are raised. Encourage everyone to be honest about any difficulty or frustration he or she faces when it comes to Bible study.

Then ask: Since we place so much importance on knowing what the Bible has to say, why are so many parts of it hard for us to understand? Let kids respond with their opinions, but hold off on reaching any conclusions until after the Bible study.

A Seedy Story

(Needed: Bibles, copies of Repro Resource 6, pencils)

Explain: **Complaints about biblical teaching are not new. As a matter of fact, as soon as Jesus began to teach, people began to notice that they couldn't quite keep up with everything He was trying to tell them. One of the first things they discovered was that Jesus' teaching was much different than that of the religious leaders they were accustomed to hearing. It was easy to believe that Jesus knew exactly what He was talking about** (Matt. 7:28, 29), **but even Jesus' disciples had trouble at times as they searched for the "real" meanings of the stories Jesus told.**

Have group members listen or follow along as you read Matthew 13:1-9 (the Parable of the Sower). This is such a frequently taught passage that it may no longer hold much intrigue for some of your group members. But ask them to listen as if they were hearing the story for the first time.

Afterward, ask: **Suppose you went to church, knowing little about the pastor—or about Christianity, for that matter. The pastor gets up, tells the story you just heard, and sits down again. What would you think? Would you go home spiritually enriched? If not, how do you think you would feel?** Some people might think they had stumbled into the Farm Bureau rather than the church. Some might be very confused as to the purpose of the story. Those who thought the pastor was a good and wise man might try to analyze what he had said, much as they would try to figure out a riddle. Others might ignore the story or treat it as a bunch of nonsense.

Explain: **Jesus' disciples took another approach—they waited until He got away from the crowd and then asked Him what He meant** (Matt. 13:10; Luke 8:9). **And what He told them is still**

OPTIONS

LARGE GROUP

FELLOWSHIP & WORSHIP

MOSTLY GUYS

EXTRA FUN

JR.HIGH HIGH SCHOOL COMBINED

very applicable to us today. But before we look at what He told them, let's see what you think the parable means.

Hand out copies of "Sower Losers" (Repro Resource 6). Have everyone fill out the sheet. Group members will be asked to examine what they think Jesus meant. They will also be challenged to come up with some specific examples as to how the things Jesus described might actually take place in their lives. Give them some time to struggle with this for a while.

If they are confused as to what they're supposed to do, give an example: **Jesus tells us that the birds represent "the evil one [who] comes and snatches away what was sown in [a person's] heart." But when this happens to a person, we don't see birds and we don't see Satan. What might we actually see in the person's life?** (Open hostility toward Christian things? A refusal to go to church at all?) **These responses are what you should put in the last column.**

When group members finish, discuss their findings. After some speculative discussion, have someone read Matthew 13:18-23 to see what Jesus actually told His disciples. See how well your kids did at coming up with Jesus' intended meaning. Use the following information to supplement your discussion of Jesus' interpretation.

According to Jesus, one of the barriers to understanding the Word of God (the Bible) is the ongoing *spiritual conflict* we face. Satan doesn't want God to communicate clearly to us. Even though we may attend church and hear God's Word on a regular basis, it may never take root. Personal examples from your group members might include any kind of temptations they face. It's always tempting to do something else rather than apply oneself to Bible study. The other activities don't even have to be "bad" in and of themselves. Any number of things (even friends and family) can "snatch away" the "seed" of God's Word and prevent it from having its intended effect.

A second barrier to understanding the Bible is the failure to mature *spiritually*. Many of your kids may know people who became Christians and seemed to be genuinely excited about it, yet who fell away from the faith after the newness of the experience wore off. Jesus explains with His agricultural parable that we need to "put down roots." We can hear God's Word, get excited about it, and let it have an effect in our lives. But until we "go a little deeper" and develop "below the surface," we won't be able to cope with the pressures of life that we face. We usually don't have to look far to find a bunch of "wilted" Christians.

A third barrier to effective Bible study is *distraction*. Few of us, upon becoming Christians, will enter a monastery or convent. We will continue to face the "real" world with "the worries of this life and the deceitfulness of wealth" (among other concerns). It's very easy to focus more on our anxieties and daily routine than it is to keep our minds set "on things above" (Col. 3:2). We become easily distracted from the Word of God—the one thing that helps us keep all of these other things in proper perspective. We must not allow anything else to "choke" out the thing that is most important. Just as we weed a garden to ensure the best growth of the flowers or vegetables, we need to weed out any activities that prevent our spiritual growth.

Your group members should make the previous observations as well as coming up with specific ways to avoid all three barriers to understanding God's Word. Let them share the things they come up with.

Then ask: **How can you tell if someone is being "successful" in his or her study of the Bible? According to Jesus, when God's Word is heard and understood, the result will be a fruitful spiritual life. Few of us can claim we never hear God's Word. (And whether or not we hear it, we still have access to the *written* Word all of the time). But it is very likely that many of us allow one of the previous obstacles to prevent us from *understanding* and *applying* it; therefore, we don't fully experience fruitful lives. We lose out on seeing what we could accomplish (with God's help), and Christianity as a whole suffers because we forfeit what we could and should be contributing to the church body.**

Tools and Tactics

(Needed: Paper, pencils, Bible reference materials)

Say: **When people complain about the Bible's being so difficult to understand, do you think most of them have already tried as hard as possible to figure out the parts that confuse them?** Let kids respond.

Then continue: **Jesus tells us that three major reasons we fail to let the Bible speak clearly to us are (1) Satan's work to prevent our grasping God's Word, (2) our own attempts to grow without being firmly rooted, and (3) our willingness to give other concerns top priority. What percent of the time do you think one of these three causes is the real reason behind our inability to comprehend something the Bible has to say?**

While these three obstacles may not account for *every* instance of biblical confusion, we need to be aware of them and make a mental note to check for them occasionally. Whenever we find that we're not getting as much as we feel we should out of Bible study, we need to examine our lives to see if one of these negative influences has crept in.

OPTIONS

SMALL GROUP

LITTLE BIBLE BACKGROUND

FELLOWSHIP & WORSHIP

MOSTLY GIRLS

EXTRA FUN

MEDIA

URBAN

EXTRA CHALLENGE

However, there is one other important principle to explain why some parts of the Bible are so much harder to understand than others.

Ask: **Could God have provided us with a Bible in a language at, say, a third-grade level? If so, why didn't He?** (While some of the theological aspects of Scripture are a bit complicated, it seems that much of the content could be a lot easier to understand.)

Why are parts of the Bible so symbolic? For example, why did Jesus use parables? Why not just come right out and say what He meant? Let kids respond.

Explain: **In between the telling of the Parable of the Sower, and His explanation of it, Jesus explains why He used parables. And in doing so, He reveals a very important principle we need to keep in mind. Listen carefully to His comments.**

Have someone read Matthew 13:10-17. Then discuss the following questions. Suggested answers are provided, but before you provide answers, first allow group members to struggle to discover them. Allow kids to feel a bit uncertain as you lead them into the activity that follows.

Why did Jesus use parables in His teaching? (Parables are a kind of "code." They hide a deeper meaning. Jesus used them so His followers would keep thinking about what He was saying until they "figured it out.")

Is Jesus trying to keep some people "in the dark" about God and His kingdom? (God desires for everyone to turn to Him [2 Peter 3:9]. Yet He knows that some people are hard-hearted and don't really care about what He has to tell them.)

What do you think verse 12 means: "Whoever has will be given more, and he will have an abundance. Whoever does not have, even what he has will be taken from him"? Sometimes people apply this verse out of context, and it sounds terribly unfair. Yet in the context of better understanding Jesus' teachings, He suggests that those who continue to use biblical knowledge will keep adding to their understanding. Those who make no effort to do so will be unable to make sense of what little they do know.

What does the rest of this passage mean—all of the stuff about "ever hearing but never understanding" and "prophets . . . longed to see what you see but did not see it"?

Keep asking hard questions until several of your group members seem somewhat confused or overwhelmed. Then say: **This is an instance of not understanding something the Bible has to say. So what can we do about it?**

Have on hand several Bible reference resources. Briefly demonstrate how each one might be used in this case. If you wish, you can divide into groups and let each group take one of the resources to better understand Matthew 13:10-17. For example:

• Dictionary—Some people may need definitions of *calloused* (vs. 15), *righteous* (vs. 17), and so forth.

- Bible dictionary—Check for the significance of parables, the meaning of "the kingdom of heaven" (vs. 11), a short biography of Isaiah (vs. 14), and so forth.
- Commentaries—See what wisdom several Bible scholars can shed on this particular passage.
- Concordance—Look up other references to *kingdom of heaven*, *seeing*, *hearing*, and so forth.
- Cross references—Find the original sources of the passages Jesus is quoting, and see what else can be discovered through references to other verses.

By the time you use most of these resources, your group's understanding of what Jesus was saying should be greatly increased. If time permits, use the references to look up some of the "Wheel of Fortune" words and phrases that seemed to confuse group members. If not, have them do so as an assignment for the next meeting.

Close with a challenge for your group members not to be so quick to give up when they find hard-to-understand passages or verses that make no sense to them. With a better knowledge of how to use Bible reference resources, and the availability of yourself and other leaders as *human* resources, your kids should soon "produce a crop yielding a hundred, sixty or thirty times what was sown."

Code Dread

Are you one of those people who enjoys a good puzzle? Or do you prefer to have things spelled out for you? Either way, here's an activity you should enjoy. As you can see, everything is spelled out. The trouble is, it's spelled in the wrong letters or other symbols. See how many of the following codes you can break. Some of them are pretty hard, but if you're extra nice (or willing to lay out a bribe) your group leader might provide you with some clues if you get stumped.

1. ·· ··−·/−·−− −−− ··−·/− ···· ·· −· −·−/− ···· ·· ···/
·· ···/−− −−− ·−· ··· ·/−·−· −−− −·· ·/−·−− −−− ··−/
·−· ·−· ·/·− −··· ··· −−− ·−·· ·· − · ·−·· −·−−/
·−· ·· −−· ···· −

2. YLK CIU QEDO CEHTKA ERBLLI WUO YDRA WK CABE CNET

NESSIH TD AERU OYFI.

3.

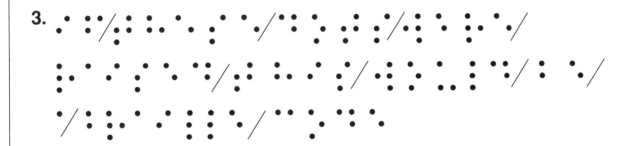

4. KP VJKU EQFG, GCEJ NGVVGT KU UJKHVGF VYQ NGVVGTU FQYP

VJG CNRJCDGV.

5. 20-8-5-19-5 3-15-4-5 14-21-13-2-5-18-19 18-5-16-18-5-19-5-14-20 20-8-5

16-15-19-9-20-9-15-14-19 15-6 20-8-5 12-5-20-20-5-18-19 9-14 20-8-5

1-12-16-8-1-2-5-20.

SOWER LOSERS

When Jesus told the Parable of the Sower (Matthew 13:1-23), He confused a lot of people—including His own disciples. Because He used symbolic images, He left a lot of people scratching their heads and wondering if they should go home and plant something. But that's not what He meant at all.

What do *you* get out of His parable? For each of the following things He describes, explain what you think He is talking about. Then after you give a general description of each problem area, get more specific about each particular problem. For example, Jesus finally explained the parable to His disciples (vss. 18-23), so you can put His "general" explanation in the first column. But even though Jesus explained *what* His symbolism meant, He didn't tell us exactly *how* those things might actually take place in our lives. That's up to you. Your specific examples should go in the second column.

Problem	In general, what do you think Jesus meant?	How might these things take place in your life?
"Some [seed] fell along the path, and the birds came and ate it up."		
"Some fell on rocky places, where it did not have much soil. It sprang up quickly. . . . But when the sun came up, the plants were scorched, and they withered because they had no root."		
"Other seed fell among thorns, which grew up and choked the plants."		

STEP 1

Have group members form pairs. As an alternative to Repro Resource 5, or in addition to it, provide the pairs with keys to Morse Code, Braille, or other codes. (These keys can be found in most encyclopedias.) Or you might give the pairs foreign language dictionaries. Then have the members of each pair attempt to send messages back and forth, with the first person asking a question and the second person answering it. Kids will quickly discover that even with the keys in front of them, it takes practice to get used to sending and receiving messages in these various codes or foreign languages. With time and practice it becomes natural and automatic; but at first, it takes some getting used to. The same may be true of Bible study.

STEP 3

Rather than having them simply stand or sit to show agreement/disagreement with the opinion statements, designate the individuals in your group as human "Jog-O-Meters." Explain that the more they agree with a statement, the faster they should run in place. Then go through each of the statements. (You may want to rephrase some of them to get more variety in the pace of your group members' activity.) Group members will probably be too busy laughing and panting to give serious thought to the statements as you are reading them; so when you're finished, be sure to review what the common opinion seemed to be for each statement. Discuss any differences of opinion at that point.

STEP 3

With a small group, you might want to replace the opinion poll with a roleplay that will accomplish the same purpose. Assign one of your group members the role of a person who is convinced that the Bible is a holy book, but that it's just too hard for "normal" people to understand. He or she has simply given up trying. The other group members should all try to convince the person of the merits of Bible reading. This roleplay should bring out many of the arguments that people give for not reading the Bible (as well as arguments *for* reading it). But in a roleplay, an honest actor may come up with some legitimate reasons that defy "the usual" reasons for Bible reading. If we're honest, we must admit that even many adults shy away from large portions of Scripture because of its difficulty or because of their own lack of knowledge of the historical context. Encourage group members to be completely open about any such feelings they have. Only then will you be able to help them deal with those feelings.

STEP 5

When you discuss tools and resources that can help your kids understand Scripture, emphasize that one good resource is other knowledgeable people. Reference materials may be readily available, yet most people tend to turn to friends for help and advice. It's much easier (and more fun) to ask someone about something we don't understand than to conduct a "research project" to find out what we want to know. However, in small groups, *human* resources may be scarce. If possible, you might want to have your youth group meet with another group (college/career, young adults, adults, or whatever). Host an informal get-together to let your group members meet and mingle with other people in your church, and to get to know them better. Help your kids see that there are additional sources of advice (and human contact) available to them beyond the small number of people in the group.

STEP 1

Prior to the meeting, gather several locks and keys (or combinations). To begin the session, give half your group members locks and the other half keys (or combinations). Have everyone try to find his or her partner. Use this exercise to point out that we may need to accumulate more than one "key" to "unlock" Scripture. Reading the Bible is certainly a good starting point. But some portions of the Bible may defy our understanding if all we do is give them a cursory read-through. We may need other "keys": prayer for wisdom, reference materials, advice from other people, Bible memorization, and so forth.

STEP 4

Have your kids form three groups. Instruct the members of each group to work together to complete Repro Resource 6. When everyone is finished, assign one "Problem" on the sheet to each group. Instruct the members of each group to create a skit that will demonstrate some of the specific applications they came up with for their assigned "Problem." (For example, it's one thing to know that the birds that ate the seed represent "the evil one [who] comes and snatches away what was sown in [one's] heart." But the group's skit should indicate some specific ways that this could happen in a person's life.) After the groups have performed their skits, discuss any questions group members have about the parable.

STEP 2

Play "Super Advanced Bible Picture Charades for Geniuses." Essentially, this is a version of Pictionary™, using the words, objects, and concepts provided in Step 2 of the session. Teams will compete to see which one can guess first what one of its members is drawing. Using such difficult words will probably be very frustrating for contestants. Perhaps your "heard it all before" group is good at *recognizing* Bible words, names, and places. But often it is quite another thing to *understand* those terms well enough to draw them so someone else can recognize them. Explain that similar distinctions can be made between hearing God's Word and applying it. Just because we hear something doesn't mean we automatically put it into practice.

STEP 3

Conduct a Christmas carol quiz. Read a line from a carol and ask kids to write down which carol the line comes from. Select lines that contain words or phrases that are somewhat difficult to understand. Here are a few to get you started:
• "He comes to make his blessing flow far as the curse is found" ("Joy to the World")
• "For lo, the days are hast'ning on, By prophets seen of old, When with the ever-circling years shall come the time foretold" ("It Came upon the Midnight Clear")
• "Veiled in flesh, the Godhead see; hail th' incarnate Deity; pleased as man with men to dwell, Jesus our Emmanuel" ("Hark! The Herald Angels Sing")
• "Word of the Father, now in flesh appearing" ("O Come, All Ye Faithful")

When you finish the quiz, discuss exactly what these lines mean. If you can stump some of your kids on a few of the carols and their messages, point out that the same principle holds true about the Bible. Sometimes we hear stories about certain passages so many times that we think we know them pretty well. Yet in reality we may be hearing without comprehending.

STEP 2

Prior to the meeting, find a contract, a professional journal, or some other resource that contains a lot of difficult-to-understand language. Or if you feel especially creative, use a dictionary and thesaurus to write a few cerebral, erudite, sagacious paragraphs of your own. Let group members struggle to understand the message that is being conveyed in the text. If they need to, let them use a dictionary to help them figure out some of the hard words. (And, by the way, there should be no eructation during this activity.) Point out that we must learn to tolerate a certain amount of difficult reading material. It's part of life. We can't avoid it, no matter how hard we try. Consequently, we shouldn't try to skip the parts of the Bible that are a little difficult to understand. Just as people aren't likely to buy a house without struggling through the "legalese" language on the contract, your group members shouldn't try to get through adolescence without starting to struggle a bit to better understand more of the Bible. Encourage them to start with what they *do* understand and move on from there.

STEP 5

If your group members don't know the Bible very well, they aren't likely to know what their options are when it comes to Bible study. Provide a variety of Bible translations and paraphrases for them to examine: *King James Version, New King James Version, New International Version, New American Standard Bible, The Living Bible, Phillips Translation,* etc. If possible, give each person a different version to examine. Choose some short passages to read from each of the versions (such as Ps. 23; Luke 2:1-7; etc.). Help group members see that understanding the Bible might begin with finding a translation that makes sense to them.

STEP 4

Depending on the season, try to bring in some wildflowers, dandelions, thistle blooms, or other kind of "pretty weeds." (If it's the middle of winter, you'll have to use your imagination.) Point out the beauty of the plants. They may be colorful, sweet-smelling, edible, or have any number of other positive characteristics. Yet if they are allowed to grow in a yard or garden, they will choke out healthy plants. And if they aren't dealt with one year, they will come back stronger the next. Use this illustration with the Parable of the Sower to point out that not all of the "thorns" in our life are easily recognized as weeds. We may have some beautiful, seemingly sweet, lovely people or habits that take our time and prevent us from growing spiritually. Challenge group members to examine their lives—relationships, use of time, habits, and so forth—to determine whether or not they may have some "pretty weeds" springing up. They may not be sure about certain things, which is fine. The important thing is that they begin to question and examine such things to ensure their continued growth. Later, close the session by praising God for the spiritual lessons He provides through nature. Ask for His wisdom in "weeding out" influences that get in the way of a better relationship with Him.

STEP 5

While it is important to try to understand as much as we can about the Bible, you might want to close by giving thanks to God that He doesn't judge any of us based on IQ or vocabulary skills. Offer praise that the most important parts of Scripture are clear and simple. Point out that as we respond to the plain truth that requires only childlike understanding and faith, God will eventually provide the wisdom we need to move ahead from there. And while we should certainly work toward knowing and comprehending whatever we can, we shouldn't feel bad or incompetent as we continue to learn.

STEP 3

Add the following agree/disagree statements to your list:

• **I'd get more out of the Bible if more women were included in it.**

• **The Bible has become outdated, especially in regard to women's rights and roles.**

• **Paraphrases of the Bible are very helpful and needed; they make it more relevant to today.**

If you have time, ask your girls to write their own agree/disagree statements on a piece of paper. After a few minutes, collect the sheets; allow the group to respond as you read the statements anonymously. (This activity may give you even further insight as to some of the frustrations your group members have about the Bible.)

STEP 5

On a large piece of newsprint or chalkboard, draw three columns. At the top of the first column, write "Satan"; at the top of the second column, write "No Roots"; at the top of the third column, write "Other Priorities." Have your girls name as many specific examples as possible for each column. Afterward, talk about the specific areas that are a struggle for your girls. For example, if some girls have a tendency to spend time on "Other Priorities"—such as over-involvement at school—brainstorm specific steps they can take to help alleviate that problem.

STEP I

Have your guys roleplay asking a girl out on a date. Set the scene so that several guys are trying to impress the same girl and convince her to go out. They should use their best lines on her and describe the kind of date they have in mind. The guys shouldn't be aware of it, but the girl (or the person roleplaying the girl) should be given a "key to her heart"—something she likes doing better than anything else. It might be eating out, horseback riding, shopping, sports, or whatever. If a guy happens to mention whatever it is she really enjoys, she should accept his offer. Otherwise, she should decline. If time permits, do a couple of similar roleplays, changing the "key" each time. If your guys are a little thick-headed when it comes to seeing the importance of finding keys to more effective Bible study, they may be able to relate to this object lesson.

STEP 4

Point out that Jesus' disciples were, for the most part, a pretty average group of guys. We tend to think that they were pretty holy and spiritual. Yet when we look closely at the Parable of the Sower, we see them pull Jesus aside and ask, "What are you *talking* about?!" Most guys ought to relate to that feeling. So ask: **What have you come across in the Bible lately that you just don't understand? If you could pull Jesus aside for a little one-on-one conversation, without any outside distractions, what would you want Him to explain to you?** After group members respond, explain that the whole purpose of Bible study and prayer is to "pull Jesus aside" and allow Him to communicate with us. It may take a bit of perseverance and effort before we finally begin to understand, but if we don't give up, usually we can start to make sense of the things that confuse us.

STEP 4

Bring in a watermelon or pumpkin. Have kids form two teams. Cut the watermelon or pumpkin into halves. Have a contest to see which team can get the most seeds out of its half in two minutes. The catch is that group members may use only *spoons* to get the seeds out—no hands or anything else. After two minutes, have both teams count their seeds. Award prizes to the team with the most seeds. Use the topic of seeds to lead in to a discussion on the parable of the sower.

STEP 5

All of the discussion in this step about using tools can sound mechanical and boring. So to show group members that tools can be our friends, conclude with a party of some kind in which all of the elements are provided except the "tools." You might have ice cream (without spoons or scoops), cans of syrup (without can openers), nuts (without nutcrackers), and so forth. The kind of food you plan will determine your need for tools. Be creative. But whatever you plan, you can begin without bowls or utensils. Then point out that just as spoons and bowls can vastly intensify the enjoyment of a hot fudge sundae, so can the appropriate reference materials enhance what we can learn from a difficult passage of Scripture.

STEP 3

After you address group members' opinions about the Bible, ask: **What can we do to better understand the difficult portions of the Bible?** Then, before kids respond, say: **Better yet, I wonder how cable television would handle the issue of making the Bible easier to understand.** Pretend to click through the channels of cable television with the assumption that each program will be devoted to explaining hard parts of Scripture. Ask: **What might the following channels do to help viewers understand and appreciate portions of the Bible that might otherwise go unread?** The channels are as follows: The Discovery Channel (which focuses on science and nature), Arts and Entertainment, The Disney Channel, ESPN, CNN, MTV, Nickelodeon (the children's network), Comedy Central, and The Nashville Network. While kids may not come up with much for all of these channels, some of the "networks" should provide fairly original approaches to the Bible. Challenge your group members to deal with Scripture at various levels as they read and reread some of the more difficult portions.

STEP 5

Wrap up the session by showing a symbolic Christian film or video. Choose one that contains clear symbolism that group members should have no problem understanding (perhaps a version of *The Lion, the Witch, and the Wardrobe*). Your kids should see that symbolism can not only be easy to understand, but may even be a better method of getting a point across than a straightforward presentation of facts. When your group members come across biblical symbolism, encourage them not to automatically resist it. Explain that perhaps the symbolism will help them understand God's truth better than they could without it.

STEP 2

Begin the session with the "Wheel of Fortune" activity in Step 2, as if it were a normal game and without any warning that the answers are very difficult. After two or three rounds, listen for any grumblings or complaints. When you begin to hear them, challenge group members to get more involved in the portions of the Bible that may seem difficult to them. Read or summarize Jesus' Parable of the Sower (Step 4) to demonstrate the importance of allowing God's Word to take root in our lives. Then spend most of your time in Step 5, discussing the intent of parables and symbolic writing, and learning how to use the right tools to better understand those portions of Scripture.

STEP 3

To make the most of the time you have, let kids come up with their own reasons for why the Bible is difficult for them to get into on a regular basis. Give kids a few minutes to come up with their reasons. Then ask for a few volunteers to pantomime some of the reasons they came up with. As each volunteer "performs," let the rest of the group try to guess what his or her reason is. For example, one person might lay down on the floor and pretend to be asleep to illustrate being too tired to read the Bible. After a few group members have performed, ask others to call out the reasons they came up with.

STEP 1

Add the following code to Repro Resource 5:

• **Or-fay od-gay o-say oved-lay ee-thay orld-way at-thay ee-hay ave-gay is-hay ee-onlay egotten-bay on-say at-thay oever-whay elieves-bay en-iay im-hay all-shay ot-nay erish-pay ut-bay ave-hay erlasting-evhay ife-lay.** (This is a Pig Latin code for the text of John 3:16.)

STEP 5

While discussing the three major reasons we fail to let the Bible speak clearly to us, it may be helpful to have your teens review Matthew 4:1-11 (Jesus' temptation in the wilderness). Discuss as a group the tactics Satan used to try to keep Jesus from focusing on His mission and the tools Jesus used to thwart Satan's plan. Then come up with an "urban equivalent" for each tactic in the story. For example, an urban equivalent of Satan's offer of all of the kingdoms in the world might be someone offering a young urban teen drugs or illicit sex. In essence, this is an appeal to a "You can have it all" mindset. Help your kids recognize what Jesus knew: the most powerful weapon against such temptations is God's Word.

STEP 1

Begin the session with the code activity on Repro Resource 5. But before you do, secretly provide your junior highers with keys to most of the codes. (The keys to Morse Code and Braille can be found in most encyclopedias. You can photocopy a key for each of your junior highers as well as letting them in on the other code secrets.) Junior highers shouldn't let high schoolers know they have the keys. When you see that most of the junior highers have worked out their codes, ask: **How many of the codes have you figured out so far?** See how your high schoolers react when the junior high kids turn out to be a lot smarter than they would ever have expected. Eventually let everyone in on the secret. Then summarize: **If you devote yourselves to regular Bible study, you will eventually figure out the "keys" to the parts of the Bible that make no sense to you now. And all of you—high schoolers as well as junior highers—can be a lot more intelligent about spiritual truths than a lot of adults you know. If you don't believe me, try it and see for yourselves.**

STEP 4

Before you study the Parable of the Sower, read or tell some of Aesop's Fables. After each one, ask: **What do you think is the moral to this story? How can you tell? How do you know that these aren't just a bunch of stories about wacky animals that relate to each other in strange ways?** Help group members—younger ones, especially—see the value of using symbolism to make an important point. Then move on to the Parable of the Sower, an example of a similar method of teaching, yet one that is a bit more difficult to understand. But since you've already established the value of the teaching style, the difference in the level of difficulty shouldn't seem to be such a major obstacle.

STEP 3

If your group members confess to having some questions about why parts of the Bible are so confusing, point out that perhaps younger kids do too. Encourage your group members to be completely honest about their feelings when it comes to the symbolic and hard-to-understand portions of the Bible. Then, as they begin to deal with their own feelings, challenge them to think of ways that they can help make the Bible more exciting to younger kids in the church. If they're ambitious enough, your group members might want to plan a "Fun-with-the-Bible Night." Not only would younger kids enjoy the opportunity to "rub shoulders" with your group of young people, but your own group members are likely to learn more from planning and teaching the younger ones for an hour than they would in a dozen regular sessions they sit through. Be creative and come up with a plan to fit your specific kids and church.

STEP 5

After kids have had an opportunity to "test drive" a variety of Bible study resources, challenge each person to become an "expert" with one of them. For instance, someone might agree to take home the Bible dictionary and get familiar with it. Someone else might spend a lot of time learning to do cross referencing. Various commentaries can be sent home with several different people, and so forth. Explain that if everyone would learn to operate one type of resource, he or she would vastly increase his or her worth as a resource to other group members. The next time someone has a problem and can't remember or find a passage he or she has heard that would apply to it, he or she can ask the concordance "expert." When someone comes across a strange word during personal Bible study, he or she can go to the Bible dictionary person. By working together, your kids may be able to help out with each others' problems.

DATE USED:

Approx. Time

STEP 1:

Tales from the Cryptogram _____
❑ Extra Action
❑ Large Group
❑ Mostly Guys
❑ Urban
❑ Combined Jr. High/High School

STEP 2:

Wheel of Biblical Confusion _____
❑ Heard It All Before
❑ Little Bible Background
❑ Short Meeting Time

STEP 3: *Peter Pollin' Mary* _____
❑ Extra Action
❑ Small Group
❑ Heard It All Before
❑ Mostly Girls
❑ Media
❑ Short Meeting Time
❑ Extra Challenge

STEP 4: *A Seedy Story* _____
❑ Large Group
❑ Fellowship & Worship
❑ Mostly Guys
❑ Extra Fun
❑ Combined Jr. High/High School

STEP 5: *Tools and Tactics* _____
❑ Small Group
❑ Little Bible Background
❑ Fellowship & Worship
❑ Mostly Girls
❑ Extra Fun
❑ Media
❑ Urban
❑ Extra Challenge

How'd That Get in the Bible?

YOUR GOALS FOR THIS SESSION:
Choose one or more

☐ To help kids recognize that the Bible contains a lot of good stories they might be missing out on, and to help them explore unfamiliar sections.

☐ To help kids brainstorm some reasons to be more thorough in their Bible study.

☐ To help kids create a list of ways to be more creative when it comes to Bible study.

☐ Other:_____
_____

Your Bible Base:

Acts 17:1-12
Various passages that deal with the importance of knowing God's Word

The Match Game

(Needed: Index cards, markers)

Give everyone a marker and several index cards. Explain that you will read a number of questions. After each one, group members should quickly write their answers (large enough to be seen at a distance), but not say aloud what they are writing. At your signal, they should then try to find everyone else who wrote the same answer. You might want to have group members imitate the action in the trading pit of a commodities brokerage—holding up their cards as they shout their response at the top of their lungs, seeking other people who are screaming the same thing over the roar of the crowd. If this isn't conducive to your setting, the same activity can be done in absolute silence as group members simply hold up their cards and *visually* search for matches.

Your questions should all have to do with Bible study, and should be phrased so that several answers are possible. For example:

- **What one word would you use to describe the Bible?**
- **Without repeating any word previously used, what other word would you use to describe the Bible?**
- **What is your favorite book of the Bible?**
- **What Old Testament book do you know the least about?**
- **What New Testament book do you know the least about?**
- **What percentage of the Bible would you say you're pretty familiar with?**
- **In your opinion, what is the most unusual Bible story?**
- **Who is a Bible character that everyone seems to know about except you?**

Though this may turn into a competition to see which group forms first, it is more important to see which are the more common responses. You should also try to see to what extent your group members are aware of the more "obscure" portions of the Bible. Do any names crop up that aren't "key players" of biblical history? Do a lot of your group members' answers tend to be the same? Do group members' responses reflect a group mentality, or does it seem that kids are reading the Bible on their own and coming across a variety of names and stories that aren't usually covered in group settings?

The Second String

(Needed: Copies of Repro Resource 7, pencils)

Explain: **If we grow up in a church, most of us hear about the "famous" people of the Bible. Our parents and Sunday school teachers tell us about Abraham, Noah, Moses, Samson, and so forth. They want us to read about them and imitate their faith. But in those second and third grade Sunday school classes they don't tell us that Abraham twice allowed a foreign king to think Sarah was his sister instead of his wife—even to the point of having the guy "date" his wife—just so his life wouldn't be in jeopardy. They don't tell us that after Noah landed the ark, he got drunk and naked. We can hardly name any of the other dozen or so judges of Israel, because Samson is the most famous one and has a really cool story to tell.**

That's the problem with "hearing" all of these good Bible stories. Until we get more involved and actually start *reading* the stories for ourselves, we miss out on a lot of the good parts. We also fail to learn about many of the other characters who may be just as important, yet aren't quite as familiar.

Hand out copies of "Who, What, and Where?" (Repro Resource 7) and pencils. Group members will get to see how much they know about some of the "second string" characters of the Bible. Without consulting their Bibles, have them try to match the character, event, and reference. After a few minutes, have each person look up one or two of the references, find the account of the character and the event, and reveal the correct matches.

The correct answers are as follows: A—17, DD; B—16, FF; C—1, EE; D—18, SS; E—4, CC; F—2, KK; G—3, TT; H—9, PP; I—20, MM; J—11, RR; K—7, LL; L—14, NN; M—5, HH; N—15, OO; O—12, JJ; P—10, QQ; Q—8, GG; R—19, BB; S—6, AA; T—13, II.

Afterward, ask: **Did anyone get all of the matches correct without having to consult the Bible—and without guessing at any of them?**

Were there any characters on the sheet that you knew absolutely nothing about? If so, which ones?

Did any of these stories sound interesting enough to check out a little more closely?

Why do you think you didn't already know all of these stories? Whose fault is it?

How do you think it will feel to get to heaven someday and meet some of these "minor" characters who did all of these incredible things, only to say, "Sorry, never heard of you"?

Books and Crannies

(Needed: Bibles)

If group members don't know a lot of the stories listed on Repro Resource 7, they may confess that it's because they aren't particularly faithful about having personal Bible study. If so, one of the reasons may be that the Bible seems foreign to many of them. Perhaps they don't know what the Bible has to offer them, or maybe they simply can't seem to find much of interest as they leaf through its pages and stumble upon the books of law or the Minor Prophets.

To help kids discover some of the things they might find in the Bible if they look a little closer—especially in regard to some of the lesser-known stories and characters they've overlooked—conduct a sword drill that will serve as the Bible study for this session. But be aware that if kids aren't comfortable with the Bible to begin with, they are likely to feel frustrated when they start to try to find their way around the 66 books and hundreds of pages. So rather than having a fiercely competitive individual sword drill, have a team competition instead. Have kids form teams that combine newcomers to the Bible with those who are familiar with it. Make sure everyone has a Bible. Then give a reference and see which team can have *all* of its members find the reference first. (When the fastest people find the verses themselves, they can help other team members.) Someone from the winning team should read the verse(s) aloud.

While competition can make the Bible study a bit more fun and exciting for some groups, keep things very loose. Don't keep score or fawn over the one or two group members who always seem to find the reference first. No one should feel bad about being slow to find a passage. Before you start, explain that many of these verses are in hard-to-find books, and that the goal is to not to see who *already* knows where they are, but to let *everyone* practice finding them. As soon as you give a reference, you can also give clues to help everyone find it (explaining where short books are located in regard to larger ones, etc.)

Point out that every verse kids look up has something to do with the importance of Bible study in general or, more specifically, the need to learn more about the "tucked away" stories in the Bible. Members of the team who read the passage aloud should also explain what they think it means.

The following are some verses you may want to use. Feel free to add your own favorite passages. These have been chosen primarily to provide an assortment of Bible books to make the sword drill more challenging. They are presented in the order they will be found in the Bible, so you'll probably want to mix them up as you conduct the sword drill.

- Deuteronomy 4:1-2—We aren't to add or take away from God's Word. (Also see Rev. 22:18-19.) If we don't learn about all of the characters of the Bible, it's like "subtracting from" God's Word.
- Nehemiah 8:9-10—While God's Word shows clearly our sinful natures and the consequences of sin, it should also be a source of great joy as we see God's provision for us.
- Hosea 14:9—We receive wisdom by understanding and applying the Word of God. We should be able to learn something about every story we read—not just the "big" ones.
- Joel 2:13—If we've strayed away from God, we shouldn't be fearful or hesitant about returning to Him. It doesn't matter how bad we are at Bible study *now* as long as we're willing to try to improve.
- Amos 3:7—We discover God's plan for us through the recorded and inspired writings of His people.
- Jonah 3:1-2—God doesn't give up on us, even when we make mistakes. (Jonah is a classic story of how God gives us second chances.)
- Micah 6:8—God's Word shows us His expectations for us. Many times such things are shown through character studies.
- Matthew 24:35—We can count on God's Word because it is eternal.
- John 13:13-15—Through Bible study we see the example set by Jesus (and others). We need to study the lives of these people thoroughly to see how we should live.
- John 15:7-8—When we live according to God's Word, God is glorified as He provides for our needs.
- I Timothy 4:12—In addition to *following* good examples, we should learn to *model* positive examples for others.

End the sword drill with Acts 17:10-11. Point out how the Bereans were commended for their willingness to "[examine] the Scriptures every day" as they tried to discover God's truth.

Ask: **Do you read the Bible every day? If not, what keeps you from it? When you read the Bible, do you examine it to see what it has to say? Or do you just put in your five minutes or so?**

Too Much of a Good Thing?

(Needed: Chalkboard and chalk or newsprint and marker, suggestion box, paper, pencils, tabloid newspapers, completed copies of Repro Resource 7)

Ask: **Since there are so many verses scattered throughout the Bible that emphasize the importance of knowing God's Word, why do you think we remain unaware of so much of what's in Scripture?** Even though you may have dealt with this issue in previous sessions—and earlier in this session—let kids respond truthfully. Several of their reasons may be quite valid. (There's a *lot* of information to read and remember; we tend to know certain parts well and keep going back to them; etc.) List all of the reasons on the board as they are mentioned and number each one.

Then place a box in the center of the room. Distribute paper and pencils. Say: **This is a suggestion box. Think about the problems we've listed and what we might be able to do to remedy any or all of these problems. Write your suggestions on these slips of paper and put them in the suggestion box. You need not sign your name, but your ideas will be read aloud—so put some thought into your responses.**

Ask group members to respond by number to save time. If they want to respond to the problems numbered 2, 3, and 6, they need only write each number and their suggestion(s) for how to deal with it. After group members have placed their ideas into the suggestion box, open it and see what they came up with. You might want to deal with the number one problem first by reading and discussing all of the applicable suggestions. Then move on to number two, and so forth.

If no one mentions it, ask: **Could one of the major reasons we stop searching the Scriptures closely be that we've ceased to be amazed at God's love and power? The Bible is full of stories that detail wonderful events and incredible miracles. Yet we read the Bible with about as much enthusiasm as we do our geometry textbooks.**

Hold up a few supermarket tabloids. Note the sensationalistic head-lines and the excitement the editors try to generate over ludicrous claims—the latest sighting of Elvis, another UFO invasion, or whatever.

Then ask: **What do you think might have happened if some of these writers had been around to cover the Bible stories we've been discussing?** In response, have group members form teams to report on any Bible story they wish—in the style of a super-market tabloid. If they can think of nothing right away, they may consult their completed copies of Repro Resource 7 for some ideas and ready references. Each team should come up with at least a headline and a lead sentence. Challenge the teams to try to capture all of the thrill of the story without stretching the truth. Their stories should demonstrate that if we don't make a point of finding and reading the lesser-known stories of the Bible and giving them our close attention, we can miss out on a lot of remarkable events that have been recorded for us.

Taking the Study Out of Bible Study

(Needed: Copies of Repro Resource 8, pencils)

Having just demonstrated one creative method of studying the Bible, challenge group members to think of other new and better ways to interact with Scripture as a whole rather than focusing on one story at a time. Use their ideas in future sessions.

One other option is a brainstorming comparison session. For example, you might ask: **What do you think is the wettest story in the Bible?** Let kids debate whether it was Noah and the flood, Jonah, Paul's shipwreck, or some other story. Then ask: **What do you think is the smelliest story?** Noah and Jonah might still be contenders, in addition to Daniel in the lions' den, the Prodigal Son feeding hogs, and so forth. You can also ask about the most violent story, the most miraculous story, the best story about a woman, the best story involving a child, and so forth. In each case, list all responses given by group members and then have kids rate the stories—perhaps forming a "Top Ten" list for each category.

Hand out copies of "NO MR E" (Repro Resource 8). Let kids try to figure out each Bible character based on his or her personalized license plate. Then let them create some of their own for other Bible characters. In some cases, kids may be able to justify more than one answer for the license plate characters, but here are the intended "drivers":

1. Nicodemus (John 3:1-21)
2. Goliath (1 Sam. 17:49)
3. Deborah (Jud. 4)
4. Peter (Matt. 14:22-33)
5. Ruth (Ruth 2–4)
6. Noah (Gen. 6–9)
7. Solomon (1 Kings 4:29-34)
8. David (1 Sam. 17:50)
9. Jonah (Jonah 1–2)
10. Absalom (2 Sam. 18:9-15)
11. Zacchaeus (Luke 19:1-10)
12. Lazarus (John 11:38-44)
13. Methuselah (Gen. 5:27)

Challenge kids to think of new and different ways to make Bible stories come alive on a regular basis. If *they* invent games or exercises, there will probably be more interest on *their* part. You may need to get them started, but usually kids can come up with some very creative ideas.

Close by thanking God for the vast variety of characters described in the Bible. And ask Him for a deeper sense of determination as your group members strive to get more involved with the *whole* Bible.

NOTES

WHO, WHAT, and Where?

So you think you know the Bible? We'll see. In the columns below, try to match each person with the correct event *and* the place in the Bible you'd find the story. Don't use your Bible at first. See how much you know without it. If you get stuck, ask your group leader for permission to "cheat" by looking up the references in the Bible.

Person	Event	Biblical Reference
___ ___ ___ A. Aaron	1. Had an unsettling conversation with his talking donkey	AA. Genesis 19:30-38
___ ___ ___ B. Achan	2. A dead man was thrown in this person's grave and came back to life after touching the bones there	BB. Genesis 29:16-30
___ ___ ___ C. Balaam	3. Fell asleep during a sermon and tumbled out of a third story window	CC. Genesis 34
___ ___ ___ D. Barnabas	4. After she was raped, her brothers plotted an elaborate revenge	DD. Numbers 17
___ ___ ___ E. Dinah	5. Hammered an opposing general's head to the ground	EE. Numbers 22:21-35
___ ___ ___ F. Elisha	6. His daughters got him drunk and had sex with him so they could have children	FF. Joshua 7
___ ___ ___ G. Eutychus	7. A shadow moved *backward* to prove to this person God's promise of fifteen more years to live	GG. Joshua 10:12-14
___ ___ ___ H. Gomer	8. While winning victories for God, he told the sun to stand still until he could wrap up a battle	HH. Judges 4:17-21
___ ___ ___ I. Haman	9. She was a prostitute who married a prophet	II. II Kings 5:8-14
___ ___ ___ J. Herod	10. Became "angry enough to die" when a worm killed his shade plant	JJ. II Kings 9:30-37
___ ___ ___ K. Hezekiah	11. Took credit for being a god, was struck down by the real God, and was eaten by worms	KK. II Kings 13:20, 21
___ ___ ___ L. Isaiah	12. Dogs devoured all of this evil person's body except for skull, feet, and hands	LL. II Kings 20:1-11
___ ___ ___ M. Jael	13. Was cured of leprosy by dipping seven times in the Jordan River	MM. Esther 7
___ ___ ___ N. Jeremiah	14. Saw God on His throne, surrounded by flying, six-winged angels	NN. Isaiah 6:1-8
___ ___ ___ O. Jezebel	15. Said God's people would be taken captive, so he was thrown into a mud pit	OO. Jeremiah 38:1-6
___ ___ ___ P. Jonah	16. Secretly stole spoils of victory and caused his whole army to lose its next battle	PP. Hosea 1:2, 3
___ ___ ___ Q. Joshua	17. Had a staff that budded, blossomed, and produced almonds—overnight!	QQ. Jonah 4:5-9
___ ___ ___ R. Leah	18. Was mistaken for Zeus by people in Lystra	RR. Acts 12:21-23
___ ___ ___ S. Lot	19. Took sister's place in wedding and spent honeymoon night with husband before he noticed	SS. Acts 14:8-18
___ ___ ___ T. Naaman	20. His evil plan backfired, and he was hanged on his own gallows	TT. Acts 20:7-12

NO MR E

Suppose you're going out cruising, driving your BMW (big mule Wilma). You're cruising the Bible expressway, where you almost always see a number of "celebrities." You can't always see their faces because of the bright sun, the veils, and the tinted glass. But the way you can tell who they are is by their personalized license plates. Here a donkey, there a camel, and occasionally a chariot goes by. You've collected the following plate numbers. How many of these Bible characters can you identify? (We also left a few blank to let you create some customized plates for other Bible characters you can think of.)

1. NIK AT NIT

2. STON 2 4HD

3. WMN JDG

4. H20 WLKR

5. ME N BOAZ

6. GR8 FLUD

7. WISEGUY

8. SLNGSHOT

9. FSH 8 ME

10. 2 MCH HAIR

11. UPATREE

12. DED 4 DAYS

13. OLLLLLD

14.

15.

STEP 1

Begin the session with an indoor scavenger hunt. Create a list of items that might be found in the place where you're meeting. If you're in a church, for example, your list might include a bulletin that's over two months old, a piece of lost-and-found clothing, a little kid's drawing, a gum wrapper, a used coffee cup, any item that has been used in a Christmas play, a cassette tape of a sermon or speaker, and so forth. Have group members form teams. Make copies of your list, provide each team with a copy, and begin the hunt. After a designated time, call everyone back together and see which team has collected the most items. Later in the session, compare the fun of searching for hard-to-find items with the potential thrill of discovering portions of the Bible that have been previously "undiscovered."

STEP 2

Rather than having group members complete Repro Resource 7 as written, use the list of names as material for charades. Have group members form teams. Instruct each team to designate one person as the clue giver. Advise teams to choose someone who knows the Bible pretty well to give the clues (and make sure each team has one or two such people). The clue giver may have to do some quick matching of people and events to figure out some of the connections. Encourage the clue givers not to linger too long on any name that his or her teammates seem unaware of. After a while, call time and see which team guessed the most names correctly. Then go down the list of names and see which ones, if any, stumped your teams. Continue your discussion with the questions provided in the session.

STEP 1

The smaller your group is, the less exciting the opening activity will be. A better option might be a "guess who wrote this" contest. Distribute index cards and pencils. Ask three of the questions from the session, and have kids write down their answers. Then collect what the cards, read them one at a time, and let group members guess who wrote what. Usually this activity reveals some surprises about several group members and helps them get to know one another better.

STEP 3

If a sword drill doesn't promise to be very thrilling due to the shortage of competitors, divide the group members into two teams. Assign each team half of the Bible references you would have used for the sword drill. Then have a contest to see which team can find all of its verses first. However, in addition to finding the verses, team members must write a brief explanation as to why each one is meaningful. The explanation must be written out before a team gets credit for finding the verse. When both teams have finished finding their passages, declare a winner. Then go through the list and discuss each passage, letting team members share what they found.

STEP 1

An alternative to the opening activity is to play "To Tell the Truth." Choose three volunteers at a time. Meet with your volunteers, and have them discuss unusual events from their past that no one else in the group would know about. Decide which volunteer's story is most unusual. Explain that each volunteer is to try to convince the group that he or she is the one who experienced that particular situation. The real person, of course, can simply tell the truth. The other two will need to do some creative bluffing and acting to try to convince the group. You should announce the situation to the group: **One of these three people, at the age of four, played "Chopsticks" for a Senator of the United States** (or whatever). Other kids will be allowed to ask a few questions. (Who was the Senator? What state were you living in at the time? How does the melody to "Chopsticks" go?) Your two bluffers will need to think quickly to answer the questions. After three or four questions, have kids vote as to which person they think is telling the truth. Try several sets of volunteers and situations to see who is best at bluffing. Then use these "secrets" from people's pasts to lead into the session goal of finding new discoveries in Scripture that may have been "hidden" until now.

STEP 4

Writing out and discussing all of the possible solutions to problems may take too long in a large group. Instead, after you come up with a list of reasons why people remain unaware of so much that's in Scripture, deal with each problem in a more immediate manner. One at a time, single out a problem and ask three kids to give you advice on how to deal with it in order to be more aware of the Bible's teachings. Then have other kids evaluate each person's advice by applauding. The person who receives the loudest applause should be the one with the best advice.

STEP 2

Prior to the meeting, find an assortment of Bible trivia books that vary in difficulty. Before you hand out copies of Repro Resource 7, have a contest to see who can get the most questions right before missing one. Start with some of the easier questions. (Try to bring out the "heard it all before" attitude of your members.) Then gradually increase the difficulty of the questions. Eventually move into the very difficult questions that no one but Bible scholars would know. Help demonstrate to your group members that there is always more to learn about Scripture. "Trivia" is only one aspect of Bible knowledge, yet the Bible is so complex that it is difficult to maintain a knowledge of even the basic *facts*. Beyond that, a more important goal should be to put into practice the things we know.

STEP 5

After group members complete Repro Resource 8, have them form teams for "The License Plate Game." Instruct the teams to create license plates for Bible characters (other than the ones mentioned on Repro Resource 8). The license plates should provide sufficient clues as to the character's identity, yet should be clever enough to stump the other team(s). Set a time limit for guessing for each license plate. If the character's identity isn't guessed within the time limit, the team that came up with the idea gets a point. If the character's identity is guessed, the team that guesses gets a point. A group that knows the Bible fairly well should be able to draw on a number of characters and have a wide variety of creative license plates. If you can channel your group members' "Been there; heard that; what's next?" attitude into challenging games and other creative outlets, they may discover they still have much to learn.

STEP 1

It's difficult to conduct a session about obscure Bible stories for kids who may not be aware of many of the major ones. So you might want to start by seeing exactly how much your group members *do* know. Ask the following questions:

- **How many of the Ten Commandments can you name?**
- **How many of the 12 disciples can you name?**
- **How many of the 27 New Testament books can you name?**
- **How many of the 39 Old Testament books can you name?**
- **How many miracles of Jesus can you name?**

Your group members may know more than they think. If so, they should be encouraged, and you can move on. If not, you may want to spend more time on some of the "basic" stories of the Bible, rather than trying to cover lesser-known ones.

STEP 2

Repro Resource 7 is likely to contain a lot of stories your group members don't know. Rather than creating a lot of confusion by trying to do the sheet as written, have kids focus on the events only. As a group, determine the three events on the sheet that sound most interesting. Then have kids form three groups. Assign each group one of the three events, as well as the Bible reference for that event. Instruct the groups to look up their assigned passages and prepare a brief report on their assigned event. While group members will only get a "sampling" of the tucked-away stories in the Bible, it will be better for them to go home knowing three of them than to still be ignorant about them all.

STEP 2

After group members have matched all of the columns on Repro Resource 7, explain that you want them to make a few more "matches." Challenge them to match other group members (and themselves) with stories they think best describe each person's personality. For example, can they see any of their peers in Balaam's place, having an "intelligent" conversation with an animal? Could any of the girls pick up a hammer and a stake to defend her nation against an evil enemy? Are any of the guys likely to be mistaken for gods? Have group members focus only on positive stories—not the ones that deal with biblical villains. Try to create a greater sense of fellowship using positive speculation. This activity should encourage group members to recognize unique traits about each other. And once such traits begin to be identified, friendships can begin to develop and grow at deeper levels.

STEP 3

As you discuss the importance of ongoing Bible study, perhaps several of your group members would be willing to commit to putting extra effort into seeing what the Bible has to say. If so, form a small study group of those who would like to give it a try. Give them a few minutes to discuss what they would like to study. (This session should provide them with a lot of possibilities.) Then help them get started, giving them suggestions on where to meet, how to conduct the study, and so forth. If a lot of group members are interested, you might want to consider having an additional group meeting every week. The regular group can continue with its emphasis on fun, personal commitment to God, and evangelistic outreach. The new group could then focus almost entirely on Bible knowledge and spiritual growth. Many groups have members who are ready to commit to more than they can get out of "regular" meetings, and this may be the opportunity they're looking for.

STEP 2

Distribute index cards and pencils. Have your girls write down several things about themselves that no one else knows. Assure them that these are for their eyes only. Then explain that just as we all have things about us that no one (or very few people) know, there are also "hidden" parts of the Bible that many people aren't aware of. Say: **Though we may not want others to know these hidden parts of ourselves, God wants us to know all parts of the Bible. He attempts to hide *nothing* from us. In fact, the more we know of the Bible, the better!**

STEP 3

Some of your girls may admit that they're not sure how to examine what they read. (And if there aren't any who'll admit it publicly, you can be sure there are some who are thinking it.) Take a few minutes to talk about what it means to "examine" Scripture. Then brainstorm a list of general questions your group members can ask themselves about a passage. Examples might include the following: "How does this relate to my life?" "Who wrote this?" "To whom was it addressed?" "Why was it written?" "What's the main point the author wants to get across?"

STEP 2

Rather than discuss all of the random stories on Repro Resource 7, this might be a good time to cover some obscure stories that could be embarrassing to deal with in mixed company. For example, the stories of Dinah and the Shechemites (Gen. 34) and Lot's daughters (Gen. 19:30-38) are both on the sheet. But there are also interesting (and sensitive) stories about Judah and Tamar (Gen. 38); Abraham, Sarah, and Abimelech (Gen. 20); Jephthah's foolish vow (Jud. 11); a Levite and his concubine (Jud. 19–21); Absalom and Tamar (2 Sam. 13); and many more. Pay particular attention to biblical accounts of loutish male behavior. Challenge your group members to take note of such actions (and their consequences) and avoid making the same mistakes.

STEP 4

The average teenage guy may not like to admit to the need for Bible study. Yet few can argue that it's not important. Perhaps some guys simply need to begin with something that interests *them*. To help find appropriate portions of Scripture where they might begin to do daily devotions, have each person describe someone he would consider a personal hero. The "hero" might be a sports figure, musician, family member, or anyone. In each case, have group members decide what specific qualities of the person are most admirable. Then, as a group, try to identify Bible stories of people with those same characteristics. Give each group member some ideas of people to look up and read about who come closest to fitting the descriptions of their personal heroes. Bible study might take on a whole new fascination if your guys can find the right starting point.

STEP 1

Play "The Obscurity Game." Let group members take turns naming categories. For each category, kids should try to think of the most obscure thing that fits the category. Categories might include things like countries, state capitols, dog breeds, insects, languages, Beatles songs, musical instruments, and so forth. Award small prizes to the people who come up with the most obscure answers for the different categories. For your final category, have each group member name what he or she thinks is the most obscure Bible story. List group members answers on the board. Later, compare their answers with the stories listed on Repro Resource 7.

STEP 5

Find the game Bible Outburst™ (© 1989 Hersch & Company) or create your own version. The object of the game is to guess as many items as possible on a category card. For example, one category from the game is "People in the Old Testament Who Saw Angels." The 10 names given on the card are (1) Hagar, (2) Abraham, (3) Lot, (4) Balaam, (5) Gideon, (6) Elijah, (7) Daniel, (8) Zechariah, (9) David, and (10) Samson's parents. These aren't the only people in the Old Testament who saw angels, but they're the only ones players can get credit for. One point is awarded for each of the listed people that players can name. A few other categories from the game are "Famous Pairs of People in the New Testament," "Names in the Bible Beginning with O," "People Associated with John the Baptist," and "Plagues Sent on the Egyptians." Most of the cards have 10 possible answers. If you can't obtain a copy of the game, you can create enough of your own cards to play. This is a good way to get into some additional "minutia" of the Bible and conclude the session with some fun and excitement.

STEP 4

An alternative to the tabloid assignment at the end of Step 4 is the video equivalent. If you have a video camera, and if your kids are more inclined to enjoy visual and verbal presentations of material rather than printed ones, let them create TV newsmagazines and send teams out to "cover" some of the biblical miracles. Some of the team members will play the roles of the newscaster and reporters. Others will play the roles of participants and eyewitnesses to the miracles. Give the teams a few minutes to prepare their material. Then, as each team gives its report, videotape the presentation. After all of the teams have reported, play back the tape, and let group members watch themselves.

STEP 5

The license plate activity on Repro Resource 8 might be just a starting point for media-minded group members. Another fun exercise would be to come up with titles of biographies (or autobiographies) for Bible characters. Have a list of recent best-selling biographies to give kids some ideas (*Me* by Katherine Hepburn, *Rare Air* about Michael Jordan, *I Had a Hammer* by Hank Aaron, and so forth). Then have group members think of Bible characters and what their life stories might be titled.

STEP 2

One way to condense the meeting time of this session is to use the two Repro Resources as the main portion of the lesson. Repro Resource 7 provides a number of potential Bible stories to follow up on after group members do the initial match-ups. Repro Resource 8 provides a creative exercise with which to wrap up the session. If time permits, end your meeting time with the problem-solving exercise in Step 4 to give group members the opportunity to share problems they face in regard to Bible study, and to receive some good suggestions to try.

STEP 5

Replace Step 5 with a shorter activity. After your group members have been inundated with story after story and character after character, it might be a good idea to let them try to put some of the pieces together. Challenge each person in your group to write the names of four characters in the Bible who are all somehow related or who all have something in common—except for one. In other words, three of the characters should have some "tie that binds"; the fourth shouldn't. The task of the rest of the group is to guess which character doesn't belong and explain why. Give group members a few minutes to come up with their four characters. Then, one at a time, have kids read their list of names to the group. If no one can correctly guess within fifteen seconds which character doesn't belong, award a prize to the person who came up with the list. A sample list might include Ahab, Boaz, Solomon, and Saul. The one who doesn't belong is Boaz, who wasn't a king like the others. (You might find that kids come up with different answers that also work. That's OK.)

STEP 2

After you go through Repro Resource 7, have your group members consider who are some of the less-familiar "heroes" in your church. Of course, everyone sees the pastor, the choir director, the organist, and the ushers. But what about the behind-the-scenes people like the custodian, the church bus (or van) driver, or the pastor's secretary? How much recognition do they get? Take a few moments at this point in the session to write brief thank-you cards to the "unsung heroes" in your church.

STEP 3

Instead of using the sword-drill activity, have your group members focus on one or more specific themes or topics in the Bible. Here are a few ideas to get you started:

• *Women in the Bible*—Sarah (Gen. 11–23); Lot's wife (Gen. 19:26); Rebekah (Gen. 24–27); Rachel and Leah (Gen. 29–35); Miriam (Ex. 2:1-10); Rahab (Josh. 2–6); Ruth and Naomi (Ruth 1–4); Esther (Es. 1–9); etc.

• *Laughter in the Bible*—Genesis 17:17; 18:12-14; 21:6; Job 8:21; Psalm 2:4; 37:13; 126:2; Proverbs 14:13; Ecclesiastes 2:2; 3:4; Luke 6:21

• *African presence in the Bible*—Ethiopians and Cushites (Gen. 10:6-9; Num. 12:1; 2 Chron. 14:9-13; 16:8; Jer. 13:23; Amos 9:7; Acts 8:27); Egypt/Egyptians (Gen. 15:18; 21:9; 45:19; Ex. 1–14; Ps. 78:12; Acts 21:38); Simon of Cyrene (Mark 15:21; Luke 23:26)

STEP 1

It may be difficult to know how much Bible knowledge your younger group members have accumulated. So rather than doing the opening activity in Step 1, try an exercise that will give you some clues. Distribute paper and pencils. Then say: **I'm going to name an object. You should then write down all of the Bible stories you know that deal with that object. For example, if I were to say, "Stone," you might write down David and Goliath, Jesus' resurrection—when the stone was rolled away from the tomb, Abraham's altar on which he offered Isaac, the stoning of Stephen, and so forth. For every story you think of, you get a point. For every story you think of that no one else thinks of, you get five points.** Start with some basic objects to see how well group members do. If they seem to be doing well, you can try some less common ones. For example, you might start out with *boat, fish, sword, bird, river*, etc. Later you might try *arrow, chariot, robe*, etc. Use a concordance if you need some additional ideas. As group members share their lists (and you add your own input), you should be able to tell how well most of your kids know the Bible, and you'll be able to lead the session more effectively.

STEP 2

Some of the stories included on Repro Resource 7 may be too intense or "mature" for younger group members. If you feel this could be a problem for your group, you need not hand out copies of the sheet. Instead, you can read selected events from the sheet and let group members try to identify the person involved with the event. You can also add other stories your group members should know to replace the ones you eliminate. The verbal presentation of Repro Resource should go quickly, so you might want to add quite a few names and events.

STEP 3

Perhaps your group members are already devoted to regular Bible reading. If so, give them the additional challenge of Bible memorization. But instead of the "big" verses of Scripture, encourage group members to memorize passages that are special to *them* in some way. Sometimes in reading a lesser-known passage, a verse or group of verses may seem to jump out as being very important. These may be verses your group members will never hear quoted or preached on. But if they seem important to the individuals doing the reading, they are certainly worth memorizing and remembering. Encourage your group members not to be so intent on quantity of reading. Make sure they are learning at a pace that allows the truths of the Bible to soak in and be recalled when needed.

STEP 5

If your group (or certain individuals) are exceptionally motivated, you might want to challenge them to begin a read-through-the-Bible program. It takes quite a commitment to read though the Bible in a single year, so you might want to consider some two-year (or longer) programs. Your local Christian bookstore will probably have some resources that will help you. If your kids don't think they have the time or energy to read through the Bible, you might want to provide them with less intensive projects (such as a verse-a-day calendar, good devotional books, etc.).

DATE USED:

Approx. Time

STEP 1: *The Match Game* _____
- ❏ Extra Action
- ❏ Small Group
- ❏ Large Group
- ❏ Little Bible Background
- ❏ Extra Fun
- ❏ Combined Jr. High/High School

STEP 2: *The Second String* _____
- ❏ Extra Action
- ❏ Heard It All Before
- ❏ Little Bible Background
- ❏ Fellowship & Worship
- ❏ Mostly Girls
- ❏ Mostly Guys
- ❏ Short Meeting Time
- ❏ Urban
- ❏ Combined Jr. High/High School

STEP 3: *Books and Crannies* _____
- ❏ Small Group
- ❏ Fellowship & Worship
- ❏ Mostly Girls
- ❏ Urban
- ❏ Extra Challenge

STEP 4: *Too Much of a Good Thing?* _____
- ❏ Large Group
- ❏ Mostly Guys
- ❏ Media

STEP 5: *Taking the Study Out of Bible Study* _____
- ❏ Heard It All Before
- ❏ Extra Fun
- ❏ Media
- ❏ Short Meeting Time
- ❏ Extra Challenge

SESSION 5

Behold! A Mystery!

YOUR GOALS FOR THIS SESSION:
Choose one or more

☐ To help kids see that all parts of the Bible are important—even those that deal with "mundane" issues such as census figures, genealogies, and strange prophecies.

☐ To help kids understand that like any other mystery, we need to search for clues to help us discover certain biblical truths that may not be as obvious as others.

☐ To help kids experience the satisfaction of solving a biblical mystery while in the group, and to challenge them to continue to try to do so on their own.

☐ Other:_____

Your Bible Base:

Daniel 2
Various passages that deal with the "mysteries" of Scripture

It's a Mystery to Me

(Needed: Trivia book, slips of paper prepared according to instructions)

Before the session, try to find a book that gives explanations for a number of odd occurrences. Select several good questions to pose to group members—questions for which the answers aren't too long or complicated. Photocopy the correct answer for each question.

To begin the session, call for several volunteers. Each volunteer will draw a slip of paper. One slip should have the answer to your question. The others should be blank. Ask the question aloud and give your volunteers time to think of an answer. (You might want to have them turn their backs so the person with the actual answer can read it without being obvious.) Those who have blank slips of paper should make up answers and try to bluff. The person with the actual answer should paraphrase his or her response so it sounds like he or she is making it up.

If you don't have a good book available, here are a few sample questions. (These are taken from the popular Imponderables™ series by David Feldman, published by HarperCollins. A couple of titles in the series are *Why Do Dogs Have Wet Noses?* and *When Did Wild Poodles Roam the Earth?*)

- **What does the Q in *Q-Tips* stand for?** (Quality.)
- **Why do you so often see tires on top of mobile homes in trailer parks?** (They prevent wind from causing the roof to pop in and out, and they reduce the noise of rain and hail.)
- **Why are paper and plastic drinking cups wider at the top than the bottom, when that makes them easier to tip over? Why not make them more like bottles?** (They need to be nested inside each other to be marketed effectively.)
- **Why do pretzels have such a strange shape?** (They were invented by a monk to reward good students. The shape was meant to resemble the arms of a child in prayer.)
- **Why do ironworkers wear their hard hats backward?** (They wear goggles much of the time and don't have to remove their hats to pull up the goggles onto their foreheads.)
- **What are male gnats doing when they swarm?** (They are males looking for female companionship.)
- **How did the grandfather clock get its name?** (From a song: "My grandfather's clock was too long for the shelf, so it stood 90 years on the floor.")

After each question, have your volunteers give their answers. Then let the rest of the group members vote for which person they think is telling the truth. Do this several times with new volunteers. See who can get the most votes for a made-up answer.

After playing for a while, point out that it is possible to have some fun, even when dealing with difficult questions. Then ask: **On a scale of one to ten—with ten being the most—how curious would you say you are about finding out why things work the way they do? In other words, do you tend to accept things as they are without questioning, or do you use the phrase, "I wonder why . . ." a lot?** The responses of your group members are likely to provide clues to their approach to Bible study. Group members who aren't naturally curious may not attempt to deal with prophetic passages or hard-to-understand portions of Scripture. They may simply move on to material that is easier to understand. The curious people, however, will take a different approach. They are likely to try to dig deeper. This can result in enthusiasm when they figure out a difficult passage, but potential frustration when they can't.

STEP 2

Clanging Symbols

(Needed: Bibles, copies of Repro Resource 9, pencils)

Before you deal with the issue of biblical symbolism, introduce the topic from a secular perspective. Explain: **Everyone needs to learn to struggle with symbolism. Classic literature is filled with symbols, similes, metaphors, and other words and phrases that aren't literal. We cannot read *Aesop's Fables*, Shakespeare's plays, or most poems and novels without having to put some thought into what the author is really trying to say. At first reading, *Moby Dick* may seem like the story of a man and a whale. But few college book reports will allow such a limited perspective of what Melville was trying to express. When Shakespeare wrote that "All the world's a stage," he didn't mean that *literally*. We have to put some brain cells to work to make the connection he intended us to make. So a personal dislike for symbolism is no reason to stop trying to figure out the portions of the Bible that aren't as clear as others.**

OPTIONS

LARGE GROUP

HEARD IT ALL BEFORE

MOSTLY GIRLS

MEDIA

SHORT MEETING TIME

URBAN

How many symbolic passages can you think of in the Bible? (Jesus' parables, much of the Book of Revelation, a lot of Old Testament imagery, etc.)

Do you ever have trouble figuring out the symbolism of these passages? Sometimes the symbolism is explained in the text itself. Sometimes we can figure out for ourselves. Other times we may guess, but be unsure about what the symbols mean.

Besides symbolic passages, what other portions of Scripture do you find difficult or perhaps irrelevant? (Genealogies, census figures, precise weights and measurements, etc.)

Why do you think all of these things are contained in the Bible? Point out that they are all there for a good reason. Sometimes we can figure out the reasons. Other times we may need to wait to discover the purpose of such passages.

If you don't understand such things, why not simply skip over them and move on to a different part of the Bible? (While these things are certainly not the most interesting or dynamic portions of Scripture and may not demand a high percentage of our Bible study time, we will never make sense of them unless we *occasionally* try to figure out why they are there.)

Explain: **God sometimes uses mysteries on purpose. If we refuse to struggle mentally with those things, we will never understand them. But if we "play detective" and look for clues, we will eventually begin to make sense of them.** If you've already done Session 3 in this book, remind kids of Matthew 13:12: "Whoever has will be given more, and he will have an abundance. Whoever does not have, even what he has will be taken from him."

Hand out copies of "One Good Mystery Deserves Another" (Repro Resource 9) and pencils. Group members are asked to figure out a number of mysteries, each of which should reveal a reference to a *biblical* "mystery." (You may want to have kids work in teams to complete the sheet.) When they finish, they should have "deciphered" and read the following passages and the mysteries that are described.

- Matthew 13:11—We can know the "secrets" of the kingdom of heaven.
- Romans 11:25—The way that God provided salvation for the Gentiles as well as the Jewish people was a mystery to the Jewish people for a while.
- 1 Corinthians 2:7-10—The work of God and His love for His people is a mystery to those who don't know Him.
- 1 Corinthians 15:51-52—The transformation that living Christians will undergo at Jesus' return is a mystery.
- Ephesians 1:9-10—God's will and purpose are a mystery to many, but have been revealed to His people.
- Ephesians 5:31-32—The "husband-wife" connection between Christ and the church is a mysterious relationship.

- Colossians 1:27—One mystery God's people learn to understand is "Christ in you, the hope of glory."
- 1 Timothy 3:16—The "mystery of godliness" is that sinful people can be made righteous through the incarnation and work of Jesus.
- Revelation 10:7—God's eventual and ultimate triumph over evil is a mystery yet to be realized.

Explain that these are by no means all of the verses that refer to the "mysteries" of God. As you can see, like any good mystery, most of these things *can* be understood. We start out confused and in the dark. But in most cases, we have been provided enough clues to follow so that if we *try*, we can solve the "mystery." In a few instances, we may not find the answer. Yet that shouldn't prevent us from waiting and searching.

STEP 3

In Your Dreams

(Needed: Bibles)

Ask: **What is the number one thing that needs to happen before we can understand the mysteries of God?** Although you've been discussing the need for effort on *our* part, even more important is God's willingness to reveal such things to us. If He didn't want us to know something, we could never figure it out on our own. (See James 1:5-8.)

Perhaps nowhere is this made clearer than in Daniel 2. It's a lengthy chapter, but not difficult to understand. And it will go quickly if you assign "parts" and read it as a play. One person should be a narrator who reads all portions that are not quotations. Other parts are King Nebuchadnezzar, astrologers (several), Daniel, and Arioch (who speaks only in verse 25).

Stop the action after verses 1-13 have been read and make sure everyone is clear on the facts. King Nebuchadnezzar has had a dream, and he wants his wise men to interpret it—*before* he tells them what the dream was. If they can tell the king his dream and its interpretation, they get "gifts and rewards and great honor." If they can't, they will be cut into pieces and their houses turned into piles of rubble. The astrologers argued that no man on earth could do such a thing—only "the gods." But that's not what Nebuchadnezzar wanted to hear, so he passed a death sentence on his staff of wise men. At this time, Daniel—along with Shadrach, Meshach, and Abednego—was on staff as well,

OPTIONS

SMALL GROUP

LITTLE BIBLE BACKGROUND

FELLOWSHIP & WORSHIP

MOSTLY GIRLS

MOSTLY GUYS

EXTRA FUN

but this passage suggests that he and his friends didn't hang out with the other wise men.

Stop the action again after verses 14-23 have been read and review the facts. When Daniel heard what was going on, he didn't panic. Instead, he gathered all of the facts he could and asked the king for a little time. He and his three godly friends then prayed for wisdom. (Hananiah, Mishael, and Azariah are the Hebrew names for Shadrach, Meshach, and Abednego.) That night "the mystery was revealed" to Daniel. And, by the way, the first thing he did was not to go running to the king. First, he stopped and praised God for providing the wisdom he had asked for. (As you read through this portion, you might want to keep a count of how many times God is referred to in connection with revealing mysteries or secret things.)

Stop the action again after verses 24-30 have been read and review the facts. Note that Daniel didn't take a bit of credit for knowing the king's dream and its interpretation. He made it very clear that the revelation came from the one God in heaven. He refers to God as "the revealer of mysteries."

You can skip the content of the dream (vss. 31-45) if you wish. While this story is a key prophetic passage and is usually the portion of Daniel 2 that people pay attention to, it's more important here to show that God is a "revealer of mysteries" in general—not specifically for Nebuchadnezzar. But be sure to focus on the king's reaction in verses 46-49. Nebuchadnezzar became convinced that Daniel served "the God of gods and the Lord of kings and a revealer of mysteries." In addition, Daniel and his friends were given positions of power in Nebuchadnezzar's kingdom.

Summarize: **Daniel truly believed that God was a revealer of mysteries, and his belief literally saved his life. While we seldom face immediate life-or-death situations to test our faith, we would certainly do better to have faith that God will help us understand "mysterious" portions of Scripture that initially confuse us.**

STEP 4

Why Bother?

(Needed: Bibles, copies of Repro Resource 10)

As you were reading Daniel 2, did anyone question who "Hananiah, Mishael, and Azariah" were (vs. 17)? Or why they had two names? (See Dan. 1:6-7.) These are the kinds of questions group members need to begin to ask if the Bible is ever going to make more sense to them.

Hand out copies of "Elementary, My Dear Methuselah" (Repro Resource 10). Have kids work on the biblical mystery: Did Methuselah die in the flood? (Answer: Methuselah had Lamech at age 187. Lamech had Noah at age 182. The flood came when Noah was 600. So 187 + 182 + 600 = 969, the age of Methuselah when he died.) This exercise should help group members see that there is some significance to the "begats" of the Bible. While we may tend to pass them over, sometimes we miss important clues by doing so.

Spend a few minutes letting kids express what they think are the least meaningful portions of the Bible. Then ask for reasons why such parts of Scripture might actually be important. Here are three common answers, with a few suggestions to explain the value of each one.

Genealogies

You might want to use Jesus' genealogies (Matt. 1:1-17; Luke 3:23-38) as examples. Group members should be able to see names they recognize: Abraham, Isaac, Jacob, Ruth and Boaz, David, Solomon, etc. While their stories are good ones, their history should mean even more when we realize they were leading up to the birth of the Savior of the world. You'll also find Rahab (see Josh. 2), a pagan prostitute who, along with her family, was spared death because she placed her faith in God. The significance of her presence in the line of Jesus should not go unnoticed.

Prophecy

Have group members thumb through the hundreds of pages from Isaiah to Malachi. Explain that the prophets were warning about (or living through) the captivity of God's people. They had much to say about the sins of His people as well as those of surrounding nations— and the whole bit may seem confusing and boring. Yet tucked away in those hundreds of pages are hundreds of wonderful promises (Jer. 33:3), hopes (Hab. 3:17-18), prophecies of Jesus (Isa. 9: 11), and stories of God's awesome love and provision for His people (Daniel and Jonah, to name just a couple).

Old Testament Laws

Sometimes people determine to read through the Bible, and they do reasonably well with Genesis and Exodus. But the Leviticus-Numbers-Deuteronomy trio of Old Testament law is enough to stop many of them in their tracks. Yet until we get a good sense of the burden it would be to live "under the law," we cannot truly appreciate what it means to live in God's grace. We also get a better understanding of the importance of *love* because Jesus sums up the entire Old Testament law in two commands: (1) Love God completely, and (2) Love our neighbors as ourselves (Mark 12:28-31). If our level of love ever got to where it *should* be, we wouldn't need all of those laws. Also, the books of law are filled with images that point to the coming of Jesus (blood sacrifices, priestly intercession, the bronze snake in the wilderness, etc.).

Your group members may come up with other portions of Scripture that don't exactly thrill them. But in each case, try to show how those portions are necessary to give us a more complete picture of God's active work among mankind. Such passages may be very mysterious now. But none of them are too hard to understand if we are willing to do a little "digging." The Gospels and other New Testament sections may seem much more relevant. Yet they are even more so when we have a good understanding of the "mysterious" portions of Scripture that are related to them.

STEP
5

Hope in the Dark

Ask: **Do you think God wants us to know *everything* He knows?** Obviously, we aren't capable of knowing all that God knows. Yet group members may come to the realization that God is always willing to teach us something new—much more than we usually attempt to know.

Continue: **When you are trying to figure something out, and you just can't seem to do it no matter how hard you try, how is your faith affected? Do you ever assume God just doesn't care? Or that you must not be "spiritual enough"?** Let group members respond.

Then explain: **God is the one and only source for true wisdom, so we need to seek His help when we come across portions of the Bible we don't understand. However, our faith** should not depend on getting answers to every question we might have. For example, one of the biggest mysteries of the Bible is when Jesus will return. People create all sorts of theories and wild guesses, and sometimes convince a lot of others to believe them. Yet Jesus Himself told His disciples, "No one knows about that day or hour, not even the angels in heaven, nor the Son, but only the Father" (Matt. 24:36).

As you can see, some things are mysteries simply because God is not yet ready to reveal them. No matter how hard we study or how much we try, we just won't figure them out—because we can't. But that shouldn't prevent us from searching the Scriptures and learning everything we can.

Close by having someone read aloud Romans 5:3-5: "We also rejoice in our sufferings, because we know that suffering produces perseverance; perseverance, character; and character, hope. And hope does not disappoint us, because God has poured out his love into our hearts by the Holy Spirit, whom he has given us."

Explain that while this promise holds true for any kind of suffering, in this case we can apply it to our struggles to understand the unclear portions of the Bible. If we struggle a bit, we learn to persevere. As we refuse to quit, we develop stronger character. And the end result of this process is that we develop a sure and certain hope that God will see us through any situation—whether we understand it or not.

OPTIONS

EXTRA ACTION

LARGE GROUP

HEARD IT ALL BEFORE

FELLOWSHIP & WORSHIP

MEDIA

URBAN

EXTRA CHALLENGE

ONE GOOD MYSTERY DESERVES ANOTHER

Sometimes during Bible study you may discover that if you figure out one thing, a lot of other mysteries fall into place as well. But other times, you may solve one mystery only to discover that it leads to new ones. The puzzles that follow are from the latter category. If you can figure them out, each reference you discover should lead you to a biblical mystery. First, solve the puzzles to discover the appropriate Bible references. Then look up the references and make a list of the biblical mysteries you find.

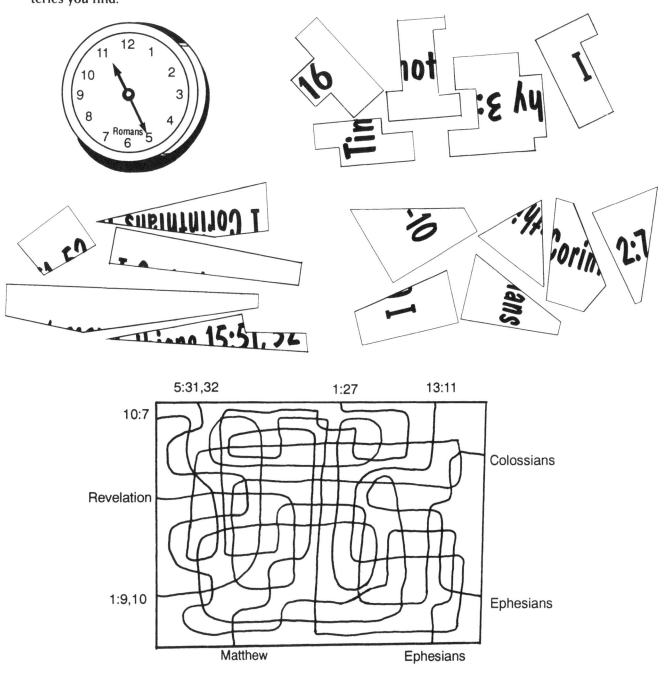

Elementary, My Dear Methuselah

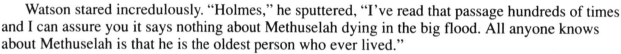

*H*olmes and Watson were having their daily devotional time (studying Genesis 5–7) when Holmes suddenly spoke: "Watson, do you suppose Methuselah was an evil person?"

Watson replied, "I say, Holmes, you come up with the strangest ideas. Whatever gave you that notion?"

"Because he died during the year of Noah's flood," said Holmes. "So it causes one to wonder."

Watson stared incredulously. "Holmes," he sputtered, "I've read that passage hundreds of times and I can assure you it says nothing about Methuselah dying in the big flood. All anyone knows about Methuselah is that he is the oldest person who ever lived."

"The oldest *recorded* person," corrected Holmes.

"Whatever," said Watson. "But the Bible says nothing about his dying in the great flood. I'm quite sure."

"I must admit," conceded Holmes, "that I cannot prove he died *because of* the flood. But he died that year, so we cannot rule out the possibility. And *if* he died in the flood, he must not have been a righteous person."

"Holmes, you always astound me," said an astounded Watson. "But you must show me how you reached your conclusion."

"It's elementary—if you read the 'begats' portion of the passage and do a little simple math," said Holmes. [NOTE: Holmes and Watson had only the *King James Version* of the Bible to work by, so they read that Methuselah *begat* Lamech and Lamech *begat* Noah.]

Watson confessed, "Ah, so that's it. I always skip those parts."

"You shouldn't," chided Holmes. "If you read Genesis 5:25-30; 7:11, 12, you should come to the same conclusion I reached."

Watson got out a pencil and paper, scratched his head a time or two, and finally said, "I say, Holmes. You've done it again!"

"Elementary, my dear Watson," Holmes replied.

How about you? Can you figure out how Holmes was able to determine that Methuselah died during the year of the great flood?

STEP 1

Have kids form two groups. Each group will create and stage a mystery for the other group to figure out. In brainstorming their mysteries, groups should think of other mysteries they've read or seen on TV. The setting may be strange and exotic. The suspects may be eccentric or normal. The victim might be one of the group members, a teacher at school, or anyone else kids choose. Several people should have motives, and the actual murderer should have an alibi (but one that can be discovered as false if the right suspects are interrogated). Each group should be able to set the scene for its mystery quickly. ("A man is found dead in bed. His butler was the last person to see him alive. The man had two children, both of whom were after his vast fortune, and a business partner whom he suspected of embezzling from the company.") Perhaps one or both of your groups will stage a thrilling experience for the other. But more likely, the result of this exercise will be to see how difficult it is to create a good mystery. Keep this point in mind as you work through the session and affirm that God's mysteries will make sense when we eventually figure them out.

STEP 5

Have kids build a human pyramid as you discuss the Romans 5:3-5 passage. When you first mention *suffering* (struggling), ask some of your larger kids to form the bottom level of the pyramid. When you get to *perseverance*, have kids form the next level up. When you mention *character*, add a third level. When you explain that all of these things are necessary to have *hope*, have a person form the top level. Point out that if our "foundational" characteristics aren't solid, neither will be the hope we have. Challenge kids to endure their sufferings, persevere through things they don't enjoy, and develop a stronger character. When those elements of their inner, spiritual "pyramid" are strengthened, their hope will be much more sure and steady.

STEP 1

If you really want to make a memorable experience out of your discussion of mysteries, you might want to take some extra time prior to the session and plan a "murder party." Bookstores and toy/game stores usually have a broad assortment of options (including "How to Host a Murder" and other series). The boxed package even contains invitations to send out. (Most murder parties require eight people.) Some have options for dinners you can plan in addition to the mystery itself. Costumes aren't necessary, but they add to the mystique of the problem-solving exercise. After all of the participants have arrived, each is given a booklet to provide clues to reveal to the others (and to alert one of the people that he or she is the real murderer). It usually takes an hour or so to do one of these roleplays, so you might need to make special arrangements in advance to ensure that everyone can be there. It won't work if one of the suspects is missing.

STEP 3

Before you read the story of Daniel, Shadrach, Meshach, and Abednego, ask your group members to think of these four guys as a small group of faithful people surrounded by a much larger group of people with no respect for God. (They were also young, so they could be classified as a youth group.) Does the situation sound familiar to them? At each pause you make in the story, discuss these questions: **How did Daniel and his friends handle being outnumbered by other people? Do you think they ever wanted to join the majority? What can we learn from them to have a more successful youth group?** Try to help your group members see that sometimes there are even advantages to being small. (They can know each other better; it's easy to get everyone together and working toward the same goals; during times of crisis, they can easily pull together for support; etc.)

STEP 2

Play "Kumquat," in which you think of a word with several definitions, replace the word with "kumquat," and then see how many clues it takes for others to guess the word. Start with hard clues and then move to easier ones. For example:
• Everyone has a kumquat.
• You never want to be accused of having two kumquats.
• One of our national monuments consists of four very large stone kumquats.
• A clock has a kumquat.
• You can kumquat the music or do an about-kumquat. (Face)
Here's another:
• To "kumquat" can mean "to put up with."
• You can under-kumquat something, but you can't over-kumquat anything.
• If you want to be noticed, you might kumquat.
• "If you don't kumquat for something, you'll fall for anything."
• A song and a movie are titled "Kumquat by Me." (Stand)

After you play a couple rounds with your kids, have them form teams and come up with some words and clues of their own to try out on the other teams.

STEP 5

After you discuss Romans 5:3-5, talk about the *importance* of hope in the lives of your young people. Then designate a "Hope Brigade." Not everyone in your group is likely to have worked through the process enough to be hopeful during trying times. So, as a group, determine some of the people who have. The more spiritually mature and optimistic people in your group should be singled out as possible contacts for other kids who are overwhelmed by stress, temptation, depression, or some other situation in which hope is needed. (The people chosen should be willing volunteers, of course.) If you can't find enough people in your group, provide a list of names and phone numbers of adults for your kids to contact if needed.

STEP 2

A "heard it all before" attitude can be a detriment to enjoying and understanding mysteries. If someone thinks he or she already knows it all, that person will place very little effort into exploring new possibilities. To demonstrate this, have group members read John 3:1-21 (the story of Nicodemus coming to Jesus). Say: **Nicodemus was an extremely educated person, yet he was confused by what Jesus was saying about being "born again." It was a mystery to him. How did Nicodemus handle his confusion?** Help group members see that Nicodemus kept challenging Jesus and asking very simple questions. He didn't mind sounding stupid. And as a result of his efforts, he was the first person to hear what is certainly the most quoted Bible verse ever (John 3:16). Today we don't think twice about being "born again," but that's only because Nicodemus persisted until he could understand that mystery. We should be less willing to assume we know it all and more eager to question and learn.

STEP 5

More than likely, your group members have some questions and doubts, whether or not they're eager to let on. As you conclude, ask: **What do you, as an intelligent person, find hardest to believe about the Bible or Christianity?** You might begin by sharing some of the questions you've struggled with. For example, the emphasis on blood sacrifice might seem strange to many people in this day and age. And certainly we should maintain a sense of wonder as to how God made it possible for people to be swallowed by large fish and vomited up three days later, or to walk on water, or to rise from the dead. If we never question such things, we never appreciate them. Perhaps you can help your group members see that some of the greatest mysteries of the Bible grow out of the simplicity of faith rather than intellectual complexity.

STEP 3

The concept of God as a "revealer of mysteries" should be an appealing one to young people who know very little about Him or His written Word. So after your discussion of Daniel, ask: **If you truly believe that no question or problem is too difficult for God, what would you like to ask Him?** Some group members may be reluctant to share their questions verbally. If so, have them write down what they would like to know. Collect the questions and discuss each one briefly. You may be able to shed some light on some of their concerns at this point. Others are likely to require longer discussions. But if you can provide some help now, you can continue to explore their mysteries together at future sessions.

STEP 4

You might want to skip this step altogether with a group that doesn't have much Bible background. But if you use it, you might want to have on hand one or more copies of *Games* magazine. Each issue usually has a feature called "Eyeball Benders," in which common objects are photographed from such unusual perspectives that they become difficult to recognize. Let your group members identify as many of the objects as they can. Then summarize: **It's important to get around to everything the Bible has to teach us—eventually. But we need to start with the basics. We need to know the major stories and learn what we can about the life of Jesus, who reveals to us exactly what God is like** (John 14:9). **To place too much emphasis on genealogies, prophecy, laws, and such before we learn the basics can cause the Bible to look distorted—like the pictures we just saw. But the whole Bible makes sense when we start with the big "clues" and advance to the other ones later on.**

STEP 3

Biblical mysteries may mean nothing compared to a young person's personal mysteries. Adolescence is a period of change and confusion. So if you want to focus more on fellowship, provide a time for group members to discuss the things they don't understand about themselves or each other. Perhaps relationships are becoming more difficult to figure out. Love and hormonal changes are certainly a mystery to most of us. But since God is a "revealer of mysteries," He should certainly be able to help us figure such things out. Challenge group members to memorize Psalm 139:23-24. Encourage them to become willing to allow God to "search," "test," "see," and "lead" them. As a result, they should begin to find some answers to their personal mysteries.

STEP 5

As wrap up the session, emphasize that it takes a great deal of faith to believe in things we don't understand. Distribute paper and pencils. Instruct group members to write an affirmation of their belief. They should title the affirmation "Faith No Matter What." Some kids may choose to write simply stated personal creeds. Others may create poetic expressions or short musical choruses. The form should be up to the person. The more important factor is the thought group members put into what they write and the content of what is expressed. Explain that since we will never understand *everything* God chooses to do in our lives, we need to learn to increase our levels of faith during confusing times. The sooner we get started, the better off our lives will be.

STEP 2

If your girls enjoy parties, you may want to take a few minutes to plan a "mystery party." (How-to kits for such parties are available wherever games are sold.) Throwing such a party, in which guests are assigned characters and clues (from which a mystery is solved throughout the course of the party), may help your girls discover how much fun solving a mystery can be. After a few minutes of planning, say: **Speaking of mysteries, let's take a look at some Bible puzzlers.** Lead in to a discussion on the "mysteries" of the Bible.

STEP 3

Ask: **Have you ever faced a situation that seemed as impossible as the one Daniel faced? If so, what was it?** Your girls may mention anything from a seemingly impossible school assignment to struggles they've faced at home. Ask them to describe how they got through the situation. Did God intervene as dramatically as He did for Daniel? This topic could lead to an insightful discussion on the many ways God works in our lives (bringing help through other people, giving us a peaceful spirit in trying times, etc.).

STEP 3

After you go through the story of Daniel's interpretation of King Nebuchadnezzar's dream, ask some tongue-in-cheek questions to your guys: **Where are the women in this story? Where was Daniel's mom, reminding him to say his prayers? Where was Abednego's wife, waking him up to make sure he went to church and became a better person? Is it really possible that a bunch of young guys could move away from home and continue to mature spiritually without begging mothers, nagging sisters, or girlfriends they were trying to impress?** Discuss to what extent your group members (or other guys they know) need to be "encouraged" or "reminded" by others to work on their spiritual growth. Remind them that maturity is an individual thing. Many of your guys might need to begin to take more responsibility for their own personal growth.

STEP 4

Ask each of your guys to think of the detective that best reflects his own personality and style. There are many to choose from: traditional (Sherlock Holmes, Charlie Chan, Nero Wolfe), private eyes (Mike Hammer, Sam Spade, Philip Marlowe, Thomas Magnum, Jim Rockford), police detectives (Columbo, Kojak, Inspector Clouseau, McCloud, Baretta, Ironside), and many more. Monitor your guys' answers for the "cool" factor. Do most of them envision themselves as strong, suave, and smart? After each person has identified with a detective, ask: **If most detectives are guys, why aren't most guys better at solving *spiritual* mysteries?** Let guys respond. Then point out that a better understanding of spiritual matters does not require a "cool factor," but rather a "humility factor." Challenge your guys to be willing to sacrifice the former to acquire the latter.

STEP 1

Trivia games seem to be perpetually popular, so open the session with one of your group members' favorites. Try to show how exciting it can be to acquire bits of knowledge about topics that no one *forces* us to learn. Some groups enjoy intellectual stimulation with games such as Trivial Pursuit. Others have favorite syndicated television shows that they can tell you *anything* about (*The Brady Bunch, Gilligan's Island, M*A*S*H,* etc.). Whatever your group members prefer, try to get them involved and enjoying themselves. Then as you go through the session, point out that they should be able to get just as excited about discovering little known facts about various portions of the Bible—including the parts that hardly anyone seems to read.

STEP 3

Have a riddle contest to see who can tell the most riddles that stump the rest of the group. You might want to be ready with a few to set the mood. Here are a couple to get you started:

- **Is a dog better dressed in summer or winter?** (In winter he has a coat, but in summer he has a coat and pants.)

- **Who is bigger: Mr. Bigger or Mr. Bigger's son?** (Mr. Bigger's son is a little Bigger.)

If possible, try to find a game called Mindtrap. It contains many challenging word puzzles and riddles that you can use. If you don't have a resource of your own, the kids will probably have plenty of riddles of their own. When you're ready to continue with the session, say: **I have a good one.** Pause. **Oh, but before you tell me the answer, I want you to tell me what the riddle is.** Then introduce the Daniel story.

STEP 2

Discuss the classic film *Citizen Kane*. If kids are familiar with it, a discussion should suffice. (Many may have seen it as a classroom assignment.) If not, you might want to have a copy of the videotape cued up in the VCR. If possible, watch the film prior to the meeting to refresh your memory about the plot line. Then, during the meeting, play the tape through the deathbed scene in which Kane speaks the word "Rosebud." Fast-forward through the rest of the movie, narrating over the speeded-up action to let kids know what's happening. Just before the end of the film, as the camera pans through Kane's vast possessions, resume real-time viewing until the secret of Rosebud is revealed and the movie ends. Point out that Kane's last word was an unsolved mystery to those who heard it; yet there was nothing mysterious about it, because *he* knew what he was talking about. Make the same comparison to some of the mysteries of God. We may be completely in the dark as to what some of those things mean, but *God* knows—and that's what matters. Some things we may be able to figure out. Other times we will simply have to trust Him until He chooses to reveal the truth to us.

STEP 5

You might want to consider concluding the session with a trip to a local arcade for video games. Or you could set up a few video games in your meeting area. Explain that we don't usually seem to mind mysteries when we're trying to figure out how to save a princess or score enough points to get to the next level. Mysteries can be challenging and fun. The same should be true about spiritual mysteries. We need to devote ourselves to the quest of learning from our mistakes and doing better as we go along—just as we do with a video game. (If you don't have access to enough video games to keep group members occupied and interested, you might consider using the VCR version of the game Clue.)

STEP 1

Bring in a "one-minute mystery" book. Such books, which contain short mysteries designed to be solved by asking only yes-or-no questions, can be found in the children's/young adult section of most bookstores. Have kids form two teams. Instruct someone from each team to call out a number at random. (Each number should correspond with a page number in the book.) The number each person calls will determine which mystery you read to his or her team. Have a contest to see which team can solve its mystery using the fewer number of questions. Use this activity to introduce the topic of mysteries in the Bible.

STEP 2

Rather than using Repro Resource 9, prepare your own worksheet for your group members. On one side of the sheet, list several symbolic phrases (e.g., "It's raining cats and dogs"; "The early bird gets the worm"; "The grass is always greener on the other side"; etc.). On the other side of the sheet, list the meanings of the phrases. Give your kids one minute to match each phrase with its correct meaning. Award prizes to those who correctly match all of the phrases and meanings within the time limit. Then quickly go through some of the passages listed on Repro Resource 9.

STEP 2

Ask your group members to close their eyes and picture the following scenes in their mind. After you set each scene, ask several volunteers to describe how they picture the scene. To set the scenes, read the following:

- Scene #1—**See Johnny run. Run, Johnny, run. Run. RUN! I said, Run!**
- Scene #2—**Broken glass everywhere . . . Can't take the smell, can't take the noise, got to move out. . . . Rats in the front room, roaches in the back, junkies in the alley with a baseball bat** (Grandmaster Flash and the Furious Five).
- Scene #3—**Suddenly the great beast beat its hideous wings, and the wind of them was foul. Again it leaped into the air, and then swiftly fell down upon Eowyn, shrieking, striking with beak and claw** (J.R.R. Tolkien).

Afterward, ask your kids to describe how they picture some of the scenes set by the symbolic language in Revelation.

STEP 5

As you wrap up the session, give your kids an opportunity to clear up some of the things they've heard about the end times. Ask volunteers to call out some of the predictions and events they've heard associated with the end times. List group members' responses on the board as they're named. The list might include things like a huge earthquake, a war probably involving Israel and the Palestinians, the rise of the Antichrist—perhaps from the European Common Market, etc. Point out that certain signs and events may lead some to believe that the end times are just around the corner. But the truth is that we won't know when the last days are coming. Have someone read aloud Matthew 24:36.

STEP 1

Begin the session by handing out paper and pencils only to your junior highers. Ask them: **What do you think are the great mysteries of life? What are some things you think you may never understand?** They may write as many questions as they can think of. When they're finished, collect their papers. Then read the questions at random, asking your high schoolers to answer them. (After all, they are so much older and wiser than the junior highers.) Goad the older kids a bit to make this a matter of pride, so they'll come up with answers that sound logical (whether or not they know what they're talking about). Then point out that certain things remain mysteries for everybody—no matter how old we are—and move on with the session.

STEP 4

Because you have some young group members, get a bit more literal as you challenge kids to get more involved with the "remote" portions of the Bible. As kids express what they think are the least meaningful portions of Scripture, use rubber bands and paper clips to show how much of the Bible they are actually talking about. For instance, if someone brings up the Minor Prophets, put a rubber band in your Bible around the books from Hosea to Malachi. When kids are finished naming "non-meaningful" portions of Scripture, use some approximate fractions or percentages to estimate how much of the Bible is left. Ask: **Why do you think God would provide us with a Bible that has _____ pages if all that's important is _____ pages? Why do you think we have so little regard for the parts of the Bible that we've sectioned off?** Point out that we will obviously miss out on a *lot* if we don't expand our Bible study interests. Challenge group members to keep reading the portions of Scripture that are particularly meaningful to them, but also to occasionally explore some of the "unknown" sections of the Bible.

STEP 4

Anticipate some of the answers your group members will give you when you ask about the "least meaningful" portions of Scripture. Be ready with some specific passages in several of the sections of Scripture that sound very confusing at first reading. Let group members struggle with these passages "on the spot." With a little direction from you, they may discover that they can do a pretty good job of figuring out what the passages are saying. Try to give them some spark of encouragement as they begin to recognize that they *can* understand some of the "mysterious" portions of the Bible—if they only try.

STEP 5

If group members seem to agree that they should be more adventurous in their approach to the Bible, challenge them to pick a book or passage to study that has always intimidated them. Perhaps one or more of those pesky Minor Prophets needs to be explored. Maybe it's time to try to figure out what Revelation is all about. Encourage kids to decide on something to *try* to study as a group. But be warned: Whatever they decide to study is something you (or someone else) will need to lead. You need to be just as enthusiastic about teaching unfamiliar sections of the Bible as group members are in learning about them.

DATE USED:

Approx. Time

STEP 1: *It's a Mystery to Me* _____
❑ Extra Action
❑ Small Group
❑ Extra Fun
❑ Short Meeting Time
❑ Combined Jr. High/High School

STEP 2: *Clanging Symbols* _____
❑ Large Group
❑ Heard It All Before
❑ Mostly Girls
❑ Media
❑ Short Meeting Time
❑ Urban

STEP 3: *In Your Dreams* _____
❑ Small Group
❑ Little Bible Background
❑ Fellowship & Worship
❑ Mostly Girls
❑ Mostly Guys
❑ Extra Fun

STEP 4: *Why Bother?* _____
❑ Little Bible Background
❑ Mostly Guys
❑ Combined Jr. High/High School
❑ Extra Challenge

STEP 5: *Hope in the Dark* _____
❑ Extra Action
❑ Large Group
❑ Heard It All Before
❑ Fellowship & Worship
❑ Media
❑ Urban
❑ Extra Challenge